The Conservative–Liberal Coa

Also edited by Matt Beech and Simon Lee

THE CAMERON-CLEGG GOVERNMENT: COALITION POLITICS IN AN AGE OF AUSTERITY

THE CONSERVATIVES UNDER DAVID CAMERON: BUILT TO LAST?

TEN YEARS OF NEW LABOUR

THE BROWN GOVERNMENT: A POLICY EVALUATION

The Conservative–Liberal Coalition

Examining the Cameron–Clegg Government

Edited by

Matt Beech
Senior Lecturer in Politics, University of Hull, UK

and

Simon Lee
Senior Lecturer in Politics, University of Hull, UK

First published 2015 by
PALGRAVE MACMILLAN

Palgrave Macmillan in the UK is an imprint of Macmillan Publishers Limited,
registered in England, company number 785998, of Houndmills, Basingstoke,
Hampshire, RG21 6XS.

Palgrave Macmillan in the US is a division of St Martin's Press LLC,
175 Fifth Avenue, New York, NY 10010.

Palgrave is the global academic imprint of the above companies and has
companies and representatives throughout the world.

Palgrave® and Macmillan® are registered trademarks in the United States,
the United Kingdom, Europe and other countries.

ISBN: 978-1-137-46136-0   hardback
ISBN: 978-1-137-50989-5   paperback

This book is printed on paper suitable for recycling and made from fully
managed and sustained forest sources. Logging, pulping and manufacturing
processes are expected to conform to the environmental regulations of the
country of origin.

A catalogue record for this book is available from the British Library.

A catalog record for this book is available from the Library of Congress.

Contents

List of Tables and Figures

Tables

Figure

Notes on Contributors

Margaret Arnott is Professor of Public Policy at the University of the West of Scotland. Her research interests include territorial politics in the UK. She has published widely on post devolution public policy in the UK. Her current research includes governing strategies of the SNP since 2007 and also the future of the UK and Unionism.

Arthur Aughey is Professor of Politics at the Ulster University. A former Leverhulme Trust Senior Research Fellow, he is now Senior Fellow at the Centre for British Politics, University of Hull. He has published widely on the politics of Northern Ireland and constitutional change in the United Kingdom. His latest publication is the *The British Question* (2013).

Tim Bale is Professor of Politics at Queen Mary University of London. He specialises in party politics and the politics of migration. He is the author of numerous articles, two books on the Conservative Party and *European Politics: A Comparative Introduction* (2013). His latest book is *Five Year Mission: the Labour Party Under Ed Miliband* (2015).

Matt Beech is Senior Lecturer in Politics and Director of the Centre for British Politics at the University of Hull. He has published widely on the history, ideas and politics of Labour, the Conservatives and the Coalition. In early 2015 he was Visiting International Research Fellow at Flinders University and is Commissioning Editor of the APSA British Politics Group http://britishpoliticsgroup.blogspot.co.uk/

James Connelly is Professor of Political Theory at the University of Hull where he teaches political philosophy, environmental politics and electoral systems. He is the co-author of *Politics and the Environment: From Theory to Practice* and many books and articles on political theory, British idealism and environmental politics.

Cathy Gormley-Heenan is the Director of the Institute for Research in Social Sciences (IRiSS) at the Ulster University. As Professor of Politics, her research interests are in the politics and public policies of divided societies. She is author of *Political Leadership and the Northern Ireland*

Peace Process (2007), co-editor of *Teaching Politics and International Relations* (2012), and *The Anglo-Irish Agreement: Rethinking Its Legacy* (2011). She is a member of the national executive committee of the Political Studies Association.

Scott L. Greer is a political scientist and is Associate Professor of Health Management and Policy at the University of Michigan School of Public Health. He is also Research Associate of the European Observatory on Health Systems and Policies in Brussels. He is author or editor of 11 books, most recently *European Union Public Health Policies* (with Paulette Kurzer) and *Federalism and Decentralization in European Health and Social Care* (with Joan Costa-Font).

Simon Griffiths is Senior Lecturer in Politics at Goldsmiths, University of London. He is interested in the links between ideology, party politics and public policy. His latest book is *Engaging Enemies: Hayek and the Left* (2014).

Holly Jarman is an Assistant Professor in the Department of Health Management and Policy at the University of Michigan School of Public Health. Jarman has published research on the development of international health law and policy, the organisation of health departments in comparative perspective, and the development of health information exchange in the United States. Her latest book, *The Politics of Trade and Tobacco Control*, is published by Palgrave.

Simon Lee is Senior Lecturer in Politics and Director of the Centre for Political Economy at the University of Hull. His teaching and research interests lie primarily in the field of political economy, with a particular focus upon globalisation, governance and national economic performance, and the politics and political economy of England.

Philip Lynch is Senior Lecturer in the Department of Politics and International Relations at the University of Leicester. His recent publications include articles on the Conservative Party and European integration, on party competition between the Conservatives and UKIP, and on the Conservatives in the European Parliament.

Christopher Martin is Senior Lecturer in War and Strategic Studies at the University of Hull. He was awarded the Julian Corbett Prize for Research in Modern Naval History in 2005 by the Institute of Historical

Research. He is currently engaged in maritime research with the Service Historique de la Défence and the Centre d'Enseignement Supérieur de la Marine (Paris). He is a member of the Groupement d'intérêt scientifique d'Histoire Maritime (Nice) and the Corbett Centre for Maritime Policy Studies. He is presently working on a book for Palgrave on afloat-support logistics and the Royal Navy.

Peter Munce is a Research Associate in the Centre for British Politics, University of Hull. He holds a PhD from the University of Ulster and from 2011 to 2014 was a Leverhulme Early Career Fellow in the CBP. His research is on British Conservatism and the protection of human rights in the UK. He has published in journals such as the *British Journal of Politics and International Relations, Parliamentary Affairs, Political Quarterly* and *Irish Political Studies*.

Philip Norton [Lord Norton of Louth] is Professor of Government, and Director of the Centre for Legislative Studies, at the University of Hull. He is author or editor of 31 books and more than 100 chapters and articles in academic journals. He was the first chairman of the House of Lords Select Committee on the Constitution and has been described in the House Magazine as 'our greatest living expert on Parliament'.

Robert M. Page is Reader in Democratic Socialism and Social Policy. He has written extensively about the post-1945 British welfare state including *Revisiting the Welfare State* (2007). His new book *Clear Blue Water? The Conservative Party and the Welfare State Since 1940* will be published in July 2015.

Rebecca Partos is an ESRC-funded doctoral researcher in Politics at the University of Sussex. Her research examines the development of post-war Conservative Party immigration policy with a focus on how periods in opposition and periods in government inform policy making. She has recently completed a placement at the Home Office, working as a researcher within Migration and Border Analysis.

Roger Scully is Professor of Political Science in the Wales Governance Centre at Cardiff University. He was Co-Director of the 2011 Welsh Election Study. Among his many publications is *Wales Says Yes: Devolution and the 2011 Welsh Referendum* (2012). He also runs the Elections in Wales blog: http://blogs.cardiff.ac.uk/electionsinwales/

Louise Thompson is Lecturer in British Politics at the University of Surrey. Her research focuses on the legislative process and the work of committees in the House of Commons. She is a member of the Study of Parliament Group and Research Associate at the Centre for Legislative Studies, University of Hull. Her forthcoming book, *Making British Law: Committees in Action* is published by Palgrave.

Rhiannon Vickers is Senior Lecturer at the Department of Politics, University of Sheffield, with research interests in British foreign and security policy. She is the author of the *Labour Party and the World, Volume 1: The Evolution of Labour's Foreign Policy 1900–51* (2004) and *Volume 2: Labour's Foreign Policy since 1951* (2011).

Centre for British Politics

The Centre for British Politics is an expert-led research centre for the study of British politics in the School of Politics, Philosophy and International Studies at the University of Hull. In particular, its subject matter is the parties, ideologies and public policies that dominate UK politics. Established in 2007 as the first of its kind in UK higher education, the Centre for British Politics has made a distinctive impact in its field of study through its annual Norton Lecture, international workshops, symposiums, media interviews, expert submissions to parliament and, of course, through its publications. The centre is led by Matt Beech. Its members are Simon Lee, Philip Norton and Ben Yong and it includes participating doctoral students, research associates, post-doctoral fellows, international visiting scholars and Senior Fellows.

This Centre for British Politics book is the fifth collection of essays, and the fourth with Palgrave Macmillan, that Matt Beech and Simon Lee have edited. They include: *Ten Years of New Labour* (2008), *The Conservatives under David Cameron: Built to Last?* (2009), *The Brown Government: A Policy Evaluation* (2010) and *The Cameron–Clegg Government: Coalition Government in an Age of Austerity* (2011). More about the research projects, activities and members of the Centre for British Politics can be found at: http://www2.hull.ac.uk/fass/politics/research/cbp.aspx

Acknowledgements

The Centre for British Politics, and his co-editor in particular, would like to thank and acknowledge Matt Beech for suggesting this project to evaluate the Conservative–Liberal Coalition and for assembling the contributors and securing the contract with Palgrave.

The editors would like to express their gratitude to all of the contributors whose excellent essays have made this volume what it is. They would also like to thank Sara Crowley-Vigneau, Commissioning Editor at Palgrave Macmillan, and her colleagues Jemima Warren and previously Andy Baird for their hard work and helpfulness along the way. The editors would like to acknowledge Stanford DTP on the production of the book, the efforts of the copy editor, Rachel Hutchings, on improving the manuscript for production and Sue Carlton for compiling the index.

Finally, Matt would like to thank his family. His wife, Claire, for her love and support during this project and their children, Joseph and Anna, for providing the very best kind of distractions from writing and editing. Simon would like to thank Elizabeth, Charlotte and Charlie for their love and support, especially in managing to move house during the production of this volume, and Rosie and Sam for sharing early morning walks on Hornsea beach, the perfect antidote to the politics of austerity.

1
The Ideology of the Coalition: More Liberal than Conservative

Matt Beech[1]

> The Conservative Party exists to conserve; it is the party of the status quo. Unfortunately for it and its adherents all things change – 'the flower withereth and the grass fadeth'.
>
> (Charmley, 1996: 1)

Introduction

For those who study British politics from a contemporary history or political science perspective the role of ideology is notable. British party ideology is diverse, fluid and contains contradictory strands. At certain times a particular expression dominates, usually from the podiums occupied by the party leadership. Of course, the role and significance of ideology is never the full story. The politics of personalities, internal management, path-dependent policy commitments and a host of external factors – chief of which is electoral calculus – all contribute to the story of a government. The work of Jim Bulpitt in relation to the primacy of statecraft in the domestic politics of Margaret Thatcher has been influential and widely cited within academic circles (Bulpitt, 1986). But Mark Garnett and Kevin Hickson are surely right to point out that ideology is a key contributing factor in the statecraft of elite politicians, including those at the apex of the oldest political party in Europe: '[W]e can see that the statecraft of the Conservative Party was not fixed but rather changed over time in the light of changed circumstances and the beliefs of the Party's leaders. On this view, ideology has always been an integral element in Conservative "statecraft".' (Garnett and Hickson, 2009: 3)

To add ballast to this point, one needs only a brief glance at post-war Conservative history from R.A. Butler's Education Act; Winston Churchill's cultivation of the 'special relationship'; Harold Macmillan's establishment of the National Economic Development Council or 'Neddy'; Edward Heath's 'Selsdon Man' manifesto; Thatcher's deregulation of the City of London; John Major's privatisation of British Rail; George Osborne's Emergency Budget and the following politics of austerity, to sufficiently demonstrate that ideology is central to British politics in general, and to Conservative statecraft, in particular.

There has been considerable academic attention to issues relating to ideology and the Coalition (McAnulla, 2010; Beech, 2011a; Hall, 2011; Kelly, 2011; Kerr *et al.*, 2011; Buckler and Dolowitz, 2012; Crines, 2013; Heppell, 2013; Lakin, 2013; Griffiths, 2014; Hayton, 2014). This essay's hypothesis suggests that the ideology of the Conservative–Liberal Coalition owes more to the well-spring of liberal political thought than conservative political thought. Due to the confines of a single essay I have selected three data points which unite the Coalition. The data are in the form of substantive policy areas and ordered in terms of import: economic liberalism, social liberalism, foreign policy (liberal interventionism). Before we proceed it is important to insert some caveats. First, the data points are areas of overlapping agreement between the two camps making Coalition possible and ideologically liberal. However, the breadth and depth of disagreement which separates Clegg's *Orange Book*[2] Liberal Democrats from Cameron's liberal Conservatives is self-evident: the European Union, immigration, defence of the realm, the constitution, aspects of environmental policy and press regulation. Second, the argument of the essay is not that the elites in both Coalition parties are of one mind. On the contrary, their frequent, ill-tempered public disagreements throughout this parliament denote two different political traditions (Ross, 2014). In addition, such disputes illustrate the electoral need to be seen to disagree with each other by their activists who can be described as partisan 'die-hards'. Without the support of such card-carrying members – 'true believers', if you will – the prospect of mounting an effective election campaign is distant.

A tale of two liberalisms rebooted

In our previous book, *The Cameron–Clegg Government: Coalition Politics in an Age of Austerity* (Lee and Beech, 2011) my focus was to explain and understand the philosophical feasibility of partnership between the Conservatives under Cameron and the Liberal Democrats under Clegg.

In other words, why should it work? This I characterised as 'a tale of two liberalisms' (Beech, 2011a: 268). In the majority partner, a modernising Conservatism comprising an economic liberal political economy passed down the generations from the materfamilias is combined with a social liberalism indicative of the metropolitan elite and, in the minority partner, *Orange Book* politics which re-emphasise the Manchester economics of old sit with the ever-present Liberal Democrat advocacy of liberal morality (ibid.: 269–70). I continue to believe that this is an accurate ideological summary of the Conservative–Liberal Coalition. In that essay I noted that Cameron's political thought is essentially a *form* of liberalism albeit communicated to the electorate as liberal Conservatism. This too I maintain. My argument has expanded to include a third liberal perspective of Cameron's Conservatives; that of liberal interventionism in British foreign policy (Beech, 2011b; Beech and Oliver, 2014). Other scholars have sought to explain and understand the role played by liberalism in Cameron's Conservatism and, relatedly, liberalism's role within the Coalition. Stuart Hall remarked that:

> Coalition set the neo-liberal-inclined *Orange Book* supporters, who favoured alliance with the Conservatives, against the 'progressives', including former social democrats, who leaned towards Labour … The Lib Dems provided the Cameron leadership with a 'fig leaf', and the banking crisis with the 'alibi' it needed. It grasped the opportunity to launch the most radical, far-reaching (and irreversible?) social revolution since the war. (Hall, 2011: 718)

For Hall, then, a neo-liberal partnership is the way to comprehend the Conservative–Liberal Coalition; with the detrimental impact of the Global Financial Crisis (GFC) on the UK 'proof' that 'emergency surgery' was required. In his piece in *British Politics*, Matthew Lakin takes a contrasting perspective on the ideological motivations of the Conservative–Liberal Coalition: '[T]he Coalition is more "muscular", or conservative, than liberal. Cameron's Conservatives, with the aid of the Liberal Democrats, have begun the process of trying to create a broad-church Centre-Right hegemony in Britain' (Lakin, 2013: 488). Lakin is correct that the partnership of Cameron and Clegg is 'broad-church Centre-Right' but off the mark with his interpretation of a '"muscular", or conservative' politics. It is difficult to identify conservative elements in Liberal Democrat policy. Even if one looks closely at the different Liberal Democrat expressions from the *Orange Book* liberals to the social liberals to the SDP liberals. While Cameron's

Conservatives exhibit some traditional conservative attitudes, compared in relation to a sizable portion of the Parliamentary Conservative Party, and many grassroots activists, they are consistently liberal. The notion of contempt felt towards Conservative activists by Cameron's coterie was given 'voice' by a source quoted by *Telegraph* journalist James Kirkup over the Conservative split on gay marriage. The source described the associations as, 'all mad swivel-eyed loons' (Kirkup, 2013). The politics of the Conservative–Liberal Coalition is essentially a right-wing liberalism.

Economic liberalism

Economic liberalism has long been the favoured economic doctrine of the Conservative Party. The DNA link between Thatcherism and the ideology of the Coalition is neo-liberalism or, emphasised slightly differently, economic liberalism. This economic liberalism is a policy continuity which trickled down the years from Thatcher's administrations to Major to Blair to Brown (before the rebirth and short second life of Keynesianism in 2008–2010) and then to the Coalition. Here, then, lies a foundational tenet of liberalism still influencing contemporary politics. Following in the footsteps of his predecessors since Thatcher, and continuing to dwell in the economic paradigm of Conservative Party thinking, Cameron too is clearly an advocate of economic liberalism (Beech, 2009). In his Commons tribute to Thatcher, on 13 April 2013, Cameron's economic liberal sympathies for her philosophy were evident:

> The air was thick with defeatism; there was a sense that the role of government was simply to manage decline. Margaret Thatcher rejected this defeatism. She had a clear view about what needed to change. Inflation was to be controlled – not by incomes policies, but by monetary and fiscal discipline. Industries were to be set free into the private sector. Trade unions should be handed back to their members. People should be able to buy their own council homes. (Cameron, 2013)

The Conservative–Liberal Coalition has sought, like Thatcher, to reduce the size of the state and cut public expenditure. The result is a slightly leaner state with the politics of austerity embedded as the *modus operandi* of our time. The authors of the austerity are equally fervent economic liberals, one a Conservative and the other a Liberal Democrat: George Osborne and Danny Alexander. The *Orange Book*

Liberal Democrats who occupy key positions in the Coalition are not reluctant partners in the politics of austerity as their voting record clearly indicates. Their leader was an *Orange Book* essayist and has given speeches where he trumpets economic liberalism as part of his party's heritage (Clegg, 2008). For their part, these Liberal Democrats desired Coalition to demonstrate that their party was fit for office and that their interpretation of liberalism possessed the economic liberal principles that were necessary to counter the profligate state that the Labour Party had used to the detriment of balanced fiscal policy. The *Orange Book* liberals were confident that – because of their commitments to a smaller state, market forces, lower taxes, entrepreneurship and less bureaucracy – their hour in British politics had come.

Therefore, it can be clearly understood that the Coalition is a project predicated on the economic (not social or foreign policy) nostrums set out in Thatcherism but they have arguably gone further in rolling-back Britain's welfare capitalism. Reductions in public expenditure, reductions of direct taxation, privatisation, and the scaling back of welfare provision are all consistent with the economic liberal conception of how to shrink the size and influence of the state and, by so doing, attain greater liberty for individuals. Some notable clues which further point to the economic liberalism of the Coalition include the scrapping of the 50p band of income tax and replacing it with a 45p band for those earning over £150,000 per annum (which is a tax cut for the most financially successful); the introduction of the spare-room subsidy or 'bedroom tax'; the rapidly increasing privatisation of NHS England services;[3] and the abolition of a range of measures, designed over many years, to support the poorest and most vulnerable citizens: the abolition of the Educational Maintenance Allowance, Community Care Grants, Crisis Loans, the Council Tax Rebate Scheme[4] and cuts to civil legal aid.

The need to reduce the deficit to sustainable proportions is uncontroversial. However, the means that are employed; the speed of the fiscal retrenchment; and the ends motivating such action are the subjects of much contestation and bitter argument. The Conservative–Liberal narrative has long been that 'Labour did not fix the roof whilst the sun was shining'. It is true that there was a deficit before the emergency measures of the Brown government to prevent the recession slipping into depression. But not only was the level of deficit manageable it was a period of reinvestment in capital infrastructure: schools, hospitals, transport, universities, social services, policing and the armed forces. Also, with a domestic reinvestment plan, the Labour governments expanded the relevant professions to staff the public services. While not every pound was spent judiciously and Labour's *penchant* for Public–Private Partnerships yielded poor value for taxpayers and many public sector employees were ground down by the incessant target culture of New Labour's managerialism, hundreds of thousands of jobs were created and ten years of consecutive growth ensued. In short, the deficits were manageable. The explosion in the deficit from 2008–2010 was, unsurprisingly, caused by the ramifications of the Great Financial Crisis. When the Conservative–Liberal Coalition was formed in 2010 the goal of deficit reduction by the end of the parliament was its priority:

> We recognise that deficit reduction, and continuing to ensure economic recovery, is the most urgent issue facing Britain. We will significantly accelerate the reduction of the structural deficit over the course of a Parliament, with the main burden of deficit reduction borne by reduced spending rather than increased taxes. (HM Government, 2010b: 15)

Without immediate action, Britain's future wealth and competitiveness would greatly suffer and the stability of the economy was precariously balanced. The Treasury set about making aggressive economies in public expenditure across the departments of Whitehall. Front-line provision of social care, policing, schools, social security, and to a lesser extent the NHS have all been structurally altered in the new era of austerity. According to the Institute for Fiscal Studies (IFS), Coalition cuts to Whitehall departmental spending from 2010 to the end of 2014–15 has been £35 billion, with an estimated further £55 billion of cuts to come between 2015–16 and 2019–20 (Johnson, 2014: 4). In 2010, the Treasury forecast that in 2014–15 the deficit would be less than £40 billion, that it is now predicted to exceed £90 billion (ibid.: 2–3). Paul Johnson, the Director of the IFS, states that: 'It is important to understand why the deficit hasn't fallen. It is emphatically not because the government has failed to impose the intended spending cuts. It is because the economy performed so poorly in the first half of the parliament, hitting revenues very hard' (ibid.: 3).

Why was this? The performance of an economy (particularly one such as the UK's) is a multifarious and complex thing. The Eurozone crisis has played a role. However, the scale of the cuts to public expenditure necessarily led to significant job losses and the knock-on effect rippled through the supply chain. This increased the welfare bill, reduced revenue from tax receipts and, simultaneously, removed much demand from an anaemic economy in the first half of the parliament. According to figures from the Office for National Statistics (ONS), published on 21 January 2015, the number of people unemployed in September to November 2014 was still 1.91 million or 5.8 per cent of the work force; and yet this is a fall of 58,000 on the previous quarter and 418,000 in the year (ONS, 2014). The Chancellor and his Treasury team's economic liberalism has forced it – somewhat ironically – to run significant budget deficits as Coalition policy has not engendered the conditions for a steady, expanding base of tax receipts. Despite the creation of many new jobs, insufficient tax revenues persist. An explanation here is that many of these positions are zero-hours and part-time contracts at low or minimum wage rates. The Conservative–Liberal Coalition with its shared commitment to economic liberalism has failed in its primary mission to clear the deficit by the end of the parliament and, despite its de-funding of what remains of the social democratic state, it has not mastered fiscal discipline.

Social liberalism

As well as sharing an economic perspective the Conservative–Liberal Coalition share a commitment to social liberalism. The *Orange Book* Liberal Democrats, like the vast majority of their party, are liberal in matters of personal and social ethics. The more interesting story is that Cameron's Conservatives are also social liberals but their beliefs place them outside of the mainstream thinking on personal and social ethics of the Parliamentary Conservative Party. Cameron and his modernisers are much more comfortable with Clegg's *Orange Book* Liberal Democrats on social issues than with many of his own parliamentary colleagues. The debate between social liberals and social conservatives in the Conservative Party is often referred to as 'Mods versus Rockers' and pertains first to the disagreements between senior modernising figures and traditionalists during the leadership of William Hague but which also caused ructions during Iain Duncan Smith's tenure (Hayton, 2010). It could be argued that the 'Mods' triumphed because the socially liberal Cameron was elected leader in 2005. Of course, social conservatism is still a key philosophical position for a majority of Conservative MPs in parliament. The battle for the soul of the contemporary Conservative Party has yet to be won.

In his attitudinal study of the 2010 Parliamentary Conservative Party, Heppell found that 50 per cent (153 MPs) are socially conservative, 20 per cent (62 MPs) are agnostic on the subject (cannot be clearly categorised), and 30 per cent (91 MPs) are socially liberal (Heppell, 2013: 345). His research indicates that of Conservative ministers serving in the Conservative–Liberal Coalition, a little below two-thirds (60.5 per cent) are socially conservative and slightly below one-quarter (22.4 per cent) are socially liberal (ibid.: 348). The philosophical divide over social and moral issues that distinguishes social liberals from social conservatives relates to marriage, adoption, gay rights, feminisation, positive discrimination, immigration, multiculturalism, penal reform, euthanasia, abortion and capital punishment. This philosophical divide is most deeply felt in the Parliamentary Conservative Party which is sharply split on such issues. On the majority of such issues Cameron's liberal Conservatives would share a liberal worldview akin to their *Orange Book* partners.

Arguably, the contemporary litmus test for whether a Conservative is more socially liberal or socially conservative is gay marriage. Of course there will be exceptions and some MPs might not hold definitive views either way. Some might have voted according to the number of emails and letters they received on the subject from their constituents and local party supporters. However, no other social issue divides the Conservative Party to such an extent. As Ben Clements notes, 'the gay marriage debate is emblematic of the main ideological divide within the contemporary Conservative Party' (Clements, 2014: 233). This was evident in the debates in the House of Commons on the Coalition's, Marriage (Same-Sex Couples) Bill during 2013. During the Bill's second reading, passionate interventions for and against were exchanged, with it passing to the next stage by 400 votes to 175; 136 Conservative MPs voted against, 127 supported, 5 abstained and 35 did not vote (BBC News, 2013a). With no party having the issue in its 2010 manifesto; it being absent from the Coalition Agreement; and knowing how divided the Conservative Party are on this subject; it appears that Cameron and his liberal Conservatives wanted this vote as a matter of principle. Furthermore, it follows that they were willing to risk losing political capital with many colleagues in the House and activists across the country. This point is heightened by the rise of UKIP as an alternative electoral option for Conservative-inclined voters who have become disillusioned with the Conservative-led Coalition. Rationally there was no need to further divide the Parliamentary Conservative Party on social issues and prompt bad feeling in the constituencies. If Cameron and his close advisors thought it would demonstrate that the Conservative Party are comfortable with alternative lifestyles they were mistaken. The fact that a majority of Conservative MPs voted against the government's

Bill at the second reading, meaning it needed support from the Liberal Democrats and the Labour Party, calls into question their judgement. It would seem, therefore, that the only reason to embark upon such a divisive, controversial and un-conservative policy is because, as social liberals, Cameron and his modernisers saw an opportunity to change a key aspect of British society – the definition of marriage – in line with their liberal ideology which is shared with their Coalition partners.

Liberal interventionism

The third and final data point which is evidence that the Coalition owes more to liberal thinking than to conservative thinking lies in the arena of foreign policy.[5] At the start of his leadership of the Conservative Party, Cameron gave a clear signal that his liberal Conservative approach to foreign policy would be different from the Blair Doctrine: 'I am a liberal conservative, rather than a neo-conservative. Liberal – because I support the aim of spreading freedom and democracy, and support humanitarian intervention. Conservative – because I recognise the complexities of human nature, and am sceptical of grand schemes to remake the world' (Cameron, 2006).

This was an attempt to reassure the electorate that the Conservative-led Coalition would not follow in New Labour's footsteps and involve the UK in further conflicts which do not affect its immediate national security. Nonetheless, with the emergence of the Arab spring and the civil war in Libya, Cameron's liberal conservative thinking took a different path. Here the influence and impact of New Labour is apparent. The fact that the Blair government had successfully intervened in Kosovo and Sierra Leone solely on humanitarian grounds, and the notion of a watching world, especially the pro-democracy protesters across the Arab region and wider Middle East, weighed heavily on Cameron and Hague. Soon, an evacuation mission for UK nationals evolved into a desire for a full-scale liberal intervention and the UK drafted UN Security Council resolution 1973 which was passed on 17 March 2011. As events unfolded Cameron and Hague each gave speeches supportive of liberal interventionism (Cameron, 2011a, 2011b, 2012; Hague, 2011, 2012).

It is of course correct that they were more circumspect than Blair, given recent British history, and Cameron addressed parliament setting out specifically his view of the appropriate parameters for military action (Cameron, 2011b). But, while conscious to distance his worldview from that of Blair, Cameron's practice owed much to New Labour's foreign policy idealism (Beech, 2011b). In addition, as Beech and Oliver demonstrate in data collected from interviews with Lords Carrington, Howe, Hurd and Sir Malcolm Rifkind MP, previous Conservative Foreign Secretaries view liberal interventionism with considerable scepticism:

> [A]ll four former Foreign Secretaries are critical of humanitarian intervention practiced by the Blair governments. They consider this form of humanitarian intervention as a potentially dangerous path for British foreign policy. It is here that one detects the innate scepticism of grand plans and idealist philosophical projects that realist Conservatives share. (Beech and Oliver, 2014: 9)

This suggests that the liberal Conservatives of Cameron have departed from some of the traditions of *realism* long practised by Conservative governments. As for Cameron's *Orange Book* partners they were supportive of the intervention in Libya as there has long been a liberal interventionist strand in Liberal Democrat foreign policy when in line with international law (Grender, 2011). The fact that he did not face opposition to his plans undoubtedly made military action politically smoother for Cameron.

The same cannot be said for the Coalition's second planned liberal intervention. As the Syrian civil war progressed, and the Assad regime deployed chemical weapons killing hundreds, the Conservative–Liberal Coalition recalled parliament and pushed for a British response. The government motion in the House of Commons on 29 August 2013 stated that it:

> agrees that a strong humanitarian response is required from the international community and that this may, if necessary, require military action that is legal, proportionate and focused on saving lives by preventing and deterring further use of Syria's chemical weapons ... believes, in spite of the difficulties at the United Nations, that a United Nations process must be followed as far as possible to ensure the maximum legitimacy for any such action. (House of Commons, 2013)

To the surprise of many, the motion was defeated by 13 votes: 285 to 272. It was the first time in modern memory that a British Prime Minister failed to win support for his government's foreign policy. Some 30 Conservatives and nine Liberal Democrats voted against the Coalition, with one MP from each party abstaining (BBC News, 2013b). The mainstay of the opposition to liberal interventionism in Syria came from the usually *idealist* Labour Party which is still recovering from the reputational fall-out of the war in Iraq. Therefore, it can be argued that Cameron's Conservatives imported a degree of liberalism in the form of liberal interventionism into contemporary Conservative foreign policy (Beech and Oliver, 2014).

Conclusion

This essay's epigraph, a quotation from the opening chapter of John Charmley's monograph on the Conservative Party, is revealing. Charmley is indeed correct that historically the Conservative Party sought to conserve and yet, as a consequence of the nature of political and social culture, they found themselves managing change and adapting as best they could. Hence his reference to the Book of Isaiah, chapter 40 verse 8,[6] though unlike the remainder of that verse, 'but the word of our God shall stand for ever' (The Holy Bible: Authorised Version, 1611) the ideology of the post-war Conservative Party has not stood firm; nor has it merely drifted a little from its traditional moorings. But, in its place, a robust *form* of liberalism has evolved over many years. The beginning of the economic liberal story in the Conservative Party is well known and its midwives are now revered in the pantheon of Conservative greats. Then, gradually with the rise of a much more secular electorate, the current Conservative elite made its peace (though sometimes begrudgingly) with social liberalism. Finally, the impact of New Labour's liberal interventionism has led to a more pro-active approach to foreign policy and human rights violations. It is this *form* of liberalism that defines Cameron's liberal Conservatives. It has enabled them to break bread with Clegg's *Orange Book* Liberal Democrats for five years and yet, in part, it has provided UKIP with the opportunity to usher in an era of four-party politics by speaking to the concerns of conservative England. Concerns that Cameron's liberal Conservatives are not trusted to address.

This then begs the question, what would a contemporary, authentic conservative politics have to say about the economy, social issues and Britain's role in the world? The following is a sketch of conservative possibilities in these arenas. The economy would, of course, be capitalist with a large, dynamic private sector but not the unbridled, free-market liberal version. Conservative capitalism would give primacy to the profit-motive but would not eschew regulation and would desire a social safety net for the sake of public order and concern for the well-being of children, the infirm and adults incapable of work. While it would be sceptical of all but the most modest state-led projects to redistribute wealth or opportunity, in the conservative mind the market is not God.

With regards to social issues, a conservative approach would place the traditional family at the heart of a stable society. This would apply to issues of marriage and adoption; the Equalities Act 2010 would be amended. Parents, not teachers or social workers, would be expected to bring up their children and take responsibility for their education, behaviour and in preparing them for adult working life. Penal policy would be predicated on custodial sentences rather than community sentences; prison places would be expanded and early-release programmes for serious offenders abolished; laws on the possession and consumption of illegal narcotics would be tightened; a debate would occur on the reintroduction of the death penalty for the most heinous crimes. Abortion on demand would be curtailed by amending the Abortion Act 1967, significantly reducing the period in which a pregnancy can be terminated from the current 24 weeks. The Human Rights Act 1998 would be repealed. Grammar schools would be re-established; traditional conceptions of educational rigour returned to core syllabuses; universities would be reduced in number. The culture of political correctness would be challenged.

In foreign affairs a realist approach would be adopted. The core driver would be the security of Britain and its national interests. Her Majesty's Royal Navy would be restored with long-term investment in aircraft carriers and destroyers. The sovereignty of nation-states would be respected, along with intolerance towards Britain's enemies within and without. Humanitarian interventions would be resisted due to the risk to service personnel and the legal and financial costs involved. Instead, traditional diplomatic means would be utilised and the United Kingdom would maintain a presence within international organisations and at elite-level summits. Membership of the EU would be renegotiated given the concerns over the diminution of parliamentary sovereignty, uncontrolled immigration, judicial activism by the European Court of Justice, the centre-left policy agenda from Brussels, and the alien desire for a federal Europe found in some quarters of the institution.

The findings of this essay are that after five years in office, the Conservative–Liberal Coalition was more liberal than conservative, and that the liberal Conservatives of Cameron and the *Orange Book* Liberal Democrats of Clegg share a particular *type* of liberalism which combines economic, social and foreign policy commitments. This tale of two liberalisms was much more than a marriage of convenience.

Notes

1. I am grateful to Kevin Hickson for reading and commenting on an earlier draft. I am especially grateful to colleagues in the School of Politics and International Studies at the University of Leeds for inviting me to give a research seminar on 27 November 2014. It was a helpful opportunity to test my hypothesis, data and arguments on the Coalition's ideology. Any errors in this chapter are, of course, my own.
2. This term is taken from the influential edited volume of the same name (Marshall and Laws, 2004).
3. For a study of the implications of the Health and Social Care Act 2012 see Jarman and Greer in this volume.
4. For an analysis of the Coalition's reforms to these and other social security matters see Page in this volume.
5. For an evaluation of Coalition foreign policy see Vickers in this volume.
6. The verse in full reads 'the grass withereth, the flower fadeth: but the word of our God shall stand forever.' (The Holy Bible: Authorised Version, 1611).

References

BBC News (2013a) Gay marriage: MPs back bill despite Conservative backbench opposition. 5 February. http://www.bbc.co.uk/news/uk-politics-21346220 last accessed 2 February 2015.

BBC News (2013b) Syria vote: Which Tory and Lib Dem MPs rebelled? 30 August http://www.bbc.co.uk/news/uk-23892715 last accessed 2 February 2015.

Beech, M. (2009) Cameron and Conservative Ideology. In S. Lee and M. Beech (eds), *The Conservatives under David Cameron: Built to Last?* (Basingstoke: Palgrave), 18–30.

Beech, M. (2011a) A Tale of Two Liberalisms. In S. Lee and M. Beech (eds), *The Cameron–Clegg Government: Coalition Politics in an Age of Austerity* (Basingstoke: Palgrave), 267–279.

Beech, M. (2011b) British Conservatism and Foreign Policy: Traditions and Ideas Shaping Cameron's Global View. *British Journal of Politics and International Relations*. 13 (3), 348–363.

Beech, M. and Oliver, T.J. (2014) Humanitarian Intervention and Foreign Policy in the Conservative-led Coalition. *Parliamentary Affairs*, 67 (1), 102–118.

Buckler, S. and Dolowitz, D. (2012) Ideology Matters: Party Competition, Ideological Positioning and the Case of the Conservative Party under David Cameron. *British Journal of Politics and International Relations*. 14 (4), 576–594.

Bulpitt, J. (1986) The Discipline of the New Democracy: Mrs Thatcher's Domestic Statecraft. *Political Studies*. 34 (1), 19–39.

Cameron, D. (2006) A New Approach to Foreign Affairs – Liberal Conservatism. Speech to the British-American Project. 11 September. http://www.theguardian.com/politics/2006/sep/11/conservatives.speeches last accessed 2 February 2015.

Cameron, D. (2011a) Speech to Kuwaiti National Assembly, Kuwait, 22 February. https://www.gov.uk/government/speeches/prime-ministers-speech-to-the-national-assembly-kuwait

Cameron, D. (2011b) Statement to the House on Libyan intervention, 21 March. https://www.gov.uk/government/speeches/pm-statement-to-the-house-on-libya

Cameron, D. (2012) Transcript of Speech: Prime Minister and Prime Minister Abdurraheim Al-Keib of Libya, Downing Street, 24 May. https://www.gov.uk/government/speeches/transcript-the-prime-minister-and-prime-minister-abdurrahim-al-keib-of-libya

Cameron, D. (2013) Tribute to Lady Margaret Thatcher by Prime Minister David Cameron. (London: Cabinet Office) https://www.gov.uk/government/speeches/tribute-to-lady-margaret-thatcher-by-prime-minister-david-cameron last accessed 29 January 2015.

Charmley, J. (1996) *A History of Conservative Politics 1900–1996* (Basingstoke: Macmillan).

Clegg, N. (2008) Speech on the reform of public services. Liberal Democrat Manifesto Conference, London School of Economics, 12 January. www.news.bbc.co.uk/1/hi/uk_politics/7187852.stm

Clements, B. (2014) Partisan Attachments and Attitudes towards Same-Sex Marriage in Britain. *Parliamentary Affairs.* 67 (1), 232–244.

Crines, A.S. (2013) The Rhetoric of the Coalition: Governing in the National Interest? *Representation.* 49 (2), 207–218.

Garnett, M. and Hickson, K. (2009) *Conservative Thinkers: The Key Contributors to the Political Thought of the Modern Conservative Party* (Manchester: Manchester University Press).

Grender, O. (2011) Here's why Lib Dems are wholly behind the Libya intervention. *New Statesman,* 22 March. http://www.newstatesman.com/blogs/olly-grender/2011/03/party-intervention-liberal last accessed 2 February 2015.

Griffiths, S. (2014) What was Progressive in 'Progressive Conservatism'? *Political Studies Review.* 12 (1), 29–40.

Hague, W. (2011) Speech to Conservative Spring Conference. Cardiff, 6 March. http://www.newstatesman.com/2011/03/foreign-policy-british-britain

Hague, W. (2012) International Law and Justice in a Networked World. London, Foreign and Commonwealth Office, 9 July. https://www.gov.uk/government/speeches/international-law-and-justice-in-a-networked-world

Hall, S. (2011) The Neo-liberal Revolution. *Cultural Studies.* 25 (6), 705–728.

Hayton, R. (2010) Conservative Modernisation and David Cameron's Politics of the Family. *Political Quarterly.* 81 (4), 492–500.

Hayton, R. (2014) Conservative Party Statecraft and the Politics of Coalition. *Parliamentary Affairs.* 67 (1), 6–24.

Heppell, T. (2013) Cameron and Liberal Conservatism: Attitudes within the Parliamentary Conservative Party and Conservative Ministers. *British Journal of Politics and International Relations.* 15 (3), 340–361.

HM Government (1967) Abortion Act (London: Stationery Office).

HM Government (1998) Human Rights Act (London: Stationery Office).

HM Government (2010a) Equalities Act (London: Stationery Office).

HM Government (2010b) The Coalition: Our Programme for Government (London: Cabinet Office).

HM Government (2012) Health and Social Care Act (London: Stationery Office).

House of Commons (2013) *Syria and the Use of Chemical Weapons*. HC Debates, 29 August, cols 1425–1426. http://www.publications.parliament.uk/pa/cm201314/cmagenda/ob130829.htm last accessed 2 February 2015.

Johnson, P. (2014) Introductory Remarks. *Institute for Fiscal Studies: Autumn Briefing 2014*, 4 December. http://www.ifs.org.uk/uploads/publications/budgets/as2014/as2014_johnson.pdf last accessed 2 February 2015.

Kelly, P. (2011) Red or Orange: The Big Society in the New Conservatism. *Political Quarterly*. 82 (s1), 22–34.

Kerr, P., Byrne, C. and Foster, E. (2011) Theorising Cameronism. *Political Studies Review*. 9 (2), 193–207.

Kirkup, J. (2013) David Cameron's Ally: Our Party Activists are 'Loons', *The Telegraph*, 17 May. http://www.telegraph.co.uk/news/politics/10065307/David-Camerons-ally-our-party-activists-are-loons.html last accessed 2 February 2015.

Lakin, M. (2013) The Ideology of the Coalition: More 'Muscular' than 'Liberal'? *British Politics*. 8 (4), 476–490.

Lee, S. and Beech, M. (2011) (eds) *The Cameron–Clegg Government: Coalition Politics in an Age of Austerity* (Basingstoke: Palgrave Macmillan).

Marshall, P. and Laws, D. (eds) (2004) *The Orange Book: Reclaiming Liberalism* (London: Profile Books).

McAnulla, S. (2010) Heirs to Blair's Third Way? David Cameron's Triangulating Conservatism. *British Politics*. 5 (3), 286–314.

Office for National Statistics (2014) Employment up 37,000 compared with the previous quarter. Labour Market Statistics January 2015 Release. http://www.ons.gov.uk/ons/rel/lms/labour-market-statistics/january-2015/sty-labour-market-statistics--january-2015.html last accessed 2 February 2015.

Ross, T. (2014) David Cameron and Nick Clegg forced to intervene in 'daily' Coalition rows. *The Telegraph*, 5 January. http://www.telegraph.co.uk/news/politics/david-cameron/10551069/David-Cameron-and-Nick-Clegg-forced-to-intervene-in-daily-Coalition-rows.html last accessed 2 February 2015.

The Holy Bible (1611) *Authorised Version*. Isaiah 40. 8. https://www.biblegateway.com/passage/?search=Isaiah+40&version=KJV last accessed 28 January 2015.

2
Indebted and Unbalanced: The Political Economy of the Coalition

Simon Lee

Introduction

On 20 May 2010, when the Coalition published its Programme for Government, two key objectives were identified which would provide the twin benchmarks for evaluating the political economy of the Coalition and its economic policy performance in office. First, and in their foreword to the Coalition's programme, David Cameron and Nick Clegg affirmed their agreement that 'the most urgent task facing this coalition is to tackle our record debts, because without sound finances, none of our ambitions will be deliverable' (Cameron and Clegg, 2010: 7). However, while they believed that '[t]ackling the deficit is essential', they also affirmed that this was not what either of them had entered politics to achieve. On the contrary, the creation of the Coalition had not only provided the means to strengthen and enhance their respective 'visions of a Britain better in every way', but also 'the potential to deliver era-changing, convention-challenging, radical reform' (Cameron and Clegg, 2010: 7). Consequently, a second key objective for the Coalition's economic policies was identified. This would be 'to build a new economy from the rubble of the old', a much broader political economy than simply the alleviation of fiscal deficits. This second objective would encompass support for 'sustainable growth and enterprise, balanced across all regions and all industries', the promotion of 'the green industries that are so essential for our future', 'radical plans to reform our broken banking system and new incentives for green growth', and 'a Britain where social mobility is unlocked' (Cameron and Clegg, 2010: 7).

This chapter uses the twin objectives of budget deficit reduction and the construction of 'a new economy' to evaluate the political economy and economic policy record of the Coalition. By drawing extensively on the reports and data published by the Office for Budget Responsibility (OBR), the most important institutional legacy of George Osborne's tenure at the Treasury, the chapter has reached a clear and definitive conclusion: the Coalition has failed to achieve either of its principal economic policy objectives. First, the Coalition has failed to tackle the budget deficit in the manner it specified in the June 'Emergency' Budget and October Spending Review of 2010. Having inherited public sector net debt of £974.2 billion (62.7 per cent of GDP) from the Brown government, the Coalition's June 2010 Budget had forecast public debt to be £1,284 billion or 69.4 per cent of GDP by the end of March 2015 (Office for Budget Responsibility, 2010: Table C6). At the end of December 2014, United Kingdom public sector net debt (excluding the 'temporary' liabilities of public sector banks) had risen to £1,483.3 billion (80.9 per cent of GDP), or £1,795.0 billion (97.9 per cent of GDP), if the effects of 'temporary' interventions to rescue United Kingdom banks were to be included (Office for National Statistics, 2015a: 37). Coalition economic policy is shown to have evolved through three phases: Plan A or expansionary fiscal contraction; second, the dilution of Plan A; and, third, the adoption of Plan B or 'the long-term economic plan'.

Second, the chapter concludes that the Coalition has failed to build a new economy. Nor has it unlocked social mobility. As the evidence published by its own Social Mobility and Child Poverty Commission has attested, the United Kingdom has remained a 'deeply elitist' society under the Coalition, where the prospects of social mobility and an escape from child poverty have been diminished by declining home ownership and the impact of cuts to welfare (Social Mobility and Child Poverty Commission, 2014: 2). Rather than an economy characterised by sustainable growth and enterprise, and balanced across all regions and all industries, the chapter uses the United Kingdom's consecutive annual current account and trade deficits in every year of the Coalition to illustrate that the economy has not been re-balanced.

Phase one: Plan A: expansionary fiscal contraction

When it was published on 20 May 2010, the Cameron–Clegg Coalition's Programme for Government immediately identified fiscal austerity as its overriding priority. It stated: 'The deficit reduction programme takes precedence over any of the other measures in this agreement, and the speed of implementation of any measures that have a cost to the public finances will depend on decisions to be made in the Comprehensive Spending Review' (HM Government, 2010). Subsequently, the conduct of economic policy under the Coalition can be understood in terms of three phases. During its initial two years in office, the first phase of economic policy was marked, in policy terms, by the announcement and implementation of the June 2010 'Emergency' Budget and the October 2010 Spending Review and Plan for Growth. This phase was the Coalition's Plan 'A' for 'Austerity'. In policy terms, it was characterised by an adherence to the notion of expansionary fiscal consolidation. In rhetorical terms, it was underpinned by the political narrative 'we're all in this together'. This theory held that a reduction in government borrowing would diminish the 'crowding-out' of private sector economic activity by the state, and therefore result in a 'crowding-in' of investment, exports, and an increase in trade's overall share of national income. In practice, GDP fell during the third quarter of 2010, and the second and fourth quarters of 2012, while household real disposable income was to fall from £17,300 in 2010 to £16,900 in 2013 (Office for National Statistics, 2015b).

The thesis that government borrowing and spending may 'crowd out' more productive economic activity by the private sector is not a new one for British politics. The first Thatcher government had tested both theses in its macroeconomic policies in general and its 1981 Budget in particular (Needham and Hotson, 2014). Consequently, when the Coalition took office in May 2010, there was already a long-standing debate among economists and political economists about the efficacy of 'expansionary austerity' or 'expansionary fiscal contraction', i.e. cutting government spending (with the promise of future lower taxes), as a means of entrenching economic recovery, while simultaneously redressing the high levels of public debt incurred during, and in the immediate aftermath of, major financial crises. However, despite several decades of vigorous debate among policy-makers and academics alike, there was far from consensus about the efficacy of fiscal austerity. Indeed, at the very point that the Coalition was announcing its intention to embrace expansionary fiscal contraction, many others, including the International Monetary Fund (IMF) were pointing out its flaws and risks.

In its October 2010 World Economic Outlook, the IMF reported: 'Fiscal consolidation typically has a contractionary effect on output. A fiscal consolidation equal to 1 percent of GDP typically reduced GDP by about 0.5 percent within two years and raises the unemployment rate by about 0.3 percentage points' (International Monetary Fund, 2010:

94). Subsequent IMF research would assert that the contractionary impact of austerity might be greater, and that a 1.0 per cent of GDP fiscal consolidation would not only reduce real private consumption by 0.75 per cent within two years, but also cut real GDP by 0.62 per cent (Guajardo *et al.*, 2011: 29). Indeed, an IMF paper co-authored by its chief economist, Olivier Blanchard, asserted that 'actual multipliers were substantially above 1 percent early in the crisis' (Blanchard and Leigh, 2013: 19).

It should also be remembered that fiscal consolidation was not a policy invented by the Coalition. As Emmerson and Tetlow have noted, in its 2010 Fiscal Responsibility Act, the Brown government was planning to cut public borrowing, as a share of national income, in every year from 2010–11 to 2015–16, and to at least halve borrowing between 2009–10 and 2013–14. As a consequence, Labour planned that public sector net debt would fall, as a share of national income, between 2014–15 and 2014–16, but this would be achieved through cuts in day-to-day public expenditure equivalent to 2.1 per cent of national income, and cuts in public investment expenditure amounting to 0.9 per cent of income (Emmerson and Tetlow, 2015: 17). Although the Coalition duly repealed Labour's Fiscal Responsibility Act, it adopted its own fiscal mandate. This sought both to balance the cyclically adjusted current budget by the end of a rolling five-year forecast horizon, and to deliver a fall in public sector net debt as a share of national income between 2014–15 and 2015–16 (Emmerson and Tetlow, 2015: 19).

In June 2010, George Osborne pledged that he would borrow £452 billion over the lifetime of the 2010–15 parliamentary term. Under his predecessor as Chancellor, Alistair Darling, whom Osborne had accused of reckless profligacy, public debt had risen by £432.4 billion, from £541.8 billion in June 2007 to £974.2 billion in May 2010 (Office for National Statistics, 2015a: 39). Osborne had planned to cut public net borrowing from £149 billion or 10.1 per cent of GDP in 2010–11 to £37 billion or 2.1 per cent of GDP by the end of 2014–15. Public sector net debt would rise from £932 billion or 61.9 per cent of GDP at the end of 2010–11 to £1,284 billion or 69.4 per cent of GDP at the end of 2014–15 (but a declining share of GDP, compared to 70.3 per cent at the end of 2013–14) (HM Treasury, 2010).

The Coalition's fiscal austerity would be achieved principally by cutting public spending by 6.2 per cent of national income more than Labour had planned in March 2010 (Emmerson and Tetlow, 2015: 25). While the Brown government's March 2010 Budget had envisaged a total fiscal consolidation of £109.1 billion, equivalent to 5.8 per cent of GDP, by 2019–20, Emmerson and Tetlow have estimated that the Coalition's November 2010 Autumn Statement had increased this total consolidation to £132.6 billion, or 7.0 per cent of GDP, by 2019–20 (Emmerson and Tetlow, 2015: 20, 21). Subsequently, the December 2014 Autumn Statement was to estimate that the total fiscal consolidation would be £201.8 billion, or 10.7 per cent of GDP. This consolidation would be composed of a net tax increase of 1.2 per cent of national income (or £22 billion in 2015–16 terms) and a net spending cut of 9.5 per cent of GDP (or £180 billion in 2015–16 terms) (Emmerson and Tetlow, 2015: 24). Furthermore, Emmerson and Tetlow have calculated that only Greece (18.3 per cent of GDP), Iceland (17.5 per cent) and Ireland (12.8 per cent) have planned a larger cut in their structural public borrowing in the period from borrowing's recent peak until 2019 (Emmerson and Tetlow, 2015: 28).

Therefore, the Coalition's decision to implement fiscal consolidation during the first phase of its economic policy was a conscious political choice, rather than an inevitable policy decision supported by uncontested economic theory or empirical evidence. Indeed, as Robert Chote, the Director of the Office for Budget Responsibility was later to point out, in a letter to the Prime Minister (dated 8 March 2013), every forecast published by the OBR from the June 2010 Budget onwards had incorporated 'the widely held assumption that tax increases and spending cuts reduce economic growth in the short term' (Chote, 2013). Furthermore, the Coalition had chosen to implement austerity by protecting some departments and programmes, with a knock-on impact on others. The Coalition planned to make real departmental spending cuts of 9.5 per cent between 2010–11 and 2015–16. Austerity would entail real cuts of 8.3 per cent to resource (non-investment) spending and 25.9 per cent to real capital expenditure. As Crawford and Keynes have noted, because inflation proved to be lower than forecast, these cuts were actually 7.8 per cent and 13.6 per cent, respectively. However, because the Coalition chose to protect real expenditure on health, schools and overseas development assistance from the full impact of fiscal consolidation, other departments were confronted with an average 20.6 per cent cut to their budgets between 2010–11 and 2015–16 (Crawford and Keynes, 2015: 151).

Phase two: the dilution of Plan A

During the Coalition's first two years of office, fiscal contraction did not fuel the expected economic expansion. The overall growth performance of the United Kingdom economy under the Coalition's austerity was disappointing. The Office for National Statistics (ONS) has estimated that GDP grew by 1.9 per cent to £1,592 billion during 2010; by 1.6 per cent during 2011 to £1,618 billion; by 0.7 per cent during 2012 to £1,628 billion; by 1.7 per cent during 2013 to £1,655 billion; and by 2.6 per cent during 2014 to £1,698 billion (Office for National Statistics, 2015c: 6). In June 2010, the United Kingdom's real GDP had been forecast to grow by 7.4 per cent from the first quarter of 2010 to the fourth quarter of 2012. In the event, it grew by 3.5 per cent – less than half the forecast rate (Office for Budget Responsibility, 2014b: 24).

Nor did austerity cut borrowing or the budget deficit by the amount or at the pace forecast. Total government activity was supposed to contract by 1.7 per cent of GDP between the first quarter of 2010 and the final quarter of 2012. In practice, it actually grew by 0.1 per cent of GDP, as the government sought to mitigate the failure of business investment, residential investment and net trade to contribute as forecast to economic growth (Office for Budget Responsibility, 2014b: 24). In the face of this disappointing economic performance, Emmerson and Tetlow have highlighted how the pace of fiscal consolidation was allowed to slow by the Coalition. During the first phase of its economic policy, in 2010–11 additional fiscal tightening had amounted to 1.5 per cent of national income, followed by a further 2.3 per cent during 2011–12. However, the realisation that a further acceleration in fiscal tightening might drive the economy into recession persuaded Osborne to loosen fiscal policy, with the result that fiscal consolidation was planned to be only 0.7 per cent of GDP in 2014–15 and 0.6 per cent in 2015–16 (Emmerson and Tetlow, 2015: 25). Furthermore, the December 2012 Autumn Statement planned borrowing of 5.2 per cent of GDP in 2014–15, compared to the Coalition's November 2010 Autumn Statement plans for public borrowing of only 1.9 per cent of national income (Emmerson and Tetlow, 2015: 22). Having also forecast in November 2010 that public sector net debt, as a share of national income, would fall from 68.8 per cent of GDP in 2014–15 to 67.2 per cent in 2015–16, the Coalition was now to forecast in December 2012 that public debt would increase from 79.0 per cent to 79.9 per cent during the same period (Emmerson and Tetlow, 2015: 23).

Welfare spending, so often the rhetorical target of ministerial attacks, actually rose by 2.3 per cent of GDP during the financial crisis and a further 0.2 per cent of GDP between 2009–10 and 2012–13 (Office for Budget Responsibility, 2014a: 97). Indeed, far from being cut back by austerity, the impact of the financial crisis and its longer term aftermath will have been to have increased welfare spending by more than 50 per cent in cash terms, and by around 20 per cent in real terms, during the period from the onset of crisis in 2007–08 towards the end of the planned period of fiscal consolidation in 2018–19 (Office for Budget Responsibility, 2014a: 97). The Coalition chose to protect benefits, including the state pension, for elderly citizens with a tendency to vote (and with a greater proclivity than the general population to vote Conservative). The other fastest rising component of general expenditure was debt interest payments. These were set to rise from their pre-crisis post-war low of 2.1 per cent of GDP to 3.7 per cent of GDP by 2018–19 (Office for Budget Responsibility, 2014a: 105).

The scale of the failure of Plan A to deliver the expected dividend for growth and budget deficit reduction was charted by the OBR's *Forecast Evaluation Report* (FER). In its October 2013 report, the OBR outlined the degree to which its initial June 2010 economic forecasts had proven to be accurate. The report disclosed that by the end of June 2013, real UK GDP had grown by only 3.2 per cent since June 2010, compared to the OBR's initial forecast of real GDP growth of 8.9 per cent (Office for Budget Responsibility, 2013: 16). The principal reason for this 5.7 per cent shortfall had been a 0.9 per cent decline in the contribution of business investment to real GDP. The OBR had recorded a 3.1 per cent expansion, and a paltry 0.7 per cent increase in the contribution of net trade to real GDP, compared to the OBR's original forecast of a 2.6 per cent contribution (Office for Budget Responsibility, 2013: 17). The very sectors of the economy which Plan A had expected to drive 're-balancing' of the economy had failed to deliver. Residential investment had also contributed only 0.6 per cent to real GDP during this period, when forecast to contribute 1.1 per cent. Even private consumption, which had at least contributed 2.2 per cent to the growth of real GDP, had failed to reach its forecast contribution of 3.4 per cent. Only government had delivered a larger contribution to real GDP than forecast (a 0.2 per cent contribution, compared to the OBR forecast of a 2.1 per cent contraction in its contribution) (Office for Budget Responsibility, 2013: Table 2.1, 17). Thus, Osborne's own stated objective of reducing the role of the state, in order to avoid the crowding-out of private investment, especially in manufacturing and exports, had been contradicted.

The OBR had forecast that nominal GDP in the UK would grow by 16.3 per cent, or around £230 billion a year, between June 2010 and the end of June 2013. In the event, the collapse in private business investment meant that nominal GDP grew by only 9.3 per cent or around £130 billion a year, leaving an annual shortfall of £100 billion

(Office for Budget Responsibility, 2013: 20, 26). This reflected the fact that real private investment, which had been forecast to grow by 33.7 per cent from the first quarter of 2010 to the end of the second quarter of 2013, had actually fallen by 10.5 per cent. Private residential investment had also failed to match forecast growth expectations, rising by 6.8 per cent, against a forecast increase of 22.9 per cent. In total, real private investment had fallen by 2.8 per cent, when it had been expected to rise by 32.9 per cent (Office for Budget Responsibility, 2013: Table 2.16, 33). Both the OBR and Osborne had underestimated the weakness of the private sector. While exports during this period had been forecast to increase by 20 per cent, they had actually grown by only 12.5 per cent. Imports had grown by 9.3 per cent, marginally faster than the 9.0 per cent OBR forecast, but this meant that 're-balancing' towards exports and private investment had not occurred (Office for Budget Responsibility, 2013: Table 2.18, 36).

In its October 2014 FER, the OBR confirmed the trends established by its report a year earlier, namely the failure of private investment and net trade to contribute to economic growth and a wider 're-balancing' of the economy. For example, in June 2010 business investment had been expected to rise by 1.7 per cent of GDP, and net trade by 0.8 per cent of GDP, in the period from the final quarter of 2012 to the second quarter of 2014. In the event, business investment had risen by a paltry 1.1 per cent of GDP and net trade a derisory 0.3 per cent of GDP (Office for Budget Responsibility, 2014b: 27). Rather than responding to fiscal consolidation, and the earlier substantial depreciation of sterling during 2008 and 2009, by boosting investment so as to be able to increase their share of export markets, the OBR concluded that United Kingdom exporters had chosen instead to boost their profit margins and not to expand, possibly because of limited confidence or an incapacity to be able to source the credit for expansion (Office for Budget Responsibility, 2014b: 36). Thus, rather than a private sector business investment- and export-led recovery, fiscal consolidation had been marked by an actual decline in the United Kingdom's market share of major export markets, most notably in the euro area (Office for Budget Responsibility, 2014b: 37).

Phase three: Plan B: the 'long-term' economic plan

On 9 September 2013, George Osborne chose to make a keynote speech on the economy from 1 Commercial Street, a private sector development in the City of London. Having begun in 2007, construction on the development had stopped in 2008, but restarted during 2012 – a symbol of the nature of the faltering economic recovery in the United Kingdom: one confined to London and the South East of England. Osborne's message had four elements. First, 'the economic collapse was even worse than we thought', an open admission of miscalculation and the Coalition's complacency in thinking it could re-balance the public finances and national economy within the confines of a single parliamentary term. Second, 'repairing it will take even longer than we hoped', not least because of the Coalition's mistaken faith in expansionary fiscal austerity, and its flawed 'crowding-out' thesis. Third, 'we held our nerve when many told us to abandon the plan', an attempt to make a virtue out of his own arrogance and Coalition obstinacy in the face of overwhelming evidence of the failure of Plan A. Fourth, 'thanks to the efforts and sacrifices of the British people, Britain is turning a corner', a highly questionable assertion which neglected the fact that the majority of the people in England would have to suffer falling real living standards for many further years, given his plans for harsher austerity (Osborne, 2013a).

Osborne's speech marked a turning point in Coalition economic policy for two important reasons. First, in the Conservative political narrative accompanying and justifying austerity, and hereafter in every major speech on the economy made by Osborne or Cameron, they would refer to their economic plan with the newly acquired pre-fix 'long-term', a simple rhetorical recognition of the obvious truth that the Coalition would fail to achieve its planned fiscal consolidation within the timeframe specified in June 2010, a fact symbolised by the earlier extension of the actual period from the originally planned 2015–16, initially to 2016–17 and latterly to 2018–19. Second, Cameron and Osborne's speeches would now include clear mention of their respective ambition to roll back the frontiers of the state further than had previously been envisaged under the Coalition's plans. In effect, they had switched to a Plan B.

This would create clear blue water, ideologically, between them and their principal political opponents, who were unlikely to sign up for such an aggressive attempt to roll back the frontiers of the state. It would also open up the possibility of a majority Conservative government after the 7 May 2015 general election, but only if the Conservatives could manage to boost their opinion poll rating from a consistent share of between 30 and 33 per cent – at least 5 per cent too small for any prospect of an overall parliamentary majority at Westminster. For Cameron, Plan B meant 'building a leaner, more effective state. We need to do more with less. Not just now, but permanently' (Cameron, 2013). For Osborne, it meant 'we will have a surplus in good times as insurance against difficult times ahead. Provided the recovery is sustained, our goal is to achieve that surplus in the next Parliament' (Osborne, 2013b).

The true scale of that ambition was not laid bare fully until the publication of the December 2014 Autumn Statement. It confirmed the new objective in fiscal policy 'to reach a small surplus of 0.2% of GDP in 2018–19 and 1.0% of GDP in 2019–20' (HM Treasury, 2014: 7). Furthermore, 'total public spending was now projected to fall to 35.2 per cent of GDP in 2019–20, taking it below the previous post-war lows reached in 1957–58 and 1999–2000 to what would probably be its lowest level in 80 years' (Office for Budget Responsibility, 2014: 6–7). Indeed, 'Between 2009–10 and 2019–20, spending on public services, administration and grants by central government is projected to fall from 21.2 per cent to 12.6 per cent of GDP and from £5650 to £3880 per head in 2014–15 prices' (Office for Budget Responsibility, 2014d: 7).

As one influential analysis of the implications of Plan B noted, if implemented, government spending would now take a lower share of national income than any year since 1945, and well below the average of 40.4 per cent of GDP in the period since 1948 to 2007–08 (Crawford *et al.*, 2015: 98). Furthermore, Osborne's plans entailed a further £92 billion fiscal consolidation, equivalent to 4.9 per cent of GDP (Crawford *et al.*, 2015: 97). This would necessitate a significant redefinition of the role of the state, unprecedented in modern times, whose shape and consequences would be more profound in its impact than any simple change in the ratio of public spending to GDP could ever convey.

During its tenure, the Coalition had apportioned fiscal consolidation upon the basis of 82 per cent by spending cuts and 18 per cent by tax increases. However, the planned additional fiscal consolidation for Plan B in the next parliament envisaged 98 per cent of fiscal consolidation would be achieved through further spending cuts, and only 2 per cent via tax increases (Emmerson and Tetlow, 2015: 10). Moreover, it was estimated that the IMF's forecast of a 3.5 per cent cut in the United Kingdom's structural borrowing between 2015 and 2019 would be the largest reduction for any of 31 advanced economies (Emmerson and Tetlow, 2015: 29). However, even if this was to be accomplished by a future government, it would in itself be a demonstration of the failure of Plan A for Austerity under the Coalition, as a means of cutting the budget deficit. After all, in 2015 only Japan would have higher structural borrowing than the United Kingdom, and this despite the Coalition having implemented the seventh largest fiscal consolidation, among 31 advanced economies, since the onset of the financial crisis (Emmerson and Tetlow, 2015: 10).

The failure to re-balance the economy

The second great strategic policy objective in the political economy of the Coalition was the construction of 'a new economy from the rubble of the old' through the support of 'sustainable growth and enterprise, balanced across all regions and all industries' (HM Government, 2010: 7). George Osborne's February 2010 Mais Lecture had envisaged 'a new model of economic growth that is rooted in more investment, more savings and higher exports' (Osborne, 2010). The October 2010 Spending Review had lamented the United Kingdom's economy for having become unbalanced, and reliant upon 'unsustainable public spending and rising levels of public debt'. Indeed, the Coalition had insisted 'For economic growth to be sustainable in the medium-term, it must be based on a broad-based economy supporting private sector jobs, exports, investment and enterprise' (HM Government, 2010: 6).

This has not happened. There has not been an investment-, manufacturing-, and export-led recovery. The Coalition has presided over parallel deteriorations in the United Kingdom's balances on its current account, its trade in goods, overall trade account, and its international investment position. For example, during the third quarter of 2014, the United Kingdom's current account deficit widened to £27.01 billion or 6.0 per cent of GDP, constituting the joint largest such deficit since the ONS records began in 1955. This was composed of parallel deficits on its accounts in trade in goods and services (£9.04 billion or 2.0 per cent of GDP in deficit during the third quarter), primary income (£12.59 billion or 2.8 per cent of GDP in deficit), and secondary income (£5.37 billion or £1.2 billion in deficit). The United Kingdom's record surplus on its trade in services (£22.86 billion or 5.1 per cent of GDP) was in no way sufficient to compensate for its deficit on trade in goods (£31.9 billion or 7.1 per cent of GDP) (Office for National Statistics, 2014a: 2, 3). Nor was the United Kingdom's £1.47 billion surplus on its current account with the rest of the world sufficient to counteract its £28.48 billion quarterly deficit with the European Union. The United Kingdom also recorded net liabilities on its international investment position of £450.7 billion at the end of the third quarter of 2014, reflecting external assets abroad of £9,706.1 billion, but larger external liabilities of £10,156.8 billion (Office for National Statistics, 2014a: 1). However it might be measured, the United Kingdom's economic performance under the Coalition had demonstrated precious little evidence of either re-balancing or enhanced international competitiveness during the Coalition's final year in office – a performance consistent with that achieved during the Coalition's previous four years.

The Coalition's greatest strategic failure, which it shares with every United Kingdom government since the mid-1970s, had been the demise of its plans to 're-balance' the economy away from an over-dependence upon financial services and a debt-led, consumer-driven, import-fuelled growth model towards one based upon private sector investment, manufacturing and exports. Every government had delivered annual deficits on the United Kingdom's current account since 1984, and on its trade account since 1982. Moreover, the UK had sustained a combined current and capital account deficit in every year since 1983, and every quarter since the third quarter of 1998. To finance that deficit, the United Kingdom squandered its North Sea Oil revenue, sold off its formerly state-owned utilities to foreign ownership, and engaged in a wider fire sale of national public and private assets which meant, by the end of 2012, no less than 53.4 per cent of United Kingdom quoted shares in the United Kingdom were owned by overseas investors (Office for National Statistics, 2013).

Between 2013 and 2014, total output from the United Kingdom's production sectors increased by 1.4 per cent, with manufacturing output increasing by 2.7 per cent – the strongest annual growth rate since 2010, when output had risen 4.7 per cent. However, during 2011, manufacturing output had grown by only 1.8 per cent, before contracting by 1.3 per cent in 2012 and 0.7 per cent in 2013. While the United Kingdom's GDP had surpassed its pre-downturn peak during the third quarter of 2013, total production output from the United Kingdom in the fourth quarter of 2014 still remained 10.6 per cent below its pre-downturn peak in the first quarter of 2008. Manufacturing output was also 5.4 per cent below its peak (Office for National Statistics, 2015d: 4). This was despite the fact that, among the Group of Seven industrialised economies, the United Kingdom had experienced the smallest decline (6.1 per cent) in its average annual output, as a consequence of the economic downturn which had followed the financial crisis of 2007–08 (Office for National Statistics, 2015d: 5).

The economy had not been re-balanced. Indeed, if anything, it has become even more imbalanced towards the interests of the financial services and overheated property markets of London and the South East of England. For example, during 2013, at the administrative regional level, London had recorded the highest Gross Value Added (GVA) (a measure of the increase in the value of the economy, arising from the production of goods and services) of £40,215 per head; Inner London, at £71,162 per head, the highest GVA at the sub-regional level; and Inner London West, at £135,888, the highest GVA at the local area level (Office for National Statistics, 2014b: 1). This meant that London's regional GVA was 171.9 per cent of the United Kingdom average. It also accounted for £338.475 billion or 22.2 per cent of the United Kingdom's total GVA. Only the South East of England, with a regional GVA of £25,843 per head was above the United Kingdom average of £23,394. All seven other English administrative regions fell below the national average for both the United Kingdom and for England itself (£24,091 per head). Indeed, the North East of England, with a regional GVA of only £17,381 per head or 74.3 per cent of the United Kingdom average was only prevented from being the poorest area by Wales, which registered a GVA per head of only £16,893 or 72.2 per cent of the United Kingdom average (Office for National Statistics, 2014b: 2). There was precious little tangible evidence of any re-balancing between the constituent nations and regions of the United Kingdom.

This failure to re-balance was further highlighted in the United Kingdom's trade figures for 2014, during which it recorded a trade deficit of £34.8 billion, following the deficits of £37.1 billion during 2010, £23.8 billion in 2011, £34.5 billion in 2012, and £33.7 billion in 2013. Thus, in every year of the Coalition, the United Kingdom had recorded an overall deficit in its trade with the rest of the world. However, these figures disguised the scale of the deficit on the United Kingdom's trade in goods. Despite George Osborne's pledge of a 'march of the makers', as part of the overall re-balancing of the national economy, during 2014 the United Kingdom had recorded a record total deficit on its trade in goods of no less than £119.9 billion, following deficits of £97.4 billion in 2010, £96.5 billion in 2011, £109.0 billion in 2012, and £112.6 billion in 2013 (Office for National Statistics, 2015e: 32). Osborne had aimed for the United Kingdom's total exports to double to £1 trillion by 2020, but in 2014 total exports were only half that total, having fallen £16 billion from their £516 billion total in 2013 (Office for National Statistics, 2015e: 32). Although the United Kingdom had achieved a record £85.1 billion surplus on its total trade in services in 2014, following surpluses of £60.4 billion in 2010, £72.7 billion in 2011, £74.5 billion in 2012, and £78.9 billion in 2013, this performance had been nowhere near sufficient to compensate for, or eliminate, the much larger deficit on the United Kingdom's trade in goods (Office for National Statistics, 2015e: 32).

The simple but unavoidable truth, demonstrated not only by the United Kingdom's economic performance under the Coalition, but by the deficits on its trade and current accounts in every year since the early 1980s, is that the United Kingdom has continued to produce too few goods and services which people in other economies wish to purchase. In particular, the size of the United Kingdom's manufacturing sector, at between 10 and 11 per cent of GDP, and upon which the Coalition's aspirations to 're-balance' the economy were founded, is too small to achieve that purpose, especially when compared with the service sector's overwhelming 78.4 per cent contribution to national output. While the United Kingdom's total exports of merchandise, which amounted in 2013 to $542 billion or a 2.9 per cent share of world merchandise trade (and a 15 per cent annual increase), were sufficient to rank it as only the eighth largest exporter in the world, its higher ranking as the world's second largest exporter of commercial services generated only $293 billion or a 6.3 per cent share of world markets (World Trade Organization, 2014: 28). Furthermore, at $4645 billion in 2013, world exports of commercial services were only 24.6 per cent of the total of $18,816 billion of world exports of merchandise goods (World Trade Organization, 2014: 26). Like it or not, for the foreseeable future, as had been the case for at least the past 30 years, the United Kingdom would need to focus upon its output from its production industries (above all, from manufacturing), if it was ever to re-balance its economy, as the Coalition had proposed.

As the Coalition's own official statistics have attested, George Osborne is but the latest Chancellor of the Exchequer to have devised a strategy for national economic recovery which began as a 're-balancing' programme for British industrial modernisation, but which soon metamorphosed into a short-term, property-led and debt-fuelled pre-general election consumer boom. He has simply followed the precedent for economic booms and busts set by Chancellors from Anthony Barber to Gordon Brown. There is precious little evidence of re-balancing away from financial speculation towards manufacturing or significant additional private investment in new enterprises, products or services. Plan A has failed in its own terms, but the developmental state piloted by the Treasury under Osborne has continued to pick the usual winners.

It has not simply been 'business as usual' for the City of London's most speculative financial market traders. On the contrary, during the Coalition's tenure, such markets have prospered as never before. Thus, the Bank for International Settlements has noted how, in the period from April 2010 to April 2013, foreign exchange turnover in London increased by 47 per cent, and London's share of the $5.3 trillion a day turnover in foreign exchange rose to 41 per cent, way ahead of the United States' 19 per cent, Singapore's 5.7 per cent and Japan's 5.6 per cent (Bank for International Settlements, 2013). Any thought that re-balancing under the Coalition might extend to reining in, or taxing more aggressively, the derivatives traders and speculators who have so generously funded the Conservative Party under David Cameron's leadership, has been belied by the Coalition's inaction on that particular front.

Osborne's interventions have also been heavily skewed in favour of asset-owning interests. The largesse shown towards private, buy-to-let landlords, heavily subsidised by taxpayer-funded housing benefits to their tenants and tax relief on their investments, has contrasted with the Coalition's strategic failure to ensure a flow of cheap credit to United Kingdom enterprises in general, and manufacturers in particular. The Bank of England's *Trends in Lending* reports have documented how, in every year of the Coalition, businesses, both large and small, have actually been net lender to the banking sector, rather than net borrowers (Bank of England, 2015a: 4). This was despite the provision of £375 billion of Quantitative Easing with the express purpose of fuelling the flow of funds to private business. Moreover, under the Bank of England's Funding for Lending Scheme Extension, statistics for the third quarter of 2014 showed that United Kingdom businesses had once more been net lenders to financial institutions, this time to the tune of £2.4 billion (Bank of England, 2015b: 4).

On 12 January 2015, and as part of the gathering general election campaign, David Cameron delivered a speech in Nottingham on the theme of 'Britain living within its means'. He claimed that in election year, the choice was clear. On the one hand, there was 'the road to recovery', 'a strong and competent team', 'a proven record', and 'a long-term economic plan that is turning our country around', offered by his Conservative Party. On the other, on offer to the electorate was 'the path to ruin', 'chaos', 'confusion', 'uncosted plans' and 'the spectre of more debt' offered by all other political parties (Cameron, 2015). Cameron's speech did not identify re-balancing among its key themes. While Cameron was delivering his speech in the East Midlands, in the English West Midlands, Jaguar Motors was announcing the creation of 1,300 new jobs to assemble Jaguar's first sports utility vehicle at its Solihull plant. Tata Motors, the Indian owner of Jaguar, had already invested no less than £1.5 billion in the Solihull plant. It had not only increased the volume of production, but also doubled the workforce in only three years to 9,450. It was a rare but welcome example of major private sector investment in manufacturing in England, but highlighted a willingness of foreign owners to invest strategically and profitably in high-technology engineering and manufacturing. In direct contrast, throughout the Coalition's tenure, British business leaders had demonstrated their preference for a business model founded upon the employment of workers on zero-hours contracts for the manufacture of low added value, low productivity products, harnessing a much lower level of private investment than their major international competitors.

Presciently, at Solihull some 39 years earlier, on 9 July 1976, the leader of a major political party had laid out a nine-point plan for industrial recovery, and issued the starkest of warnings to an audience of industrialists: 'The recovery and expansion of British industry is the most important single task of the next Government. On that everything else depends'. Indeed, the speech had reached the most chilling of conclusions: 'we must export or die ... we must manufacture, or die even quicker' (Thatcher, 1976). The author of that speech had been none other than Margaret Thatcher. She had failed to deliver the recovery and expansion of British industry, the single most important task her government faced. The United Kingdom had not exported. Two million jobs in manufacturing had died with her governments' failure. In failing to re-balance, the Coalition had simply repeated this strategic failure in industrial modernisation.

Conclusion

Any evaluation of the political economy of the Coalition must acknowledge that many of the trends in the United Kingdom's economic policy and performance which the Coalition's policies failed to reverse had long predated the Coalition's formation in May 2010. Indeed, the flaws and failures of the Coalition's particular British model of political economy, were very much those of all previous state-led programmes of British modernisation attempted by successive governments since 1970 (Lee, 2015). The 2010 Conservative Party general election manifesto promised to create a more balanced economy by giving 'strong backing to the growth industries that generate high-quality jobs around the country' (Conservative Party, 2010: 11). In practice, the Coalition continued to base economic recovery on debt- and property market-fuelled consumption. It offered 'strong backing' only to the City of London and to the very banks whose reckless lending led to the 2007–08 financial crisis. Decisions on major infrastructure funding continued to show the same London and South East-centric bias. The £375 billion Quantitative Easing programme provided banks with a plentiful supply of cheap credit to rebuild their balance sheets, and asset-owning billionaires with the opportunity to transform London's skyline in a binge of upmarket property developments, cementing London's status as one of the world's principal tax havens for capital. Credit did not reach private sector manufacturing companies or exporters who were expected to invest, innovate and expand their output to re-balance the economy. Instead, cheap credit fuelled lending to an overheating property market in London and other property 'hotspots' elsewhere in England.

The Coalition's Programme for Government and June 2010 'Emergency' Budget envisaged that George Osborne's 'Plan A' for fiscal consolidation would be sufficient to have balanced the budget by the end of 2015–16. In practice, Plan A has failed. By the end of March 2015, the Coalition had implemented fiscal consolidation amounting to 5.8 per cent of GDP (Emmerson and Tetlow, 2015: 31). However, this meant that, of its planned fiscal consolidation, the Coalition had only achieved just over half (as measured as a share of national income) or around one third (if measured in cash terms). Around 60 per cent of the further cuts to public spending envisaged by David Cameron and George Osborne's Plan B 'long-term economic plan' would have to be during the next parliament (Office for Budget Responsibility, 2014b: 6).

The Coalition's fiscal and economic legacy was to leave the United Kingdom facing a further four years of fiscal consolidation until 2019–20. Indeed, the supplementary data supplied by the OBR to accompany the December 2014 Autumn Statement once more highlighted the extent to which future economic recovery was planned to be built upon the accumulation of further private indebtedness and consumption, rather than private investment, manufacturing and exports. The OBR's March 2014 *Economic and Fiscal Outlook* had forecast that total household liabilities would increase from £1,685 billion at the end of the second quarter of 2015 to £2,251 billion by the end of the first quarter of 2019 (Office for Budget Responsibility, 2014c). However, OBR data in December 2014 suggested instead that the increase in private indebtedness would be even larger. Total household liabilities were now forecast to soar by £883 billion from £1,756 billion at the end of June 2015 to £2,639 billion by the end of March 2020, and less than two months before the 2020 general election. In other words, Osborne's future economic recovery would depend upon individual consumers' willingness to borrow more and spend an average of more than £170 billion a year (Office for Budget Responsibility, 2014d: Table 1.11). However much austerity was expected to apply to public finances in the next parliament, it would not be expected to apply to personal private finances. A reduction in cheaper, public debt and borrowing would be accompanied by a projected increase in more expensive, private debt as 'Generation Debt' was once more expected to engage in sustained consumption.

As Tom Clark and Anthony Heath have reminded us in *Hard Times: The Divisive Toll of The Economic Slump*, their important analysis of the political economy of austerity and social security reforms, 'there is no getting away from the fact that the decision to defend or cut this expenditure remains a political choice' (Clark and Heath, 2014: 227). Austerity was the wrong political choice in 2010. It remained the wrong political choice in 2015. It was a flawed strategy, implemented in England by a failed and failing British state.

References

Bank of England (2015a) *Trends in Lending: January 2015* (London: Bank of England).

Bank of England (2015b) *Funding for Lending Scheme Extension: Usage and Lending Data* (London: Bank of England). www.bankofengland.co.uk/markets/Pages/FLS/extensiondata.aspx (accessed 12 February 2015).

Bank for International Settlements (2013) *Triennial Central Bank Survey of Foreign Exchange and Derivatives Market Activity in 2013* (Basle: Bank for International Settlements).

Blanchard, O. and Leigh, D. (2013) *Growth Forecast Errors and Fiscal Multipliers*. IMF Working Paper 13/1 (Washington, DC: International Monetary Fund).

Cameron, D. (2013) Speech to Lord Mayor's Banquet Mansion House, City of London, 12 November.

Cameron, D. (2015) Speech, Nottingham, 12 January.

Cameron, D. and Clegg, N. (2010) 'Foreword' to HM Government, *The Coalition: Our Programme for Government* (London: The Cabinet Office).

Chote, R. (2013) Letter from Robert Chote to Prime Minister, 8 March. www.budgetresponsibility.org.uk/letter-from-robert-chote-to-the-prime-minister/ (accessed 1 February 2015).

Clark, T. and Heath, A. (2014) *Hard Times: The Divisive Toll of The Economic Slump* (New Haven, CT: Yale University Press).

Conservative Party (2010) *Invitation to Join the Government of Britain: The Conservative Manifesto 2010* (London: Conservative Party).

Crawford, R. and Keynes, S. (2015) Options for further departmental spending cuts. In Emmerson, C., Johnson, P. and Joyce, R. (eds) *The IFS Green Budget, February 2015* (London: Institute for Fiscal Studies).

Crawford, R., Emmerson, C. and Tetlow, G. (2015) Public finances: a dicey decade ahead? In Emmerson, C., Johnson, P. and Joyce, R. (eds) *The IFS Green Budget*, February 2015 (London: Institute for Fiscal Studies).

Emmerson, C. and Tetlow, G. (2015) Public finances under the coalition. In Emmerson, C., Johnson, P. and Joyce, R. (eds) *The IFS Green Budget*, February 2015 (London: Institute for Fiscal Studies).

Guajardo, J., Leigh, D. and Pescatori, A. (2011) *Expansionary Austerity: New International Evidence*. IMF Working Paper 11/158 (Washington, DC: International Monetary Fund).

HM Government (2010) *The Coalition: Our Programme for Government* (London: The Cabinet Office).

HM Treasury (2010) *Budget 2010*, HC 61 (London: The Stationery Office).

HM Treasury (2014) *Autumn Statement*. Cm.8961 (London: The Stationery Office).

International Monetary Fund (2010) *Recovery, Risk, and Rebalancing: World Economic Outlook October 2010* (Washington, DC: International Monetary Fund).

Lee, S. (2015) *The State of England: The Nation We're In* (London: Palgrave Macmillan).

Needham, D. and Hotson, A. (eds) (2014) *Expansionary Fiscal Contraction: The Thatcher Government's 1981 Budget in Perspective* (Cambridge: Cambridge University Press).

Office for Budget Responsibility (2010) *Budget Forecast: June 2010* (London: Office for Budget Responsibility).

Office for Budget Responsibility (2013) *Forecast Evaluation Report: October 2013* (London: Office for Budget Responsibility).

Office for Budget Responsibility (2014a) *Welfare Trends Report: October 2014* (London: Office for Budget Responsibility).

Office for Budget Responsibility (2014b) *Forecast Evaluation Report: October 2014* (London: Office for Budget Responsibility).

Office for Budget Responsibility (2014c) *Economic and Fiscal Outlook: March 2014*, Cm8820 (London: Office for Budget Responsibility).

Office for Budget Responsibility (2014d) *Economic and Fiscal Outlook: December 2014*, Cm8966 (London: The Stationery Office).

Office for National Statistics (2013) *Ownership of UK Quoted Shares, 2012* (Newport: Office for National Statistics). www.ons.gov.uk/ons/dcp171778_327674.pdf (accessed 12 January 2015).

Office for National Statistics (2014a) *Balance of Payments, Q3 2014* (Newport: Office for National Statistics).

Office for National Statistics (2014b) *Regional Gross Value Added (Income Approach), December 2013* (Newport: Office for National Statistics).

Office for National Statistics (2015a) *Public Sector Finances, December 2014* (Newport: Office for National Statistics).

Office for National Statistics (2015b) *Personal and Household Finances in the UK* (Newport: Office for National Statistics). http://visual.ons.gov.uk/ uk-perspectives-personal-and-household-finances-in-the-uk/ (accessed 13 February 2015).

Office for National Statistics (2015c) *GDP Preliminary Estimate, Q4 2014* (Newport: Office for National Statistics).

Office for National Statistics (2015d) *Index of Production: December 2014* (Newport: Office for National Statistics).

Office for National Statistics (2015e) *UK Trade: December 2014* (Newport: Office for National Statistics).

Osborne, G. (2010). A New Economic Model: 2010 Mais Lecture, Cass Business School, London, 25 February.

Osborne, G. (2013a) Speech on The Economy, Commercial Street, London, 9 September.

Osborne, G. (2013b) Speech to The Conservative Party Annual Conference, Manchester, 30 September.

Osborne, G. (2014) Chancellor George Osborne's Budget 2014 speech, 19 March.

Social Mobility and Child Poverty Commission (2014) *Elitist Britain?* (London: Social Mobility and Child Poverty Commission).

Thatcher, M. (1976) Speech to the Industry Conference ('A Programme for Industrial Recovery'), 9 July.

World Trade Organization (2014) *International Trade Statistics 2014* (Geneva: World Trade Organization).

3
Education Policy: Consumerism and Competition

Simon Griffiths

Introduction

In December 2010, Michael Gove, the Secretary of State for Education, wrote that it had become fashionable 'to refer to the Coalition as a Maoist enterprise. Not so much because the government is inhabiting the wilder shores of the Left but because of the relentless pace of modernisation being pursued across government' (Gove, 2010). Over the next four years, the government undertook one of the most radical periods of structural reform to the English education system in recent history, driving through a decentralising, marketising agenda from the centre. In this chapter, I focus on the Coalition's policies on schools and higher education in England. Education is a devolved responsibility in the UK, with Scotland, Wales and Northern Ireland operating different systems. There is much else that could have been written about developments in education policy in England since 2010: 'early years' intervention; the raising of the school leaving age; apprenticeships; the scrapping of the Educational Maintenance Allowance; the 'bonfire' of quangos such as the General Teaching Council for England and the Qualifications and Curriculum Development Agency; or assessment reform to GCSE and 'A' levels. However, it is the radicalism of the Coalition's reforms to the system of schools and higher education in England that is likely to be the most significant legacy of the Coalition.

'Academisation': trying to let go

Schools policy in England has been dominated by the devolution of power from local authorities to Academies and Free Schools. The

Academies Act (2010) was one of the first pieces of legislation to be passed by the Coalition. The Act made it possible for all state schools in England to gain Academy status. Academies are publicly funded independent schools which are, to some degree, free from local authority and national government control. Other freedoms include setting their own pay and conditions for staff, freedoms concerning the delivery of the curriculum, and the ability to change the length of their terms and school days (Department for Education, 2010a). Schools can either convert to Academies on their own or as part of a 'chain', run by private or charitable organisations such as ARK Schools, Harris Federation or the Priory Federation. Most Academies are at secondary level, although there are some at primary level too. In May 2010, Gove wrote to every head teacher in England to encourage them to apply for Academy status (Shepherd, 2010).

The Academies Act also made possible the introduction of 'Free Schools'. This was part of the Coalition Agreement, which agreed to 'promote the reform of schools in order to ensure that new providers can enter the state school system in response to parental demand' (HM Government, 2010: 28). Derived from Charter Schools in the United States and Free Schools in Sweden, English Free Schools are all-ability state-funded schools, free of local authority control. Under the plans it became much easier for charities, businesses, or groups of parents, for example, to set up new schools (Department for Education, 2010b).

To some degree, 'academisation' is an extension of the Grant Maintained Schools introduced by former Conservative Secretary of State for Education Kenneth Baker in 1988 (Baker, 2010), and a continuation of the Academies brought in by New Labour from 2000. Under New Labour, Academies were largely an attempt to give 'a fresh start' to struggling schools. However, the Coalition has pushed forward the idea more strongly than the previous Labour administration and seems more relaxed about the lack of central control upon Academies than many in the Labour Party (Griffiths, 2009: 107). The result has been a dramatic rise in the number of Academies. By late 2014 there were around 4,000 Academies, almost 20 times as many as in 2010. In addition, 250 Free Schools have been created by parents or community groups, with another 112 pending, all with the same freedoms as Academies, although often smaller in scale (*The Economist*, 2014). 'Academisation' under the Coalition is on a different scale to anything that went before.

Critics of the Academy model have, among other things, attacked the freedoms these new schools have – described by one critic as their ability to teach 'creationism instead of literacy' (Sellgren, 2010). The curricular freedom afforded to Academies jarred with Gove's own beliefs on the ways in which certain subjects should be taught. Other critics have worried that Academy schools increase segregation in a variety of ways, including introducing covert selection to screen out pupils less likely to be successful (Sellgren, 2013; Wiborg, 2010: 14–15). For some analysts, the Academy Programme, with its extensive use of private companies to run schools, combined with a politics of austerity, means the 'privatisation' of education in England (West and Bailey, 2013). To some of these critics, academisation marks 'the beginning of the end of state education' (Ball, 2012).

Michael Gove carried out this academisation alongside a conflicting and arguably contradictory battle with teachers about the way in which some subjects, particularly history, are taught. This reflected much older tensions within Conservative policy (Exley and Ball, 2011: 97). On the one hand, there had been a strong belief in 'letting go' and devolving power away from the state to schools and parents. Margaret Thatcher's Secretary of State for Education and Science, Sir Keith Joseph, for example, was influenced by neoliberal arguments for education vouchers, which give parents a choice of school and allow them to 'top up' their vouchers to send their children to fee-paying schools should they wish. Gove's devolution of power to Academy schools became part of this decentralising, anti-centralist tendency in the Conservative Party. On the other hand, Conservatives have often believed in the power of the state to set standards and create social norms. Kenneth Baker, Joseph's successor at the Department for Education, provided an example of this rather more centralist line of thinking, establishing a National Curriculum in England, Wales and Northern Ireland in 1988.

At times, Gove was also prone to these centralising tendencies. For example, he put his weight firmly behind the new draft national curriculum for history, launched in February 2013, which focused on chronological narratives, 'great' men and women, and fostering British national identity. Gove's proposals were met with derision by professional historians and teachers. This is history taught to promote the idea of 'The Wonderfulness of Us', as the historian Richard J. Evans argued (Evans, 2011). Evans reminded Gove that 'history isn't a form of instruction in citizenship. It's an academic subject in its own right' (Evans, 2013). During his time in office, Gove was torn between devolving power to schools and determining what they should be teaching and how. In office, Gove was not entirely able to 'let go'.

The Pupil Premium: markets for social justice

A second significant policy development was the introduction of a 'Pupil Premium'. The policy had been put forward by both Coalition partners in their 2010 manifestos, although details varied. The Premium was described as a 'priority policy' by the Liberal Democrats (Liberal Democrats 2010: 7, 34, 101), while the Conservatives argued 'we can't go on giving the poorest children the worst education' and saw the Pupil Premium – 'extra funding for children from disadvantaged backgrounds' – as the solution (Conservative Party, 2010: 53). Given the agreement over a policy of this kind, plans for a Pupil Premium were set out in the Conservative and Liberal Democrat Coalition Agreement, reached on 11 May 2010. The agreement stated that the Coalition would 'fund a significant premium for disadvantaged pupils from outside the schools budget by reductions in spending elsewhere' (Conservative Party and Liberal Democrats, 2010: 1).

The introduction of the Pupil Premium was confirmed in the Comprehensive Spending Review (CSR) on 20 October 2010, committing government to 'a substantial new premium worth £2.5 billion targeted on the educational development of disadvantaged pupils' (HM Treasury, 2010: 7). This was expanded upon in the Schools' White Paper, *The Importance of Teaching*, published two days later, which argued that reforms to the way in which England's schools are funded were needed, both to 'help the most disadvantaged and encourage new providers into the state school system' (Department for Education 2010c: 80). The White Paper confirmed that the new Pupil Premium would provide 'additional money for each deprived pupil in the country' and that '£2.5 billion a year on top of existing schools spending will be spent on the Pupil Premium by 2014–15'. The government argued that the policy would mean

head teachers [would] have more money to spend on offering an excellent education to [poorer] children: it will also make it more likely that schools will want to admit less affluent children; and it will make it more attractive to open new Free Schools in the most deprived parts of the country. (Department for Education, 2010c: 81)

However, the White Paper also noted: 'This money will not be ring-fenced at school level, as we believe that schools are in the best position to decide how the premium should be used to support their pupils' (Department for Education, 2010c: 81).

The redistributory nature of the Pupil Premium also means that some schools with pupils from better-off backgrounds will have to make significant cuts. This was made explicit by Gove, when he admitted that 'there will be some schools that will have less' (Prince, 2010). Indeed, the independent economic research centre, the Institute for Fiscal Studies (IFS) has estimated that 87 per cent of secondary pupils and 60 per cent of primary pupils are in schools where funding will fall (Harrison, 2010). A leaked Treasury report suggested that as many as 40,000 teaching jobs could be lost (Stratton, 2010). The extent of the changes in the schools' budget led to a backlash against the Pupil Premium, particularly in the right-wing press – which strongly associated the scheme with the Liberal Democrats, despite its existence in both Coalition partners' manifestos. *The Daily Mail*, for example, argued that schools in 'middle-class' areas were being hit twice, from cuts to the building programme (the news of which was mismanaged by the Department and caused Gove early difficulties in his role) and from the redistribution of money as a result of the Pupil Premium (Shipman, 2010).

Support for the policy was stronger in theory than in practice. The IFS was cautious, arguing that while

> in principle, a Pupil Premium could narrow the achievement gap between advantaged and disadvantaged pupils ... Schools are unlikely to actively recruit more disadvantaged pupils as a result of the Pupil Premium: the premium would need to be very high to sufficiently reduce the disincentive for schools to attract such pupils, and schools' ability to select pupils is also limited to some extent by the School Admissions Code. The Pupil Premium may lead to a small reduction in covert selection by schools but is unlikely to significantly reduce social segregation. (Chowdry *et al.*, 2010: 2)

The latest available research at the time of writing argued that, 'It is too early to measure the impacts of the Pupil Premium on attainment', which 'constitutes a relatively small proportion of schools' total income' (3.8 per cent for primary schools with high levels of free school meals in 2011/12, for example). However, case studies have shown that the Pupil Premium was often significant when it was earmarked for spending on disadvantaged pupils or to help schools to support these pupils, in the face of pressures on budgets (Carpenter *et al.*, 2013).

Schools policy: conclusions

There is some degree of policy continuity between the Coalition and New Labour on schools policy. The introduction of a Pupil Premium and of Academies and Free Schools can be seen as part of the increasing use of market mechanisms in the school system. Academies and Free Schools mark a long-term move from a (theoretically) universal service to one in which the school system is shaped by parental choice, with the quasi-market subsidised by a premium for poor pupils to increase social justice. A more radical application came from the comedian Paul Merton, who once joked that it would sometimes be easier if parents were given choice of children, rather than just schools. The idea for the Pupil Premium is said to have originated from Julian Le Grand in the 1980s, writing at the time as a 'market socialist', who originally described a 'positively discriminating voucher' (Freedman and Horner, 2008: 4). From 2003 to 2005, Le Grand was a senior policy adviser to Tony Blair, focusing on introducing choice and competition into education and health care, and there are obvious overlaps between Blair's public service agenda and that of the Coalition. In this respect, the Gove reforms mark a continuation of the 'marketisation' of the school system through allowing a greater diversity of provision of schools to increase parental choice and the use of market incentives to persuade schools to compete for poorer pupils. However, it is the scope and radicalism of Gove's reforms – rolling a market-based system to all schools – that constitutes a step-change from anything that went before. This marketising approach is consistent with the radical reform of higher education undertaken during the same period.

Higher education reform: the Browne Review

The Coalition government has carried out radical reforms to higher education in England, marketising the system in a way that raises several difficult questions about the nature of the higher education system. In November 2009, John Browne, the former Group Chief Executive of BP and a cross-bench peer, agreed to lead a report making 'recommendations to Government on the future of fees policy and financial support for full and part-time undergraduate and postgraduate students' (The Browne Report, 2010). Browne had been approached by Lord Mandelson, then Labour Secretary of State for Business, Innovation and Skills. Mandelson discussed the Review's membership with David Willetts, at the time the Conservative Shadow Universities Secretary, to ensure Conservative 'buy-in' and to make sure that both parties were 'committed to ensuring its independent nature' (Gill, 2009). The Coalition Agreement committed the government to waiting for Lord Browne's final report into higher education funding in England before setting policy (the other nations of the UK having different funding arrangements).

The Browne Report – more formally *Securing a Sustainable Future for Higher Education: an independent review of higher education funding and student finance* – published its findings on 12 October 2010. Among other things, the Review argued that there should be no limit on fees charged by universities and that government should underwrite fees up to £6,000, with universities subject to a levy on all fees charged above that level. In addition, a new body, the Higher Education Council, would be responsible for investing in priority courses, setting and enforcing quality levels and improving access. It should have the power to bail out struggling institutions and would be able to explore options such as mergers and takeovers if institutions faced financial failure. There was also scope for new providers to enter the system and offer higher education teaching. In terms of how this affected students, Browne proposed that students should not have to pay any tuition fees up front, but would begin to pay their loans back (with interest) after graduation when their earnings reached £21,000. Browne assumed that 'if fees can be deferred, then participation can be protected' (The Browne Report, 2010: 26). Browne's claim appears to be holding out so far, with an Independent Commission on Fees' report in 2014 finding a slight increase in the number of people from disadvantaged backgrounds going to university since 2010 (Independent Commission on Fees, 2014: 10–13), although this might be partly due to a lack of employment opportunities elsewhere in the economy.

David Willetts, then Minister of State for Universities and Science, announced the government's response to the Browne Review on 3 November 2010. Although the thrust of the Review was accepted, there were some differences. In particular, the government put forward an absolute cap on fees of £9,000 per year. This cap was in the face of opposition from some elite universities which were threatening that any cap would lead to them opting out of the state system entirely and going private (Garner, 2010: 22). Oxford, in particular, has continued to push for a £16,000 a year cap, and it is possible that these reforms will find their way into Conservative policy should the party win the next election (*The Telegraph*, 2014). In an effort to mitigate criticisms that the Review would discourage poorer potential students from applying, the government also proposed that universities charging fees of over £6,000 per year would have to contribute to a National Scholarships program and that there would be a stricter regime of sanctions encouraging high-charging universities to increase participation. Despite government assurances that this would lead to price variation in the market, the overwhelming majority of universities charge fees at the top rate (Grove, 2013). While early policy had allowed universities unlimited recruitment of students with AAB grades or above at 'A' level, it was announced in the 2013 Autumn Statement that there would be no limits at all on student recruitment after 2015 (Morgan, 2013). It remains to be seen whether and how this reshapes the higher education landscape, although a significant rise in student numbers and a fall in academic quality of student are both predicted (Hillman, 2014). By and large, however, it was recognisably a 'Revised Browne Review' that found its way into legislation. In the 2014 Autumn Statement, the system of loans was also extended to postgraduate students (Coughlan, 2014).

The consequences of the Browne Review

The adoption of a 'Revised Browne Review' has several consequences: party political, fiscal and socio-economic. In party political terms, the Review caused severe problems for the Liberal Democrats. In courting the party as potential partners in the Coalition, the Conservatives recognised that the future funding of higher education was a divisive issue. The Liberal Democrats went into the 2010 general election on a manifesto pledge to 'scrap unfair university tuition fees' (Liberal Democrats, 2010: 33) with every Liberal Democrat MP elected in 2010 – much to their subsequent discomfort – signing a pledge stating that they would 'vote against any increase in fees in the next parliament and to pressure the Government to introduce a fairer alternative' (National Union of Students, 2010). Opposition to increased tuition fees was a potent vote winner for the party, especially among student voters. As such, the Coalition Agreement noted that 'If the response of the Government to Lord Browne's report is one that Liberal Democrats cannot accept, then arrangements will be made to enable Liberal Democrat MPs to abstain in any vote' (Conservatives and Liberal Democrats, 2010: 5). Liberal Democrats were therefore not bound to the increase in tuition fees.

Yet, despite these promises, the Liberal Democrat leadership supported the government's proposals. It split the party. In December 2010, 28 Liberal Democrats voted in favour of the government's proposals, despite their pre-election pledge. Breaking with the government line, 21 Liberal Democrat MPs voted against the government's proposals to raise tuition fees in higher education. It was the most serious split the Coalition had faced and destroyed many voters' trust in the Liberal Democrats. The party had polled 34 per cent shortly before the 2010 General Election – above both the Conservatives and Labour (their actual May 2010 General Election result had given them 23 per cent of the vote). By January 2011, the same polling organisation gave the party just 7 per cent of the vote. In 2012, Nick Clegg apologised for breaking the pledge to oppose any increase in tuition fees (Wintour and Mulholland, 2012). In made no difference to his party's fortunes: the damage had been done and the legislation remained in place. The Liberal Democrats have flat-lined in the polls since that date. At the time of writing (December 2014), their polling figures were 6 per cent in one poll. The party faces an uncertain future.

Second, the new university funding system appears to have created long-term fiscal problems. The combination of high student debt and a 30-year write-off for student loans means that many graduates will never fully repay their debt. The IFS has estimated 73 per cent will have some debt written off at the end of the repayment period, compared with 32 per cent under the old system. The average amount written off will also be substantial – about £30,000 (Crawford and Jin, 2014). This is threatening to create a funding 'black hole' in future, in which government, as the underwriter, will end up indirectly subsidising higher education by writing off billions of pounds in student debt. This is ironic, given that the Coalition reforms were designed to make universities less reliant on the taxpayer. Ironically, the government is likely to find it has saved little or no public money by trebling fees to £9,000 and scrapping the direct grant. In November 2014, the Commons Business, Innovation and Skills Select Committee argued that the UK was reaching a 'tipping point' for the loan system's financial viability and called for an urgent review of the system's sustainability, a request the government refused (House of Commons Business Innovation and Skills Committee, 2014). The same month a cross-bench committee described the new funding system as the 'worst of all worlds': government is investing heavily but getting no credit for it; students feel they are paying substantially more despite having debts written off; and universities are seen as rolling in money from fees when their grant has been cut and fee income has failed to rise with inflation (Weale, 2014).

Finally, in socio-economic terms, the 'Revised Browne Reforms' introduced a model of marketised higher education. While earlier reforms under New Labour ended 'free' university education, the Coalition has gone far further in turning students into consumers. This has radical implications for the way in which higher education is provided in England. The literary critic and intellectual historian, Stefan Collini, noted that:

> Essentially, Browne is contending that we should no longer think of higher education as the provision of a public good, articulated through educational judgment and largely financed by public funds (in recent years supplemented by a relatively small fee element). Instead, we should think of it as a lightly regulated market in which consumer demand, in the form of student choice, is sovereign in determining what is offered by service providers (i.e. universities). (Collini, 2010)

In particular, Collini highlights the almost complete withdrawal of the present annual block grant that government makes to universities to underwrite their teaching. This, he argued, 'signals a redefinition of higher education and the retreat of the state from financial responsibility for it' (Collini, 2010).

The marketisation of higher education also raised worries about those institutions that fail. Thompson and Bekhradnia argue that:

> It is too simplistic to argue, as the report does, that those universities that are not as popular as others will 'raise their game' if they see their numbers falling, or will be allowed to fail. Those universities may be doing a perfectly good job, but be less well endowed, have less appeal, may be geographically disadvantaged ... But nevertheless the national interest would be ill served if they were to fail. (Thompson and Bekhradnia, 2010: 56)

Students as consumers determine which institutions, departments or modules survive, not – in the main – a decision about what research and teaching is in the public interest. A university, like any other business, can now fail if it does not attract students as consumers, regardless of whether it was carrying out work in the public good.

Conclusion

In July 2014, Gove was replaced as Education Secretary, ending one of the most radical periods of reform to the structure of the education system in England in recent history. Gove's 'Maoist' zeal for revolution, in the face of opposition from many in schools and universities, was seen to have created too many enemies in the educational establishment in the run up to a general election. By the time he left office, Gove had taken to referring to his opponents as 'the Blob', after the 1950s science fiction film about an unstoppable amoeba-like alien mass. Gove saw himself, as the introduction to this chapter has shown, as a hero fighting this group's 'progressive' grip over education (Robinson, 2014). His replacement, Nicky Morgan, has taken a more pacifying approach to her critics.

The Coalition's legacy in education will be significant. The administration has used the power of a strong central state to marketise the education system in England. Market-based approaches have also been used to promote social justice, as is the case with the Pupil Premium. It remains to be seen if the incentive structures encouraging good schools to take disadvantaged pupils have been successful in improving educational attainment for the least well off. Above all else, the Coalition is likely to be remembered for the Academies programme, which is increasingly severing the link between schools and the democratically accountable local authorities that once ran them. In many cases, the local authority has been replaced by private companies, which run chains of Academies, effectively privatising some schools. This marks a radical departure from the politics of the recent past.

In higher education, this marketising approach has gone even further. This agenda has created enormous problems for the Liberal Democrats, whose electoral popularity never recovered from their decision to accept the Browne Report after running in 2010 on a promise to reject any rise in university fees. If the current fees arrangements survive, it is uncertain that they will save the Exchequer money in the long run. It is likely that the state will end up paying off significant student debt. What is striking is that recent reforms have turned higher education into a commodity. Little regard has been shown by the Coalition for the argument that the market will not adequately defend subjects, departments or institutions that it would be in the broader public interest to protect, but which student demand will not. In office, Cameron's Coalition has used the strong central state to push through market-based reforms that are, in this case, fundamentally changing the structure of education in England.

References

Baker, M. (2010) Gove's academies: 1980s idea rebranded?, *BBC News*, 1 August. www.bbc.co.uk/news/education-10824069 (accessed 24 December 2014).

Ball, S. J. (2012) The reluctant state and the beginning of the end of state education. *Journal of Educational Administration and History*, 44(2): 89–103.

Carpenter, H., Papps, I., Bragg, J., Dyson, A., Harris, D., Kerr, K., Todd, L. and Laing, K. (2013) *Evaluation of pupil premium* (London: Department for Education). www.gov.uk/government/publications/evaluation-of-pupil-premium (accessed 24 December 2014).

Chowdry, H., Greaves, E. and Sibieta, L. (2010) *The pupil premium: assessing the options* (London: Institute for Fiscal Studies). www.ifs.org.uk/publications/4776 (accessed 24 December 2014).

Collini, S. (2010) Browne's Gamble. *London Review of Books*, 32(21), 4 November: 23–5. www.lrb.co.uk/v32/n21/stefan-collini/brownes-gamble (accessed 24 December 2014).

Conservative Party (2010) *Invitation to Join the Government of Britain: The Conservative Manifesto 2010* (London: The Conservative Party).

Conservative Party and Liberal Democrats (2010) *Conservative Liberal Democrat Coalition Negotiations – Agreements reached – 11 May 2010*. www.conservatives.com/~/media/Files/Downloadable%20Files/agreement.ashx?dl=true (accessed 24 December 2014).

Coughlan, S. (2014) Postgraduate student £10,000 loans, *BBC News*, 3 December. www.bbc.co.uk/news/education-30293964 (accessed 24 December 2014).

Crawford, C. and Jin, W. (2014) *Payback time? Student debt and loan repayments: what will the 2012 reforms mean for graduates?* (London: Institute for Fiscal Studies). www.ifs.org.uk/comms/r93.pdf (accessed 24 December 2014).

Department for Education (2010a) *Academy Conversion Process* (London: Department for Education). www.education.gov.uk/schools/leadership/typesofschools/academies (accessed 24 December 2014).

Department for Education (2010b) *Opening a Free School* (London: Department for Education). www.education.gov.uk/schools/leadership/typesofschools/freeschools (accessed 24 December 2014).

Department for Education (2010c) *The Importance of Teaching: The Schools White Paper 2010, Cm.7980* (London: The Stationery Office). www.education.gov.uk/publications/eOrderingDownload/CM-7980.pdf (accessed 24 December 2014).

Evans, R. (2011) The Wonderfulness of Us: The Tory Interpretation of History. *London Review of Books*, 33(6), 17 March: 9–12. www.lrb.co.uk/v33/n06/richard-j-evans/the-wonderfulness-of-us (accessed 24 December 2014).

Evans, R. (2013) Michael Gove's history curriculum is a pub quiz not an education. *New Statesman*, 21 March. www.newstatesman.com/culture/culture/2013/03/michael-gove%E2%80%99s-history-curriculum-pub-quiz-not-education (accessed 24 December 2014).

Exley, S. and Ball, S. J. (2011) Something old, something new ... understanding Conservative education policy. In H. Bochel (ed.), *The Conservative Party and Social Policy* (Bristol: Policy Press).

Freedman, S. and Horner, S. (2008) *School Funding and Social Justice: A Guide to the Pupil Premium with a Foreword by Julian Le Grand* (London: Policy Exchange).

Garner, R. (2010) LSE raises spectre of private universities. *The Independent*, 27 October. www.independent.co.uk/news/education/education-news/lse-raises-spectre-of-private-universities-2117396.html (accessed 24 December 2014).

Gill, J. (2009) Lord Browne to lead fees review. *Times Higher Education*, 9 November. www.timeshighereducation.co.uk/news/lord-browne-to-lead-fees-review/409011.article (accessed 24 December 2014).

Gove, M. (2010) Michael Gove: my revolution for culture in classroom. *The Telegraph*, 28 December. www.telegraph.co.uk/education/8227535/Michael-Gove-my-revolution-for-culture-in-classroom.html (accessed 24 December 2014).

Griffiths, S. (2009) Cameron's Conservatives and the public services. In M. Beech and S. Lee (eds), *The Conservatives Under David Cameron: Built to Last?* (London: Palgrave Macmillan).

Grove, J. (2013) Nine out of 10 universities opt to charge maximum fee. *Times Higher Education*, 11 July. www.timeshighereducation.co.uk/news/nine-out-of-10-universities-opt-to-charge-maximum-fee/2005624.article (accessed 24 December 2014).

Harrison, A. (2010) Most pupils in schools which will face cuts, claims IFS, *BBC News*, 22 October. www.bbc.co.uk/news/education-11607269 (accessed 24 December 2014).

Hillman, N. (2014) A guide to the removal of student number controls. (London: Higher Education Policy Institute). www.hepi.ac.uk/wp-content/uploads/2014/09/Clean-copy-of-SNC-paper.pdf (accessed 24 December 2014).

HM Government (2010) *The Coalition: Our Programme for Government – Freedom, Fairness, Responsibility* (London: The Cabinet Office).

HM Treasury (2010) *Spending Review 2010*. Cm. 7942 (London: The Stationery Office).

House of Commons Business, Innovation and Skills Committee (2014) Student loans system reaching tipping point – News from Parliament, 22 July. www.parliament.uk/business/committees/committees-a-z/commons-select/business-innovation-and-skills/news/report-student-loans/ (accessed 24 December 2014).

Independent Commission on Fees (2014) *Analysis of Trends in Higher Education Applications, Admissions, and Enrolments* (London: Independent Commission on Fees). www.independentcommissionfees.org.uk/wordpress/wp-content/uploads/2014/08/ICoF-Report-Aug-2014.pdf (accessed 24 December 2014).

Liberal Democrats (2010) *Liberal Democrat Manifesto 2010: Change that works for you – building a fairer Britain* (London: Liberal Democrats).

Morgan, J. (2013) Undergraduate numbers cap 'to be abolished' – Osborne, *Times Higher Education*, 5 December. www.timeshighereducation.co.uk/news/undergraduate-numbers-cap-to-be-abolished-osborne/2009667.article (accessed 24 December 2014).

National Union of Students (2010) Lib Dem MPs sign the pledge. http://web.archive.org/web/20101212020612/http://www.nus.org.uk/Campaigns/Funding-Our-Future/Lib-Dem-MPs-sign-the-pledge (accessed 3 February 2015).

Prince, R. (2010) Schools in better-off areas will lose cash to aid poor, *The Telegraph*, 24 October. www.telegraph.co.uk/education/8084535/Schools-in-better-off-areas-will-lose-cash-to-aid-poor.html (accessed 24 December 2014).

Robinson, N. (2014) Gove – Battling 'The Blob', *BBC News*, 3 February. www.bbc. co.uk/news/uk-politics-26008962 (accessed 24 February 2014).

Sellgren, K. (2010) Tory free schools 'barking mad' says teachers' leader: BBC News education reporter at the ATL conference, *BBC News*, 31 March. www. bbc.co.uk/news/1/hi/education/8597572.stm (accessed 24 December 2014).

Sellgren, K. (2013) Academies could 'fuel segregation'. *BBC News*, 10 January. www.bbc.co.uk/news/education-20960500 (accessed 24 December 2014).

Shepherd, J. (2010) English primary and secondary schools offered chance to become academies. *The Guardian*, 26 May. www.guardian.co.uk/ education/2010/may/26/primary-secondary-schools-academies (accessed 24 December 2014).

Shipman, T. (2010) School cash cuts hit middle classes twice as government reveals funding and building programmes will be slashed. *The Daily Mail*, 25 October. www.dailymail.co.uk/news/article-1323438/School-cash-cuts-hit-middle-classes-twice-government-reveals-funding-slashed.html (accessed 24 December 2014).

Stratton, A. (2010) Spending review will lead to loss of 40,000 teaching jobs. *The Guardian*, 20 October. www.guardian.co.uk/politics/2010/oct/20/spending-review-loss-teaching-jobs (accessed 24 December 2014).

The Browne Report (2010) *Securing a Sustainable Future for Higher Education: An Independent Review of Higher Education Funding & Student Finance* (London: Department for Business, Innovation and Skills).

The Telegraph (2014) Fees at Oxbridge could rise to £16,000 a year. *The Telegraph*, 3 August. www.telegraph.co.uk/education/educationnews/11009244/Fees-at-Oxbridge-could-rise-to-16000-a-year.html (accessed 24 December 2014).

The Economist (2014) The new school rules, *The Economist*, 11 October. www. economist.com/news/britain/21623766-academies-programme-has-transformed-englands-educational-landscape-new-school-rules (accessed 24 December 2014).

Thompson, J. and Bekhradnia, B. (2010) The Independent Review of Higher Education Funding: an analysis (London: Higher Education Policy Institute). goo.gl/EqCsy1 (accessed 3 February 2015).

Weale, S. (2014) Student loan system 'worst of all worlds'. *The Guardian*, 18 November. www.theguardian.com/education/2014/nov/18/higher-education-commission-funding-challenges-sustainability (accessed 4 December 2014).

West, A. and Bailey, E. (2013) The development of the academies programme: 'privatising' school-based education in England 1986–2013. *British Journal of Educational Studies* 61(2): 137–59.

Wiborg, S. (2010) *Swedish Free Schools: Do they work? LLAKES Research Paper 18* (University of London: Centre for Learning and Life Chances in Knowledge Economies and Societies).

Wintour, P. and Mulholland, H. (2012) Nick Clegg apologises for tuition fees pledge. *The Guardian*, 20 September. www.theguardian.com/politics/2012/ sep/19/nick-clegg-apologies-tuition-fees-pledge (accessed 24 December 2014).

4
The Big Bang: Health and Social Care Reform under the Coalition

Holly Jarman and Scott L. Greer

The May 2010 Coalition Programme for Government was full of what seemed to be fresh ideas, including promises about how the new government would reform and improve the NHS. The document suggested a great synergy between Conservative and Liberal Democratic ideals, almost going so far as to outline an ideology that could guide future NHS reforms:

> [T]ake Conservative thinking on markets, choice and competition and add to it the Liberal Democrat belief in advancing democracy at a much more local level, and you have a united vision for the NHS that is truly radical: GPs with authority over commissioning; patients with much more control; elections for your local NHS health board. Together, our ideas will bring an emphatic end to the bureaucracy, top-down control and centralisation that has so diminished our NHS. (HM Government 2010a: 8)

In hindsight, the problems are obvious. The 'Conservative thinking on markets, choice and competition' is not just Conservative and far from new – it represents the continuation of a bipartisan consensus on how to fix the NHS that grew out of reforms under Thatcher, Major, Blair and Brown. And while these ideas have been implemented in a wide-ranging reform programme that is, indeed, 'radical', the 'Liberal Democrat belief in advancing democracy at a much more local level' has not been embedded in current health policy structures and ideas.

The NHS has seen greater centralisation under the Cameron government, combined with a fragmentation of the centre. The Cameron government has followed and extended the path laid out by

Labour, and, like Labour, has searched for but failed to find a set of governance structures that separate NHS management from political influence. As one Secretary of State is replaced by another, one structural reform agenda is layered over the previous reforms, often at breakneck speed (Jarman and Greer, 2010). The result is a series of rapid, yet largely unproven, structural changes in the organisation of health services in England.[1]

Taken together, the reforms led by the Cameron government have radically altered the nature of health and social care policies and structures, moving faster and further along the trajectory laid out by previous governments. Strongly infused with Conservative ideology, these reforms were improbable, are likely to be unstable, and continue to cast a shadow of uncertainty over the future of the NHS.

Grand reform in the style of New Labour: Andrew Lansley, 2010–2012

The Coalition's first Health Secretary, Andrew Lansley, came into office with a grand reform agenda developed in Opposition. His term in office was dominated by the interaction between austerity and his reforms. On entering office, the Coalition promised to increase spending in real terms in each parliamentary year, implying that other departments' budgets would be cut to compensate for that additional spending (HM Government 2010a: 24); this is certainly more money than was allocated to other departments such as local government, but given the tendency of health expenditure to increase as a percentage of GDP in every society it felt like an annual cut to many in the NHS.

In the government's first White Paper on health, *Equity and Excellence: Liberating the NHS* (HM Government, 2010b), the Coalition pledged to do what every government since 1979 had pledged, but failed, to do: create a stable and long-lasting organisational structure for the NHS that could improve the quality of care and make the NHS more efficient by introducing greater competitive elements, all while devolving power to local communities and patients. Strikingly, the White Paper and draft Bill were both more radical than the Conservative Party document Lansley had written in Opposition; his responses to snags that civil servants identified (e.g. questions about the position of Strategic Health Authorities (SHAs)) appear to have been the most radical ones available (e.g. abolition of SHAs). Notably, the White Paper stated that 'the debate on health should no longer be about structures and processes, but about priorities and progress in health improvement for all' (ibid.: 6).

This agenda seemed radical to many. To Lansley (and many in his party leadership), these were incremental, not radical reforms (Timmins, 2012). Core ideas contained in the White Paper, such as the notion that the NHS could achieve huge efficiency savings by simplifying its management structures and concentrating spending on 'front line' services, a reduction in the number of arm's length bodies and executive agencies, a move towards greater numbers of foundation trusts, and shifting functions carried out by the Department of Health (DH) to centralised quangos, maintained continuity with the previous government's reform agenda (HM Government, 2010b; Gershon, 2004; Department of Health, 2007; Greer and Jarman, 2007).

Drawing on this White Paper, the government put forward its first major reform legislation, the Health and Social Care Bill, in January 2011. The Bill contained a range of measures designed to address some very familiar complaints and assumptions about the NHS that stretch back to the narratives of the Thatcher governments during the 1980s. In terms of structure, the proposals criticised central 'top-down' control of the NHS, as well as putatively wasteful intermediate territorial units; in terms of expertise, the familiar refrain of 'managers not politicians' was a core part of the proposal; and in terms of ideals, the Bill clung closely to the assumption that greater competition and commissioning would improve the quality and efficiency of care (Greer *et al.*, 2014).

Despite the Coalition's stated aim to avoid the frequent and extensive structural reforms of previous governments, the proposals aimed to fix perceived problems largely by creating new organisational units and abolishing others. The government promised that Clinical Commissioning Groups (CCGs) made up of local GPs would be able to access expanded budgets to buy care on behalf of local patients, proposed to make all NHS trusts into foundation trusts (privatising or merging those deemed incapable), and to eliminate SHAs and Primary Care Trusts (PCTs).

At the centre, the English NHS would be managed differently, with core responsibilities of the DH moved to four new agencies: (1) An executive non-departmental body, the NHS Commissioning Board (later named NHS England, or NHSE for short) would take on central commissioning and overall system maintenance, e.g. interventions when providers go bankrupt; (2) An executive agency, Public Health England (PHE), would be responsible for national-level public health functions not devolved to local government; (3) The Care Quality Commission (CQC) would ensure quality; while (4) Monitor would be responsible for market regulation, preventing 'anti-competitive' practices, and (together with NHSE) setting the national tariff.

Confronting criticism

The proposal ran into serious trouble. At the Liberal Democrat Spring Conference in March 2011, members rebelled against the party leadership, opposing aspects of the Bill related to sub-contracting services to private companies and fears that companies would be able to 'cherry pick' lucrative contracts, leaving other essential services underprovided (Wintour and Stratton, 2011). A March 2011 Special Conference of the BMA called for the Bill to be withdrawn (GPonline, 2011). Sean Donnelly, an enterprising MC, created an 'Andrew Lansley Rap' that mixed criticism of 'Equity and Excellence' with derogatory comments about the Health Secretary and drew even more attention to the reforms.

Over the course of the Bill's passage, the opposition, if anything, increased. In February 2012, Channel Four News reported that the Health and Social Care Bill was opposed outright by the Royal College of GPs, Royal College of Nursing, Royal College of Midwives, Royal College of Pediatrics and Child Health, Royal College of Physiotherapy, Faculty of Public Health, British Geriatric Society, Chartered Society of Physiotherapy, and the Community Practitioners and Health Visitors Association. Other groups, including the Royal College of Radiologists, British Psychological Society and the Patients' Association, were unwilling to support the Bill in its existing [February 2012] form (Channel Four News, 2012; Hart, 2012). In addition to the official positions adopted by professional associations, many more votes, polls and surveys of members indicated opposition to the reforms (Hart, 2012; Golding, 2012). Even some Clinical Commissioning Groups (Oxford City Locality, Tower Hamlets, and City and Hackney CCGs) opposed the Bill on the grounds that it would distract from, or even harm, efforts to improve patient care (Hart, 2012; Rogers, 2012; Pulse, 2012; Rimmer, 2012). The Bill received unqualified support from the National Association of Primary Care. Other organisations, including the NHS Alliance, NHS Confederation and the Foundation Trust Network, expressed qualified support, raising some concerns about how the proposals would be implemented (Channel Four News, 2012; Hart, 2012).

What was the criticism about? Rudolf Klein divided the numerous critics into the indignant and the incredulous (Klein, 2013). The incredulous, including the bulk of political observers, focused on the lack of an obvious reason to make such big changes. The NHS was performing extremely well by historical standards and was facing very large effective budget cuts (since health care cost inflation tends to be above general inflation, even a real-terms increase can feel like a cut). Conservatives rarely poll well as stewards of the NHS; there was an obvious case for leaving the NHS alone, taking credit when possible, and focusing political energy elsewhere. Instead, the government was pursuing an enormously disruptive reorganisation that could not help but reduce NHS efficiency and effectiveness during the transition, with no obvious justification.

The indignant felt they had an answer: a combination of right-wing ideology and personal desire for profit was motivating the Conservatives to break up the NHS and replace it with something that would have more individualised financial exposure for patients (less redistribution) and more private sector profit. They focused on the extent to which the NHS reforms promised to introduce the private sector: for commissioning support (i.e. managing CCGs) and as providers of services across the NHS, from telephone support (NHS 111, replacing a national service with local contractors) to cancer care management. They also focused on the extent to which the reforms fit with long-standing Conservative plans to break up the NHS as a single organization (Reynolds *et al.*, 2011; Reynolds and McKee, 2012), and the extent to which the reforms would allow private sector provision to enter the system and 'cream-skim' lucrative services (Hunter, 2013; Peedell, 2011; Reynolds *et al.*, 2012). Critics' complaints included cataloguing the large number of Conservative MPs and party leaders, and supportive figures from other parties, who had interests in firms that stood to profit from more pluralist NHS provision.[2]

Widespread criticism of the reform proposals forced the Cameron government to take an unusual step. In April 2011, despite the legislation having already passed the committee stage, the government announced that there would be a 'pause' in pushing the measures forward (Lansley, 2011).

A committee of experts named the NHS Future Forum and led by Steve Field, former Chair of the Royal College of GPs, would lead this 'listening exercise' (Triggle, 2011). It was promptly criticised for not including the many important health groups that had flatly opposed the Bill. The 'Future Forum' reported in June, and the government accepted all but one of its recommendations. Lansley said that his 'red lines' had not been crossed, and in June the BMA called for Lansley's resignation on the grounds that he had misled them about the Bill and its effects

(King's Fund, 2013; Jaques, 2012). The Health and Social Care Bill passed the Commons in September after over 1,000 amendments. After more opposition and amendment in the Lords, the Health and Social Care Act passed through the House of Lords and received royal assent in March 2012. One effect of this convoluted and much-amended passage was that the original relative clarity of the White Paper was diluted; while it remained possible to characterise the main architecture of the system in Lansley's terms, important details such as 'failure regimes' for when a provider goes bankrupt, and ultimate responsibility for service provision, were changed quickly and quietly.

Conclusion

For most outside observers, Klein's 'incredulous', the great puzzle surrounding the Lansley reforms is how they came to be at all (d'Ancona, 2013). They were not promised in the Coalition Programme for Government; they contravened the expressed intention of the Coalition to avoid major NHS reorganisation; they were a major distraction from fiscal and redistributive agendas that really interested the government; they came when the NHS was performing as well as it ever had (creating a problem for spin doctors who had to reinterpret excellent performance in light of their proposal for complete reorganisation) and they attracted the opposition of essentially everybody in the health politics arena. Almost any theory of British politics suggests that some hurdle – the civil service, the Treasury, the Prime Minister (or the Deputy Prime Minister), the interest groups, or parliament – would have stopped it.

The most popular explanations include a lack of oversight from the centre of government in Number 10 and the Treasury; Lansley's personal stubbornness and hold over his fellow ministers (many of whom had worked for him when he was research director for the Conservative Party); Lansley's reputation for health expertise, supplemented by his long stay in the Shadow Health portfolio; Cameron and Nick Clegg's aversion to the micromanagement they associated with New Labour; and Lansley's conceptual case that his plans were a continuation of Labour's health policies though he seemed to assume full implementation of things Labour had only considered, such as widespread practice-based purchasing (d'Ancona, 2013; Timmins, 2012).

Standing back, the striking thing is how personalistic and agency-focused these explanations are. Neither institutional constraints on government such as parliamentary scrutiny, nor administrative ones such as risk registers, nor political ones such as massive opposition from interest groups and even the minority Coalition party, were able to block the reforms. It is popular to comment on the constraints facing UK governments. This thoroughgoing reform of the NHS, carried out essentially because Cameron, George Osborne and perhaps Clegg supported or failed to control Andrew Lansley, is a reminder that such talk can be taken too far. Seen in comparative terms, a Westminster government can be tremendously powerful; its structure and lack of veto points leaves tremendous agency for a few people at the centre and magnifies any failings in their interpersonal relations and thought patterns (Butler *et al.*, 1994; King and Crewe, 2013). If they choose to blunder, they are unusually capable of it.

Social care

While it is common to discuss NHS politics in isolation from social care, the distinction has always been difficult to manage. Social care budgets are separate, as are the organisations tasked with social care and the scale on which it is planned (the DH and NHS on one side, versus the Department for Work and Pensions, Department for Communities and Local Government, and local government on the other). The people, analysts and political profile are all different. Nevertheless, the connection between social care and health care is vitally important in the lives of people who interact with them and to the budgets of the organizations involved.

This issue has long been condensed down to the catchphrase 'bed blocking', in which an expensive NHS bed is occupied by somebody who requires some level of personal or nursing care but not the health care resources of the NHS. In theory these patients, for their own benefit (hospitals are infantilising and dangerous places filled with infectious diseases) and for very large public savings, should move as quickly as possible to social care of some sort, as organised by the local government. In theory, good social care can inexpensively keep some people (such as many elderly or disabled) from entering hospital in the first place, e.g. by minimising trip hazards at home.

Under the Coalition and its reduced local government and benefits budgets, the relationship between health and social care began to deteriorate more dramatically. One reason is that the long-predicted ageing of the English population is happening; there are more people in various states of physical disrepair who need some level of care every year. They are not necessarily more expensive, but they do require different kinds of care. The other main reason is that the Coalition has been especially hard on local government budgets; as has long been the case, routing social care through local government budgets makes it easy for the central government to make cuts and for local governments to prioritise something other than social care. Budgetary constraint in local government social care (exacerbated by other changes to the benefit system) eventually feeds back into increased health expenditure. These two reasons led to increased reports and activity, which exposed the budgetary and political difficulties that the Coalition faced.

In the same month as the introduction of the Health and Social Care Bill (July 2010), the Commission on Funding of Care and Support, led by Andrew Dilnot, began its work. The Commission was tasked with making recommendations 'on how to achieve an affordable and sustainable funding system or systems for care and support' of adults in England (Dilnot Commission, 2010: 1). In July 2011, the Dilnot Commission released its final report (Dilnot Commission, 2011). The Commission's recommendations were (by design) very much in line with those put forward by the previous government (HM Government, 2009).

The Commission recommended capping the lifetime contribution to adult social care costs at somewhere between £25,000 and £50,000, ideally £35,000. Above this cap, each individual would receive support from the state. They recommended that means-tested support should continue for those with 'lower means', and that the asset threshold for those in residential care should be increased from £23,250 to £100,000. For those in residential care, there should be a standardised expectation set for the amount that they contribute to their general living costs of between £7,000 and £10,000 per year. Regarding eligibility for care services, the Commission recommended that rules should be set centrally rather than at the local level, calling for more objective eligibility criteria. Those who entered adulthood with care needs should be eligible for state support and not subject to means testing. To tackle the problems associated with the complexity of the system, the Commission recommended that assessment of carers should be rationalised, with carers assessed alongside the person they are caring for, and more information provided to help carers understand the system. Adult social care and health services should be better integrated. Finally, the government should implement a new information and advice strategy to raise public awareness of the care system and how it works.

In July 2012, the government simultaneously published a White Paper on care and support, a draft Bill on social care, and a 'progress report' on social care funding reform, was also published, outlining the government's preferred options for social care reform (HM Government, 2012). The progress report took a very different tone to the Dilnot

Commission's recommendations. It lacks the Dilnot Commission's emphasis on fairness and de-emphasises issues key to the Dilnot recommendations, such as housing sell-offs and means-testing thresholds (ibid.). Instead, the report emphasises individual choice, ownership and responsibility, and relies heavily on stimulating community support as a means to reduce the number of older people in crisis (ibid.).

Nevertheless, the White Paper *Caring for Our Future* retains the Dilnot Commission's core recommendation that the government should establish national standards for service eligibility. In it, the government 'agrees that the principles of the Commission's model would be the right basis for any new funding model' – a cap on lifetime earnings and an increase in the threshold at which means-tested support is taken away (HM Government, 2012: 6). Principled agreement did not mean money, however. The Commission estimated that implementing the reforms with a lifetime contribution cap of £35,000 would cost the government £1.7 billion (Dilnot Commission, 2011). The Cameron government was nervous about committing to more spending, stating 'Given the size of the structural deficit and the economic situation we face, we are unable to commit to introducing the new system at this stage' (HM Government, 2012: 6).

Accountability by telephone: Jeremy Hunt – 4 September 2012 to present

If the original mystery surrounding Andrew Lansley was how he was allowed to do what he did, there was less mystery when a September 2012 reshuffle moved him from Health and into the much less important role of Leader of the House of Commons. He was replaced by Jeremy Hunt, who was moved out of the Department of Culture, Media and Sport where he had been entangled with the business interests and travails of Rupert Murdoch. In the history of NHS reorganisations, there has been a long-standing pattern in which ministers associated with major reforms were followed by ministers whose job was to manage implementation and keep it from major political crisis. Hunt's brief was clearly to do that: keep the NHS from being a major political problem before the 2015 election. He was not the most obvious figure to do this. He had co-authored two books calling for the NHS to be replaced with arrangements that transfer responsibility to individuals.[3]

Conservative efforts to argue that the NHS did indeed need their major reform were buttressed by the Mid-Staffordshire Inquiry, called by the incoming Coalition to re-investigate a case of bad care in a Midlands hospital that had already been the subject of an inquiry. It reported in February 2013 with an astounding 290 recommendations.[4] Despite its sheer volume of evidence and ideas, it failed to make it clear that something demonstrably terrible was happening at the hospital (due to a dispute about how to adjust death rates in order to identify an excessive death rate). Then, despite cataloguing failures by everybody from the DH to MPs' surgeries, it settled blame on a few hospital managers. This report diffused many ideas and actions into health debate and led to increased nurse–patient ratios, but as a political moment compared to other NHS scandals such as the Bristol heart surgery scandal it fizzled.

The reorganised NHS was to go live on 1 April 2013, with a few months of (expensive) parallel running as the new structure developed. The NHS Commissioning Board was formally launched in October 2012 and renamed itself NHS England (NHSE). By April 2013 Monitor had undergone a major shake-up, with most of its old staff replaced by a mixture of management consultants and antitrust lawyers. Public Health England largely inherited staff from the old Health Protection Agency, and much of the old DH moved over to NHSE (Greer *et al.*, 2014).

Monitor and NHSE were clearly supposed to be the dominant actors in the new NHS. They jointly set the tariffs for NHS procedures. The two had a somewhat unclear relationship, and each had an ingrained theory of the NHS and its role. On one hand, Monitor – staffed by people from outside the NHS, mostly with management consulting or antitrust backgrounds – was responsible for financial controls within trusts, and a competitive market. The basic theory is that the NHS has purchasers (CCGs and NHSE) who will do best if they can enjoy multiple bids from financially sound providers. This theory suggests the strict application of competition policy and law, and a focus on market entry (since more competition produces better results). The 'Any Willing Provider' policy entrenches this, making it clear that NHS organisations should not have advantages over outside and private sector bidders. It also creates a tension within Monitor: is it there to enforce competition, or to assure financial balances?

NHS England also has dual responsibilities: for commissioning a huge volume of centrally commissioned services; and for ensuring that commissioning works. This means that as the dominant purchaser it can shape the NHS; no hospital can ignore its commissioning, and a CCG that diverges from its broad direction will have trouble implementing its preferences. NHSE is also primarily staffed by people who had been doing NHS management work in the DH and presumably brought their outlooks and ideas along. Both Monitor and NHSE are, therefore, in a position to produce broad direction for the NHS, but neither is clearly superior and they have different orientations and tools.

In October 2014 the new Chief Executive of NHS England, former Blair advisor and private sector health lobbyist in the US Simon Stevens, produced an effort to articulate a vision for the NHS backed by the power of NHSE, a 'Five year forward view'. Articulated in a language of priorities and management to which the NHS is accustomed, and welcomed by NHS managers looking for a central direction, it was not intellectually radical in its focus on support for prevention and care outside of hospitals, but was striking for the form it gave and for the echoes of Labour priorities. It also took the government's promises of autonomy seriously, laying out an agenda for advocacy as well as commissioning. It called for a 'radical upgrade in prevention and public health' and said NHSE would 'advocate for stronger public health-related powers for local government and elected mayors' (NHS England, 2014: 3). Within the NHS, it promised more support for carers, better partnership with voluntary organisations and local communities, and more power for patients over their care. The vehicle would be a menu of 'radical new care delivery solutions' that the CCGs could select and work with their local trusts to provide (ibid.: 4).

The key bet in the 'FYFV' as it is often called is on integrated systems, a model that is heavily espoused by American health management thinkers but generally unimplemented by other health care systems, and which rests on a surprisingly thin evidence base. The idea is to cut through older debates about the roles of GPs, commissioning, and hospital care by transitioning to systems in which an organisation, presumably built out of a foundation trust, takes on more and more primary care services, using its flexibility to improve primary care and thereby reduce the costs of hospitalisation. Whether this can work well within the existing legislative framework is unclear; at a minimum, Monitor might well develop an interest in trying to maintain an NHS market by forcing competition between integrated systems.

On the ground, meanwhile, the reforms meant that the NHS underwent serious disruption that coincided with the start of the serious financial constraints. Foundation Trusts have been winners over several NHS reforms; Trusts (self-governing hospitals or systems) have become the most solid part of the architecture of the NHS since their first creation in 1989. On the commissioning side, the elimination of PCTs has, if anything, increased Trust power. PCTs were always weak and inexpert, with remarkably high executive turnover. CCGs are substantially still PCTs, but with a severely disrupted organisation and an extra link called Commissioning Support Units (CSUs) that the GPs on the CCG hire to commission for them. One CSU staffer commented to Greer in June 2014 that he and his colleagues regard the GPs as having the expertise and influence of lay board members (Anonymous, 2014). Studies suggest that while GPs often have some good skills at choosing doctors and hospitals for their patients, they have neither time nor expertise to do system-wide commissioning, and so in each NHS reform commissioning duties have fallen on somebody else, such as public health officers or professional managers. As was foreseen, GPs mostly want to do clinical, not managerial, work (Black, 2010).

Even a well-funded and relatively stable NHS, such as that of 2010, produces problems and complaints and a desire for government intervention. The unstable, politicised, reorganised, and less well-funded NHS of the Coalition years produced many more. Like its predecessor governments, the Coalition has failed to avoid the trap of demanding compliance from the centre. Unlike its predecessor governments, however, the Coalition had left itself few tools for intervention. Self-restraining legislation had left the Secretary of State with the crudest of tools – literally, calling the NHS to account on the telephone. By mid-2013, NHS managers were complaining about government demands for frequent, in-depth progress reports. In 2013 it emerged that Hunt had personally telephoned the Chief Executives of five hospital trusts that had failed to meet Accident and Emergency waiting times. Such demands for compliance and explanations of failure are at odds with the Coalition's stated intent to separate management of the NHS from the fickle, short-term demands of politics and politicians (Clover, 2013; Clover and Barnes, 2013; Greer *et al.*, 2014: 9).

Meanwhile, the tension between health and social care policy and finance has been causing increasingly large problems. If the start of the Coalition suggested that the government might take a new direction, the end of the Coalition was centred around the quite predictable difficulties with people who were in expensive NHS accommodation rather than local authority social care; a squeezed NHS, a tightly squeezed local government sector, and a failure to develop a new funding or administrative structure. Local authorities and the NHS were complaining about breakdowns in patient pathways and the resulting expense; it was possible to argue that the real-terms increases for the NHS had been more than consumed by the costs of delayed transfers of care, not to mention people with health problems that could have been avoided with better social care. The government responded with a Better Care Fund, given jointly to local authorities and the local NHS; while the joint architecture was promising, the amount of money was very small compared to the scale of the problem. The impact of social care problems on the NHS is a mainstay of NHS politics, but the dramatic scale of cuts in local government, and the Coalition's general lack of sympathy for most populations who require social care, have led to both bigger NHS and human problems than normal.

Conclusion: five remarkable things before the election

The first remarkable thing about health policy under this government has been its sheer improbability. Of all the problems facing the UK in 2010, the organisation of the NHS could not have been a big one. Of the issues discussed here, long-term social care was probably the most pressing, and it is the one where there has been the least change (despite the interest that long-term care holds for core blocks of Tory voters).

The second remarkable thing is what the indignant highlighted: the shift to 'welfare pluralism' in which the state is not a uniform provider but rather contracts with organisations that do not make profits, such as foundation trusts, to provide its services. That is what the NHS would have looked like had Aneurin Bevan not held the Health portfolio in the Attlee government (Klein, 2013). It does not mean, however, that the private sector will do well. The problem is that it still seems difficult to make money out of the NHS (Greer and Rauscher, 2011). Major firms whose core business is outsourced public sector work, such as Serco, are drawing back from NHS business.

Hinchingbrooke hospital in Huntingdon turned out to be the iconic case of privatisation. It had never been a high-performing hospital, and under Labour a consensus developed among the regional management (East of England Strategic Health Authority) that it would be a good case for privatisation, meaning transfer of its plant and staff to a private sector firm that might run it better. The Labour government, always interested in the idea of 'constructive discomfort' (Stevens, 2004) and impressed by the ability of private sector competition to squeeze more efficiency out of the NHS, was supportive. Hinchingbrooke was finally handed over to a firm called Circle in February 2012. It started out with good publicity and high ratings in customer service scores, but collapsed dramatically in January 2015. The CQC issued a report about as negative as it has ever given (Care Quality Commission, 2015); Circle, rather than waiting and showing contrition, as NHS trusts do, 'pre-butted' the report with a hostile press release complaining about

(NHS-wide) budget constraints and the CQC's procedures (Circle, 2015). Then, taking advantage of a clause in the contract saying it could break the contract if it lost more than £5 million pounds, Circle announced that it would hand back Hinchingbrooke.

What lessons can we take away from Hinchingbrooke's story? One is that the urge to introduce the private sector – and an increasing acceptance of private involvement in the NHS, complete with conflicts of interest – dates to the Labour government as much as to Conservatives. But the main lesson is that it is very difficult to make money out of the NHS; an efficiently run health care system has very few pockets of activity so wasteful that a private sector firm, with private sector cost of capital, can find enough efficiencies to be worthwhile. Finally, it seems that the NHS is not as bad at negotiating as one might imagine. Pluralistic provision in pre-NHS England was mostly by charities unconcerned with profit and mostly unable to raise serious capital; that might well be the case now, in which case the NHS is likely to remain a dominant provider.

The third remarkable thing about the reform has been its centralisation; instead of seeing the Coalition as a story about marketisation, it could be better understood as a story about centralisation. If we follow the civil servant's dictum that the content of a proposal is the opposite of its title, we might note that the title of Lansley's original proposal was *Autonomy and Accountability*, and yet the system he created combined a very high degree of centralisation with weak accountability. Centralisation – because the old NHS structure of territorial units such as District and Regional Health Authorities had finally been broken in favour of a direct relationship between the centre (DH, Monitor, CQC) and the NHS frontline (trusts and CCGs). But lack of accountability – it is very crowded in the centre of Lansley's panopticon with ministers, the DH (including its Trust Development Authority), Monitor, NHSE and the CQC all squashed in and squabbling. The Coalition eliminated territorial units and established powerful regulatory powers over and information about the NHS while creating a centre too fragmented to hold the NHS to account or be held to account itself. That is how a government that has made such claims to authority over health care can, in the words of a junior minister, find that 'with the Lansley act we pretty much gave away control of the NHS' (Helm, 2014).

The fourth remarkable thing about the NHS structure that the Cameron government created is its instability. The NHS can operate quite well with improbable or inefficient structures; that has often been the case. The distinctive thing about the Conservative architecture is that it has ıdamental instabilities at each level, ones exacerbated by the tight funding (and tighter funding promised should the Conservatives be returned to office in 2015). On one hand, the centralisation is inefficient, producing great demands on the centre, and removing shock absorbers such as regions or SHAs that could mediate between central policies and local conditions. On the other, the centre's fragmentation means that there is no central planning or market-making authority, and the very different visions of the NHS found in Monitor, NHSE, and the DH are all equally valid and enforceable. For example, NHSE and many health policy analysts call for integration between providers; it is not clear how that fits with Monitor's fealty to competition.

Fifth and finally, it is worth making clear what might have been evident all along: the government might be a Coalition, but its health policy is Conservative. Explanations of the Health and Social Care Act all focus on Conservatives, whether for their putative conflicts of interest or for their interpersonal politics. Liberal Democrat ideas had almost no influence on the key policies. For health policy purposes, this was a Conservative government; if Liberal Democrats are to be held accountable for anything, it is for a failure to influence it.

Notes

1. The best history of this episode is Timmins (2012).
2. E.g. http://www.nhsforsale.info/database/impact-database/conflict-of-interest.html
3. One book lists Hunt as one of many co-authors, led by Daniel Hannan MEP: (Hannan, 2005). Its health policy ideas are on pp. 74–80; they clearly advocate for eliminating the NHS though the shape of its replacement is unclear. A later and more clearly written book that proposes individual accounts is formally written only by Douglas Carswell MP (who later defected to UKIP) and Hannan, but lists Hunt (p. 195) as one of the people on behalf of whom it speaks (Carswell and Hannan, 2008): the health policy discussion is on pp. 97–106. A desire to abolish the NHS is not rare in the Coalition government; David Laws, in the Orange Book summarising the preferences of the current Liberal Democrat leadership, called for a transition to what he understood as a 'social insurance' model of health care finance (Marshall and Laws, 2004). Oliver Letwin was reported to have said that the NHS would cease to exist under a Conservative government (see McSmith, 2004).
4. The Mid Staffordshire NHS Foundation Trust Public Inquiry (Chaired by Robert Francis QC) (2013) *Report of the Mid Staffordshire NHS Foundation Trust Public Inquiry*, HC.947 (London: The Stationery Office). http://www.midstaffspublicinquiry.com/report

References

Anonymous (2014) Interview with CSU staffer. Birmingham, June.

Black, N. (2010) 'Liberating the NHS' – another attempt to implement market forces in English health care. *New England Journal of Medicine*, 363: 1103–05.

Butler, D., Adonis, A. and Travers, T. (1994) *Failure in British Government: The Politics of the Poll Tax* (Oxford: Oxford University Press).

Care Quality Commission (2015) *Hinchingbrooke Health Care NHS Trust: Report* (London: Care Quality Commission).

Carswell, D. and Hannan, D. (2008) *The Plan: Twelve Months to Renew Britain* (Lulu.com).

Channel Four News (2012) FactCheck: Who supports the health bill? Available at: http://blogs.channel4.com/factcheck/factcheck-who-supports-the-health-bill/9674.

Circle (2015) A Statement on Hinchingbrooke. Press release, 9 January. Available at: http://www.circlepartnership.co.uk/about-circle/media/a-statement-on-hinchingbrooke.

Clover, B. (2013) Regulator chiefs summoned to Number 10 over winter pressures. *Health Service Journal*, 30 October.

Clover, B. and Barnes, S. (2013) Hunt demands explanations from A&E underperformers. *Health Service Journal*, 22 November.

d'Ancona, M. (2013) *In it Together: The Inside Story of the Coalition Government* (London: Penguin).

Department of Health (2007) Departmental Report. Available at: http://webarchive.nationalarchives.gov.uk/20130107105354/http://www.dh.gov.uk/prod_consum_dh/groups/dh_digitalassets/@dh/@en/documents/digitalasset/dh_074766.pdf.

Dilnot Commission (2010) Terms of reference for the Commission on the funding of care and support. Available at: http://webarchive.nationalarchives.gov.uk/20130221130239/http://dilnotcommission.dh.gov.uk/files/2010/11/Tor-final.pdf.

Dilnot Commission (2011) Fairer care funding: the report of the Commission on funding of care and support. Available at: http://webarchive.nationalarchives.gov.uk/20130221130239/http://dilnotcommission.dh.gov.uk/files/2011/07/Fairer-Care-Funding-Report.pdf.

Gershon, P. (2004) Releasing resources to the front line: independent review of public sector efficiency. July. Available at: http://webarchive.nationalarchives.gov.uk/+/http:/www.hm-treasury.gov.uk/d/efficiency_review120704.pdf.

Golding, N. (2012) 'PM defends health reforms amid growing pressure to scrap bill', *Local Government Chronicle*, 9 February. Available at: http://webarchive.nationalarchives.gov.uk/20130107105354/http://www.dh.gov.uk/prod_consum_dh/groups/dh_digitalassets/@dh/@en/documents/digitalasset/dh_074766.pdf.

GPonline (2011) Doctors demand withdrawal of Health Bill. 15 March. Available at: http://www.gponline.com/doctors-demand-withdrawal-health-bill/article/1060148.

Greer, S. L. and Jarman, H. (2007) *The Department of Health and the Civil Service: From Whitehall to Department of Delivery to Where?* (London: The Nuffield Trust).

Greer, S. L., Jarman, H. and Azorsky, A. (2014) *A Reorganisation You Can See from Space: The Architecture of Power in the New NHS* (London: Centre for Health and the Public Interest).

Greer, S. L. and Rauscher, R. (2011) When does market-marking make markets? EU Health services policy at work in the UK and Germany. *Journal of Common Market Studies*, 49(4): 797–822.

Hannan, D. (2005) *Direct Democracy: An Agenda for a New Model Party* (Lulu.com).

Hart, T. (2012) The Health and Social Care Bill – Where do they stand? Available at http://www.theguardian.com/news/datablog/2012/mar/19/health-social-care-bill-visualised.

Helm, T. (2014) NHS is out of control, says Tory health minister. *The Observer*, 21 June.

HM Government (2009) Shaping the Future of Care Together (Cm7673). Available at: https://www.gov.uk/government/uploads/system/uploads/attachment_data/file/238551/7673.pdf.

HM Government (2010a) The Coalition: our programme for government. Available at: http://www.gov.uk.

HM Government (2010b) *Equity and Excellence: Liberating the NHS*. White Paper, Cm7881 (July). Available at: http://www.gov.uk.

HM Government (2012) Caring for our future: reforming care and support, Cm8378. Available at: www.gov.uk.

Hunter, D. J. (2013) Will 1 April mark the beginning of the end of England's NHS? Yes. *BMJ* 346: f1951.

Jaques, H. (2012) BMA calls for resignation of English health secretary Andrew Lansley. *BMJ* 344: e4473.

Jarman, H. and Greer, S. L. (2010) In the eye of the storm: civil servants and managers in the Department of Health. *Social Policy and Administration*, 44(2): 172–92.

King, A. and Crewe, I. (2013) *The Blunders of Our Governments* (London: Oneworld).

King's Fund (2013) The Health and Social Care Act: A tale in a timeline. Available at: http://www.kingsfund.org.uk/topics/nhs-reform/health-and-social-care-act-2012-timeline.

Klein, R. (2013) The twenty-year war over England's National Health Service: a report from the battlefield. *Journal of Health Politics, Policy and Law*, 38(4): 849–69.

Lansley, A. (2011) NHS Reform. *Hansard* HC Deb, 4 April 2011, vol. 526, col. 767.

Marshall, P. and Laws, D. (2004) (eds) *The Orange Book: Reclaiming Liberalism* (London: Profile).

MCNxtGen. (2011) 'Andrew Lansley Rap'. Available at: https://www.youtube.com/watch?v=Dl1jPqqTdNo (accessed 29 January 2015).

McSmith, A. (2004) Letwin: 'NHS will not exist under the Tories', *Independent*, 6 June, http://www.independent.co.uk/life-style/health-and-families/health-news/letwin-nhs-will-not-exist-under-tories-6168295.html

NHS England (2014) *Five Year Forward View* (London: NHS England).

Peedell, C. (2011) Further privatisation is inevitable under the proposed NHS reforms. *BMJ* 342: d2996.

Pulse (2012) More GP commissioners withdraw support from health bill. 13 March. Available at: http://www.pulsetoday.co.uk/newsarticle-content/-/

article_display_list/13604675/more-gp-commissioners-withdraw-support-from-health-bill.

Reynolds, L., Lister, J., Scott-Samuel, A. and McKee, M. (2011) *Liberating the NHS: Source and destination of the Lansley reform.* Available at: pcwww.liv. ac.uk/~alexss/toryattackonnhs.pdf.

Reynolds, L. and McKee, M. (2012) Opening the oyster: the 2010–2011 NHS reforms in England. *Clinical Medicine*, 12(2): 128–38.

Reynolds, L., Attaran, A., Hervey, T. and McKee, M. (2012) Competition-based reform of the National Health Service in England: a one-way street? *International Journal of Health Services*, 42(2): 213–17.

Rimmer, A. (2012) CCGs' leaders call on Cameron to drop the Health Bill. *GP*, 1 March. Available at: http://www.gponline.com/News/article/1120121/CCGs-leaders-call-Cameron-drop-Health-Bill/.

Rogers, S. (2012) Health and social care bill: who's against (and for) it? Full list visualised. *The Guardian*, March 19. Available at: http://www.theguardian.com/news/datablog/2012/mar/19/health-social-care-bill-visualised.

Stevens, S. (2004) Reform strategies for the English NHS. *Health Affairs*, 23(3): 37–44.

Timmins, N. (2012) *Never Again? The Story of the Health and Social Care Act 2012: A study in coalition government and policymaking* (London: Nuffield Trust).

Triggle, N. (2011) PM seeks to allay fears, but insists change is needed. *BBC News*, 6 April. Available at: http://www.bbc.co.uk/news/health-12981370.

Wintour, P. and Stratton, A. (2011) NHS reforms face overhaul after Liberal Democrats' rebellion. *The Guardian*, 13 March. Available at: http://www.theguardian.com/politics/2011/mar/13/nhs-reforms-overhaul-liberal-democrats.

5

The Coalition, Poverty and Social Security

Robert M. Page

In 1965 the British pop group The Animals had a top ten hit single containing the memorable lyric 'I'm just a soul whose intentions are good. Oh Lord please don't let me be misunderstood'. This sentiment is likely to resonate with the Work and Pensions Secretary (and former Conservative leader) Iain Duncan Smith when he reflects on his tenure as Secretary of State for Work and Pensions in the Conservative-led Coalition government of 2010–15. His self-professed aim as Secretary of State was to create a more effective, socially just, social security system which would be 'fair to both the people who use it and the taxpayers who pay for it' (Duncan Smith, 2013: see also Department for Work and Pensions (DWP) 2014b; HM Government, 2012, 2013). However, this pledge has been treated with scepticism by many claimant groups and critics who contend that he has merely continued the harsh neo-liberal approach to social policy associated with both the Thatcher (1979–90) and Major (1990–97) governments (Toynbee and Walker, 2013).

This chapter will explore the Cameron-led Coalition government's record on social security with a view to determining whether a more socially 'progressive' approach can be detected. To this end attention will be given to the Coalition's approach to child poverty, its flagship initiative Universal Credit, the Work Programme, Work Capability Tests and benefit sanctions, and the impact of austerity cutbacks on various claimant groups. In order to provide a context to this discussion this chapter starts by considering the social security system bequeathed to the Conservative-led Coalition government and the 'progressive' social narrative mapped out by David Cameron and his fellow modernisers prior to the 2010 general election.

Background

The social insurance system that was set up in the UK along 'Beveridgean' lines following the Second World War has proved unable, during the intervening decades, to provide adequate levels of income security for all those in need by virtue of contingencies such as unemployment, sickness or old age. This failure reflects ideological divisions between the main parties over the relative merits of universal and selective provision, work incentives and the level of state financial support required to prevent poverty. In addition, like other nations, the British social security system has had to cope with changes in the labour market and in household formations as well as the impact of an ageing population. It can be argued that successive post-war Labour and Conservative governments have been unable or unwilling to resolve these difficulties with the result that Beveridge's vision of an effective universal social insurance scheme failed to materialise. Instead a complex, patchwork scheme has emerged with a far more significant role accorded to means-tested support than was envisaged by the post-war welfare pioneers.

While all post-war Conservative governments have always been sceptical of the merits of universal welfare provision (Raison, 1980; Page, 2015 forthcoming), it was arguably not until the premierships of Margaret Thatcher and John Major that decisive action was taken to steer the social security system in a residual direction in an effort to constrain costs and prevent what came to be known as 'welfare dependency' (Hill and Walker, 2014; Taylor-Gooby, 2014). Active steps were taken to pare back social insurance entitlements and slow the growth in social security occasioned by rising unemployment and growing numbers of dependent lone parents and pensioners. During the Major era, for example, National Insurance rights accorded to Job Seekers Allowance were restricted to six months, discretionary grants were reduced (most claimants seeking additional financial support had to rely on repayable loans rather than grants) and benefits for young people were cut. The Child Support Agency was also introduced, albeit to limited effect, in an effort to ensure that parents took greater financial responsibility for all their dependent children whether from a current or past relationship (King and Crewe, 2013).

The return of a Labour government in 1997 did not lead to any concerted attempt to resurrect the more egalitarian, universal approach to social security that had been pursued by previous Labour administrations (Francis, 1997; Piachaud, 2008; Thornton, 2009). Instead, New

Labour attempted to emulate the political success that the US Democratic Party enjoyed under Bill Clinton by adopting a more muscular response to the growth in working-age dependency on means-tested benefits. This involved the pursuit of a work-first, conditionality strategy which aimed to increase labour market participation through programmes such as the New Deals for specific claimant groups as well as more demanding eligibility requirements for Income Support claimants, particularly lone parents (Gregg, 2008). The introduction of the minimum wage and tax credits were also seen as vital components of this strategy. Although successive New Labour governments have been criticised for failing to protect the living standards of working-age adults without dependents, they did make significant progress in tackling both pensioner and child poverty (Joyce and Sibieta, 2013). Indeed, in the case of the latter, the Brown administration (2007–10) introduced the Child Poverty Act in 2010 which mandates future Secretaries of State to meet both absolute and relative child poverty targets as well as to publish an annual progress report and set out a three yearly child poverty strategy.

Adopting a more sympathetic approach to the problem of poverty was one of the components of the modern Conservative agenda that Cameron developed in Opposition after being elected as party leader in 2005. Cameron sought to distance the contemporary Conservative Party from the illiberal, harsh, politically tainted rhetoric directed towards disadvantaged and minority groups during the Thatcher era. Cameron was determined to show that the Conservatives were a compassionate party committed to bolstering the social, as well as the economic, fabric of society. This change of tack took a number of forms including the adoption of a more sympathetic narrative in relation to those who opted for alternative, non-harmful, lifestyles. Lone mothers and non-heterosexual couples were now, for example, to be viewed as part of the Conservative 'family' rather than as threatening outsiders. Cameron's determination to press ahead with legislation paving the way for gay marriage, despite some vociferous objections from socially conservative party members, was indicative of his desire to modernise the party. Cameron accepted that poverty should be measured in relative rather than absolute terms and that the pursuit of social justice and greater social mobility were legitimate Conservative tasks (Bercow, 2002; D'Ancona, 2012; Hickson, 2008, 2010). Government was seen as having an integral role to play in steering society in this direction by providing where necessary the funds for non-state, rather than state, providers to becoming the driving force of a civic 'Big Society' revolution (Letwin, 2008; Norman, 2010; Blond, 2010). In the case of poverty, for example, Cameron's modern Conservatives sought to move away from what they regarded as Labour's narrow, outmoded state-dominated remedies which focused on income poverty and concentrate instead on innovative non-state forms of provision that would tackle the underlying causes of deprivation such as family breakdown and poor schooling.

Significantly, however, Cameron's social modernisation has not been complemented by economic modernisation. Neo-liberal economic nostrums were regarded as sacrosanct and there was no appetite to return to interventionist remedies of the past. Prior to the gathering global economic storm in the summer of 2007, this adherence to a neo-liberal economic strategy was not seen as incompatible with the Conservatives' new social strategy, not least because the previous New Labour variant of this hybrid had proved electorally successful. Indeed, while in Opposition the party committed itself initially to using future growth dividends for both income tax cuts and enhanced social spending (Dorey, 2009). However, following the banking crisis, the narrative changed. Rejecting Labour's attempt to link the crisis to unpredictable global events, the Conservatives developed an alternative, and highly effective, counter narrative in which New Labour was held to blame for Britain's economic malaise because of their addiction to statism, their profligate approach to public spending and their inability to provide adequate regulation of the financial sector.

By the time of the formation of the Coalition government, there was unanimity between both partners that neo-liberal remedies to the budget deficit were required, including significant cuts in public spending rather than increased taxes or 'unsustainable' forms of borrowing. The adoption of this more orthodox neo-liberal economic policy by the Conservative-led Coalition government has, however, made it far more difficult for modernising Conservatives to present themselves as a party seeking socially just solutions to poverty and disadvantage. How then has the Conservative-led Coalition government attempted to square this circle in relation to social security?

The Conservative-led Coalition's social security strategy, 2010–15

Poverty reduction

New Labour's long-term commitment to ending child poverty by 2020 was welcomed by the Coalition in its programme for government (HM Government, 2010). The remit of the proposed Child Poverty

Commission was even extended to include the broader issue of social mobility under the Welfare Reform Act of 2012 (HM Government, 2011; Social Mobility & Child Poverty Commission, 2013, 2014). The Conservatives' desire to match Labour's anti-poverty pledge was seen as a key way of demonstrating to the electorate that the party's 'progressive' policy agenda amounted to something more than rhetoric. The Coalition published its first child poverty strategy in April 2011 and a second in 2014 (DWP and Department for Education (DFE), 2011; HM Government, 2014). Although the goal of reducing acute financial need was acknowledged in both documents, there was an attempt to move towards a more holistic approach to poverty prevention. This was reflected in a range of complementary publications where the focus was on the underlying drivers of poverty (DWP, 2014a, 2014b). For example, a report from the Labour MP Frank Field on a longer-term poverty prevention strategy recommended that greater emphasis be given to integrated 'foundation' services (from pregnancy to the age of five), which would provide support for parents and improve the long-term prospects of disadvantaged children, rather than to 'unaffordable' and 'unrealistic' anti-poverty income targets (HM Government, 2010).

While Duncan Smith's desire to tackle the underlying causes of poverty has drawn support from 'progressives' within his own party, it has proved to be more problematic for a cost-conscious Chancellor and his Treasury team. Influenced by the paternalist conservative ideas of the US poverty expert Lawrence Mead (Mead, 1986; Mead and Beem, 2005), Duncan Smith supported the idea that imposing greater demands on those in poverty to ensure their speedy return to financial independence was the right course of action even if it required additional public spending in the short term. This appeared to suggest a rejection of some of the harsher, cost-cutting remedies recommended by the neo-liberal American social scientist Charles Murray, whose warnings about the emergence of a British 'underclass' had proved so persuasive during the Thatcher era (Murray, 1984, 1994).

Duncan Smith has found it difficult to convince Treasury sceptics that his more holistic approach would bring about a long-term reduction in levels of state dependency (D'Ancona, 2013). This impasse came to public attention when the Treasury vetoed a plan devised by Duncan Smith, and his Liberal Democrat Coalition colleague David Laws, to include new poverty indicators[1] (as required by the Child Poverty Act of 2010) in their Child Poverty Strategy for 2014–17 on the grounds that it was likely to incur additional expenditure (Wintour, 2014). Treasury concerns over the additional costs associated with these new poverty measures were compounded, in part, by the cost over-runs associated with the introduction of the Coalition's flagship social security initiative, Universal Credit.

Universal Credit

The Centre for Social Justice, the think-tank that Duncan Smith helped to create in 2004, was instrumental in preparing the way for the introduction of a 'fairer' and 'simpler' form of financial support – Universal Credit – for working-age adults in low-paid work or seeking to re-enter the labour market. The Centre became the administrative and policy hub for the Conservative Party's Social Justice Policy Group (headed by Duncan Smith) which was one of the six specialist policy forums established by Cameron in 2005. The Group's proposals (Centre for Social Justice, 2006, 2007) for tackling the growth of poverty and welfare dependency in Britain formed part of the Green Paper *21st Century Welfare*, which was published shortly after the Coalition came into office in July 2010 (DWP, 2010a). A subsequent White Paper *Universal Credit: Welfare That Works* (DWP, 2010b) based on these initial proposals paved the way for the passage of the Welfare Reform Act in March 2012.

Universal Credit is designed to reduce benefit dependency by providing targeted support for unemployed working-age adults as well as supplementary financial assistance for low-paid workers. It will replace a number of existing benefits such as Income Support, income-based Jobseeker's Allowance, income-related Employment and Support Allowance, Housing Benefit, Child Tax Credits and Working Tax Credits. Other benefits such as Attendance Allowance, Cold Weather Payments, Pension Credits, Child Benefit and Carers' Allowances will be retained although the eligibility criteria will be subject to 'modifications' (DWP, 2012).

Although there has been broad cross-party support for the introduction of Universal Credit, a number of reservations have been voiced about some of the administrative processes that the Coalition has introduced as part of its implementation programme. These include concerns about the on-line application process as many claimants do not have internet access or IT skills; the payment system, as claimants are likely to find it difficult to budget with the new 'monthly in arrears' arrangement; and the withdrawal of the option for rent to be paid directly to landlords, which increases the risk of arrears and possible eviction. Questions have also been raised about whether the rates set for Universal Credit will be able to lift all households out of poverty

(Hirsch and Hartfree, 2013). Like many major policy initiatives of this kind, the introduction of Universal Credit has proved problematic. The scheme has exceeded its initial administrative set-up costs and has been criticised in a report from the Head of the National Audit Office for having weak management, ineffective control and poor governance (National Audit Office, 2013). As a consequence, the roll-out of the programme has been much slower than originally envisaged. By the end of May 2014 the total caseload for Universal Credit in the four north-west 'pathfinder' and six 'hub' Job Centres areas[2] stood at just 6,570 individuals. The majority of these were young people under 25 who do not have the most complex needs. It had been previously estimated that 184,000 claimants would be enrolled on the scheme by April 2014 (ibid.). Political sensitivities about the administration of the scheme were heightened in 2014 when the Cabinet Office's Major Project Authority took the extraordinary step of 'resetting' the negative 'amber/red' official rating that had been awarded to the programme. This led the Public Accounts Committee to suggest that this step had been taken solely with a view to stifling proper public scrutiny of the escalating costs of the project (Syal, 2014).

The Work Programme

Like the previous New Labour governments, the Coalition has emphasised the importance of paid work as the principal means of tackling long-term benefit dependency among working-age adults. In 2011 it replaced New Labour's various welfare-to-work schemes with the Work Programme, which was deemed to be a more cost-effective way of assisting those who have experienced a lengthy period of unemployment (nine to 12 months) to find, and retain, paid work. This £2.8bn scheme was designed to help over two million people over the lifetime of the scheme – June 2011 to March 2016. The support is provided by prime contractors,[3] which can be private, public or third sector organisations, on a payment by results basis. Higher payments are given for those groups who are likely to need more extensive support in securing a job, such as those receiving Employment and Support Allowance.[4]

As with Universal Credit, questions have been raised about both the efficacy, particularly in relation to harder-to-help groups, and cost of the Work Programme during its initial phase. By 2014, for example, just 27 per cent of Jobseeker's Allowance claimants aged 25 and over who had completed the programme had secured employment lasting six months or more – a figure that was markedly less than initial departmental (39%) and contractor (42%) estimates. Flaws in the DWP's contractual arrangements and performance measures are also estimated to have resulted in contractors being 'overpaid' to the tune of £11m in the first three years of the scheme, with further losses of £25m envisaged by the end of the programme unless remedial action is taken (National Audit Office, 2014b).

One of the other schemes[5] introduced by the Coalition to help young people find paid work, the Work Experience Programme, involved companies providing a voluntary unpaid work placement of between two and eight weeks for young people aged between 16 and 24 who would continue to receive Jobseeker's Allowance during their participation in the scheme. This programme provoked considerable media interest when cases came to light suggesting that some participants had been 'coerced' into participating in this supposedly voluntary scheme for fear of losing their benefits[6] (Malik, 2011). Concern has also been expressed about the operation of Work Capability Tests and the sanctioning of benefit recipients.

Work Capability Tests and benefit sanctions

First introduced by the New Labour government under the Welfare Reform Act of 2007, Work Capability Tests have formed a key part of the Coalition's social security reform agenda. Working-age adults claiming Employment and Support Allowance, Incapacity Benefit, Severe Disablement Allowance or Income Support on grounds of illness or disability have been subjected to a Work Capability Assessment which aims to distinguish between those whose medical condition is so severe that they are unable to work and those who are able, with appropriate support, to return to the labour market. These assessments, which have been administered by private contractors such as Atos and Capita have proved controversial. Claimants have voiced concerns about the impersonal and mechanistic approach of Jobcentre Plus staff and private sector assessors. They have also drawn attention to the lack of transparency, poor official decision making and the complexity of the procedures (Harrington, 2010, 2011, 2012; Litchfield, 2013). There have been a large number of appeals relating to Work Capability Assessments, with 37 per cent of these being upheld (DWP, 2013b). One of the firms that has been heavily criticised for sub-standard Work Capability Assessments – Atos Healthcare – eventually withdrew from this area of activity in 2014 following adverse publicity from claimants and negative statements from DWP officials. The firm has, however, retained its contract to provide assessments for those seeking Personal Independent Payments.[7]

The Coalition has also run into trouble in relation to the rising number of benefit sanctions being imposed by the DWP (Gentleman, 2014). In a report on the sanctioning of Jobseeker's Allowance claimants by Matthew Oakley (a former economic adviser at the Treasury and ex-Head of Economics and Social Policy at the right-leaning Think Tank Policy Exchange), it was noted that some 1,015,000 Jobseeker's Allowance claimants were referred for possible withdrawal of benefits in 2013 (Oakley, 2014). Just under a third – 291,000 or 28.7 per cent – of these claimants were eventually sanctioned in this way. Although Oakley concluded that the sanctions scheme was costly at £60m per annum and in need of improvement, he believed that the system was not fundamentally broken. He made a number of recommendations including improved forms of communication between officials and claimants; letters sent to claimants who are to be sanctioned should, for example, be clear and easy to understand; improved dialogue between Jobcentre Plus staff and contractors was also highlighted so that unwarranted and distressing referrals could be avoided; improvements in the quality of information provided for claimants in relation to their conditionality requirements and the sanctions process, including the appeals system and the availability of hardship payments, were recommended (ibid.). Concern about the Coalition's administration of claimant sanctions was such that three 'disgruntled' former DWP civil servants decided to launch a free specialist website providing emergency advice to claimants who believed that they had been sanctioned unfairly (Morris, 2014).

In addition, changes and delays in relation to benefit payments have been identified as two of the principal reasons for the rising number of people seeking support from the 423 food banks in the UK in 2014. According to a joint report from Church Action on Poverty, the Trussell Trust and Oxfam there were 913,138 applications for a three-day emergency supply of food and support in 2013–14 compared to 346,992 in 2012–13 and 127,697 in 2011–12 (Cooper *et al.*, 2014).

Austerity cutbacks

The Coalition has also imposed cuts on the living standards of working-aged claimants as part of its 'socially just' deficit-reduction strategy. It is contended that poorer people should not be exempted from making a proportionate financial contribution to help reduce the deficit following the financial crisis of 2007. Accordingly, a uniform £500 per week benefit cap has been applied to all claimant couples from April 2013 and the annual benefit increase for non-pensioner claimants has, following the passage of the Welfare Benefits Up-Rating Act of 2013, been restricted to 1 per cent per annum for the next three years. Following the Chancellor's Spending Review in 2013, a seven-day wait for benefit payments and an annual overall cap on non-pensioner DWP spending have also been introduced. Finally, in his speech to the annual Conservative Party Conference in September 2014, the Chancellor announced that the benefits for working-age claimants – 50 per cent of whom were in low-paid work – would be frozen for an additional two years from 2016 following the end of the 1 per cent phase.

One of the most controversial of the Coalition's cost-saving measures relates to Housing Benefit. Claimants deemed to be under-occupying their home have had their so-called spare room subsidy withdrawn with a 14 per cent reduction for one spare bedroom and 25 per cent for two spare bedrooms. This has resulted in tenants facing the unenviable choice of remaining in their current accommodation and funding the resulting rent shortfall out of their capped benefits or seeking, where possible, more affordable, less spacious accommodation. According to the DWP's own data, some 11 per cent of those living in social housing – 522,905 households in August 2013 – have been affected by the removal of the spare room subsidy now commonly referred to as the 'bedroom tax'. Although discretionary housing payments were put in place to allow local authorities to assist those who might unjustly incur a reduction in their subsidy, such as disabled people who require an additional room to store medical equipment, early evidence suggests that this has failed to prevent hardship in a number of cases (DWP, 2014g). Injustices of this kind led the Liberal Democrats to break ranks with their Coalition partner and support a Private Members' Bill in September 2014 aimed at reforming the spare room subsidy rules to provide better legal safeguards for vulnerable tenants.

The abolition of the national Council Tax rebate scheme, which came into effect in 2013, was yet another measure which had an adverse effect on the weekly incomes of some claimants. This is particularly the case for those living in financially impoverished local authorities[8] which have been forced to pare back the support they can offer. For example, all working-aged adults in one of London's most deprived boroughs, Newham, are now required to pay at least 20 per cent of their Council Tax bill. Initial evidence suggests that this has resulted in significant increases in Council Tax arrears because of the inability of poorer local residents to meet their new financial obligations, with consequent negative knock-on effects for council budgets. It has been estimated that Liverpool City Council has, for instance, only been able to collect 61 per cent of council payments from low-income families, leaving it with a projected shortfall of £3.5 million in 2013–14 (Ramesh, 2014). The Coalition has also abolished Community Care grants and Crisis Loans which formed part of the national Social Fund scheme with effect from April 2013. As a consequence those seeking help to live independently within the community, or who need an emergency loan, must now apply for less well resourced, discretionary, local council welfare assistance (Royston and Rodrigues, 2013).

In an effort to demonstrate the fairness of their approach Coalition ministers have drawn attention to other austerity initiatives which have been targeted at better-off taxpayers. For example, Child Tax Credits were withdrawn from families with incomes above £26,000 per annum (the threshold had previously been £41,300 in 2013) and Child Benefit was withdrawn from households with one higher rate taxpayer. In addition, the Coalition has made great play of its determination to minimise both illegal forms of tax evasion and legal but 'aggressive' forms of legal avoidance (Osborne, 2011). In the summer of 2012 Cameron named and shamed the comedian Jimmy Carr, who was alleged to have been involved in an elaborate offshore tax avoidance scheme (*The Times*, 2012). However, the Chancellor's decision to reduce the top rate of income tax, which had been temporarily raised to 50 per cent in 2010, to 45 per cent with effect from 2013–14, ostensibly on the grounds that the higher rate failed to generate much, if any, additional revenue, served to create the impression that some of the pro-poor rhetoric might conceal a longer-standing desire to favour the 'haves' rather than the 'have-nots'.

Pensioners are one of the groups that the Conservatives have been particularly keen to protect from the worst effects of the financial crisis. As their 2010 general election manifesto made clear, 'We strongly value the role older people play in families and in society, and will not let them suffer because of the economic mistakes of others' (Conservative Party, 2010: 42). Accordingly, they pledged to realign the Basic State Pension with earnings and protect universal pensioner benefits such as winter fuel payments, free bus passes, free TV licences, free eye tests and free prescriptions, as well as maintain those benefits that many older people claim such as Disability Living Allowances, Attendance Allowance and the Pension Credit. These commitments were included in the Coalition Agreement (HM Government, 2010) and have formed the cornerstone of Coalition policy for pensioners.[9] A new, simpler, single-tier state pension scheme is to be introduced in April 2016 with a so-called triple-lock mechanism (DWP, 2013a).[10] This will ensure that the state pension will increase by a minimum of 2.5 per cent per year. Those with a full contribution record will be entitled to a pension in the region of £7,500 per annum at current prices with pro-rata reductions.[11] Importantly, though, this will still leave the UK with one of the least generous state pension schemes in Europe (International Longevity Centre, 2014).

Although both Coalition partners have made no firm commitment to retaining the full range of universal benefits for older people,[12] their current support to this section of the electorate has placed pressure on the Labour Party, who are committed to withdrawing some universal benefits such as the Winter Fuel Allowance from better-off pensioners, to provide details of the level of protection they will afford to older citizens.

Tainted love? Socially just Conservative social policy from rhetoric to reality

Early evidence that the impact of the Conservative-led Coalition's austerity measures have been most acute for some of the poorest groups in society (Brewer *et al.*, 2011; Poinasmy, 2013; Social Security Advisory Committee, 2014; Browne and Elming, 2015) gives rise to the suspicion that Cameron's pre-election progressive rhetoric might have amounted to little more than electoral window dressing designed to disguise an attempt to complete the unfinished 'Thatcher revolution' by shrinking the state and extinguishing any possibility of a return to the egalitarianism of the immediate post-1945 period (Kwarteng *et al.*, 2011, 2012). While there has not been an explicit retreat from the socially just narrative developed in Opposition, there have been glimpses of iron hands, rather than velvet gloves, in some public pronouncements made by Conservative ministers.[13] The apparent decline in public sympathy for the plight of working-age claimants (Park *et al.*, 2012, 2014; Kellner, 2012a, 2012b) which is likely to have been reinforced by a plethora of negative media portrayals of claimants (McEnhill and Byrne, 2014),[14] certainly appears to resonate with the neo-liberal sympathies of George Osborne. In a number of public pronouncements he has been keen to distinguish between undeserving shirkers who are deemed to be content to stay at home with the curtains drawn, and deserving strivers who are willing to make the effort to get up at the crack of dawn to go to work for modest rewards (Osborne, 2012). Although Duncan Smith and Osborne (2014) have remained steadfast in their public commitment to the principle of social justice and for proportionate, rather than disproportionate, austerity sacrifices on the part of those at the foot of society, it seems clear that, in practice, social security policy appears to be heading in a Thatcherite neo-liberal direction.

One of the reasons why Conservative ministers have been able to rebuff criticisms about their supposedly shallow commitment to social justice so effectively is because both their junior Coalition partner, the Liberal Democrats, and the Labour Opposition have proved reluctant to present more radical policy alternatives for fear of the adverse electoral consequences that might ensue from being tagged as welfare parties.[15] As we approach the 2015 General Election it is possible that clearer points of difference will emerge between the main parties. Certainly there has been increased opposition from the Liberal Democrats and Labour in relation to the 'bedroom tax', which both parties are now committed to abolish. Significantly, the Liberal Democrats have been at pains to emphasise that they were the true voice of Coalition progressivism, citing their decisive role in initiatives such as the raising of the income tax threshold for lower paid workers, universal free school meals and the introduction of the Pupil Premium. However, given that both the Liberal Democrats and Labour have accepted the need for continued spending constraints, it seems unlikely that either of these parties will unveil radical social security agendas that involve sizeable increases in public spending or a return to universalist principles. As a consequence, those who have experienced benefit cuts and tighter eligibility rules under the 'real' or 'faux' progressive Conservative-led Coalition government are unlikely to be very optimistic about the prospects of significant improvements in their financial well-being as a result of the future election of a One Nation Labour or a Labour/Liberal Democrat Coalition government.

Notes

1. Duncan Smith wanted to focus on families on low incomes with an entrenchment factor such as long-term unemployment and compare their situation over time. He also wanted to identify children at greater risk of remaining in poverty as they grow up by tracking the GCSE attainment of those receiving free school meals.
2. The Pathfinder areas are Ashton-under-Lyme, Wigan, Warrington and Oldham. The hub job centre areas are Hammersmith, Rugby, Inverness, Harrogate, Bath and Shotton.
3. There are two prime contractors in each of the 18 geographical areas operating the scheme. These contractors can sub-contract some or all of the work they are commissioned to provide.

4. Employment and Support Allowance is payable to working-age adults whose ability to work is impaired by illness or disability.

5. Other schemes include: (i) sector-based work academies under which participating companies provide training, work experience and a guaranteed job interview for those who have been unemployed for over three months; and (ii) Community Activity pilot programmes under which those experiencing long-term unemployment [over two years] are provided with 30 hours unpaid work for six months in an effort to develop the disciplines and skills needed for sustained employment.

6. Under this programme, benefits could be withdrawn from a young person who, having volunteered to participate in the scheme, subsequently decided (after the one-week cooling-off period had expired) to leave the placement. Adverse publicity surrounding the case of Cat Reilly, a recent Birmingham University graduate who took legal action against DWP on grounds of violation of her human rights, led to several firms withdrawing from this scheme until they had received greater clarity about its operation.

7. Though the National Audit Office (2014a) has been critical of Atos' work in this area as well.

8. Under the new arrangements local authorities have, since April 2013, been responsible for running their own Council Tax Reduction or Council Tax Support scheme. In one instance Sandwell Borough Council attempted, unsuccessfully, to introduce modern settlement laws by restricting eligibility for Council Tax reductions to those who had lived in the borough for at least two years.

9. The Liberal Democrat Coalition Minister Steve Webb (a former Professor of Social Policy) has played a leading role in drafting these measures.

10. These new pensions will be paid to those who satisfy the minimum contribution rules and who were born on or after 6 April 1951 (men) or 6 April 1953 (women).

11. If either wages or prices increased to, say, 4 per cent then the pension would also be raised by an equivalent amount (i.e. 4 per cent).

12. At the time of writing (January 2015).

13. Lord Freud's off-the-cuff remarks about the low economic worth of some disabled people at a fringe meeting of the Conservative Party Conference in 2014 was seized on by critics to suggest that the neo-liberal leopards had not changed their spots (Dearden, 2014).

14. There has been a plethora of TV programmes in recent years highlighting the lifestyles of benefit claimants including *Saints and Scroungers* (BBC 1, 2009 – now in its fifth series), *Britain on the Fiddle* (BBC1, 2011), *Benefits Street* (Channel 4, 2014), *Benefits Britain: Life on the Dole* (Channel 5, 2014), *On Benefits and Proud* (Channel 5, 2013), *Gypsies on Benefits and Proud* (Channel 5, 2014), *Benefits Britain 1949* (Channel 4, 2013).

15. The Conservatives' social strategy has been influenced by the Swedish Moderate Party which declared that it had become the authentic Workers' party (See Page, 2014: Watt, 2014).

References

Bercow, J. (2002) 'Tories for social justice', *The Guardian*, 13 December.

Blond, P. (2010) *Red Tory*. London: Faber and Faber.

Brewer, M., Browne, J. and Joyce, R. (2011) *Child and Working-Age Poverty 2010–2020*. London: IFS.

Browne, J. and Elming, W. (2015) *The Effects of the Coalition's Tax and Benefit Changes on Household Incomes and Work Incentives*, IFS Briefing Note BN 195, London: IFS.

Centre for Social Justice (2006) *Breakdown Britain*. London: Centre for Social Justice.

Centre for Social Justice (2007) *Breakdown Britain: Ending the Costs of Social Breakdown: Overview*. London: Centre for Social Justice.

Cooper, N., Purcell, S. and Jackson, R. (2014) *Below the Breadline: The Relentless Rise of Food Poverty in Britain*. Oxford: Church Action on Poverty/The Trussell Trust and Oxfam.

Conservative Party (2010) *Invitation to Join the Government of Britain. The Conservative Manifesto 2010*. London: The Conservative Party.

D'Ancona, M. (2012) 'Cameron won't let the socialists have fairness all to themselves', *The Sunday Telegraph*, 8 January.

D'Ancona, M. (2013) *In It Together: The Inside Story of the Coalition Government*. London: Viking.

Dearden, L. (2014) 'Lord Freud: past gaffes on welfare, food banks and "bedroom tax"', *The Independent*, 15 October.

Department for Work and Pensions (2010a) *21st Century Welfare*, Cm. 7913, London: Stationery Office.

Department for Work and Pensions (2010b) *Universal Credit: Welfare That Works*, Cm. 7957, London: Stationery Office.

Department for Work and Pensions and Department for Education (2011) *A New Approach to Child Poverty: Tackling the Causes of Disadvantage and Transforming Families' Lives*. Cm. 8061, London: Stationery Office.

Department for Work and Pensions (2012) *Social Justice: Transforming Lives*, Cm. 8314, London: Stationery Office.

Department for Work and Pensions (2013a) *The Single-Tier Pension: A Simple Foundation for Saving*, Cm. 8528, London: Stationery Office.

Department for Work and Pensions (2013b) *Work Capability Assessments – Fairer and More Accurate*, Press Release, 30 April 2013. London: DWP.

Department for Work and Pensions (2014a) *An Analysis of the Drivers of Child Poverty Now*. London: DWP.

Department for Work and Pensions (2014b) *DWP Reform: DWP's Welfare Reform Agenda Explained*. London: DWP.

Department for Work and Pensions (2014c) *Independent Review of the Operation of Jobseeker's Allowance Sanctions Validation by the Jobseekers Act 2013* (The Oakley Report). London: DWP.

Department for Work and Pensions (2014d) *Government's Response to the Independent Review of the Operation of Jobseeker's Allowance Sanctions Validation by the Jobseekers Act 2013* (The Oakley Report), Cm. 8904, London: DWP.

Department for Work and Pensions (2014e) *DWP Reform: DWPs Welfare Reform Agenda Explained*. London: DWP.

Department for Work and Pensions (2014f) *Universal Credit – Experimental Official Statistics to May 2014*. London: DWP.

Department for Work and Pensions (2014g) *Evaluation of Removal of the Spare Room Subsidy*, Interim Report, London: Stationery Office.

Dorey, P. (2009) ' "Sharing the proceeds of growth": Conservative economic policy under David Cameron', *The Political Quarterly*, 80(2): 259–69.

Duncan Smith, I. (2013) 'I'm proud of our welfare reforms', *The Guardian*, 28 July.

Duncan Smith, I. and Osborne, G. (2014) 'The Conservatives' child poverty plan tackles poverty at source', *The Guardian*, 26 February.

Gentleman, A. (2014) 'No one in Britain should die penniless and alone', *The Guardian*, 4 August.

Gregg, P. (2008) 'Give up the clichés,' *Guardian Unlimited*, http://www.theguardian.com/commentisfree/2008/dec/10/welfare (last accessed 4 November 2014).

Harrington, M. (2010) *An Independent Review of the Work Capability Assessment*. London: Stationery Office.

Harrington, M. (2011) *An Independent Review of the Work Capability Assessment – Year Two*. London: Stationery Office.

Harrington, M. (2012) *An Independent Review of the Work Capability Assessment – Year Three*. London: Stationery Office.

Hickson, K. (2008) 'Conservatism and the poor: Conservative Party attitudes to poverty and inequality since the 1970s', *British Politics* 4(3): 341–62.

Hickson, K. (2010) 'Thatcherism, poverty and social justice', *The Journal of Poverty and Social Justice*, 18(2): 135–45.

Hill, M. and Walker, A. (2014) 'What were the lasting effects of Thatcher's legacy for social security? The burial of Beveridge?', in S. Farrall and C. Hay (eds), *The Legacy of Thatcherism*. Oxford: Oxford University Press, pp. 77–99.

Hirsch, D. and Hartfree, Y. (2013) *Does Universal Credit Enable Households to Reach a Minimum Income Standard?* York: Joseph Rowntree Foundation.

HM Government (2010) The *Foundation Years: Preventing Poor Children Becoming Poor Adults* (the Field Report). London: Stationery Office.

HM Government (2011) *Opening Doors, Breaking Barriers: A Strategy for Social Mobility*. London: Stationery Office.

HM Government (2012) *Social Justice: Transforming Lives*, Cm. 8314, London: Stationery Office.

HM Government (2013) *Social Justice: Transforming Lives One Year On*. London: Stationery Office.

HM Government (2014) *Child Poverty Strategy*. London: Stationery Office.

International Longevity Centre (2014) *Europe's Ageing Demography*. London: ILC.

Joyce, R. and Sibieta, L. (2013) 'An assessment of Labour's record on income inequality and poverty', *Oxford Review of Economic Policy*, 29(1): 178–202.

Kellner, P. (2012a) 'A quiet revolution', *Prospect*, March, 30–4.

Kellner, P. (2012b) 'What do we want?', *Prospect*, June, 38–9.

King, A. and Crewe, I. (2013) *The Blunders of Government*. London: Oneworld.

Kwarteng, K., Patel, P., Rabb, D., Skidmore, C. and Truss, L. (2011) *After the Coalition*. London: Biteback.

Kwarteng, K., Patel, P., Rabb, D., Skidmore, C. and Truss, L. (2012) *Britannia Unchained*. London: Palgrave Macmillan.

Letwin, O. (2008) 'From economic revolution to social revolution', *Soundings*, 40, Winter, 112–22.

Litchfield, P. (2013) *An Independent Review of the Work Capability Assessment – Year Four*. London: Stationery Office.

Malik, S. (2011) 'Young jobseekers told to work without pay or lose unemployment benefits', *The Guardian*, 16 November. http://www.theguardian.com/society/2011/nov/16/young-jobseekers-work-pay-unemployment (last accessed 4 October 2014).

McEnhill, L. and Byrne, V. (2014) '"Beat the cheat": portrayals of disability benefit claimants in print media', *Journal of Poverty and Social Justice*, 22(2): 99–110.

Mead, L. M. (1986) *Beyond Entitlement*. New York: Free Press.

Mead, L. M. and Beem, C. (eds) (2005) *Welfare Reform and Political Theory*. New York: Russell Sage.

Morris, N. (2014) 'Former DWP staff go rogue to help benefit claimants', *The Independent on Sunday*, 3 August.

Murray, C. (1984) *Losing Ground*. New York: Basic Books.

Murray, C. (1994) *Underclass: The Crisis Deepens*. London: IEA.

National Audit Office (2013) Report by the Comptroller and Auditor General, *Universal Credit: Early Progress*. HC.621, Session 2013–14, 5 September 2013. London: Stationery Office.

National Audit Office (2014a) *Personal Independence Payment: Early Progress*. HC.1070, Session 2013–14, 27 February 2014. London: Stationery Office.

National Audit Office (2014b) *The Work Programme*. HC.266, Session 2014–15, 2 July 2014. London: Stationery Office.

Norman, J. (2010) *The Big Society*. Buckingham University Press: Buckingham.

Oakley, M. (2014) *Independent Review of the Operation of Jobseeker's Allowance Sanctions Validated by the Jobseekers Act 2013*. London: DWP.

Osborne, G. (2011) 'Tax cheats have no hiding place under this coalition', *The Guardian*, 27 August 2011. http://www.theguardian.com/commentisfree/2011/aug/27/tax-cheats-coalition-george-osborne (last accessed 4 October 2014).

Osborne, G. (2012) Speech to the Conservative Party Annual Conference, Birmingham 2012.

Page, R. M. (2014) 'Running out of road? Dilemmas and issues for the British Labour Party and the Swedish Social Democratic Party in their search for a "modern" welfare state narrative', *Journal of International and Comparative Social Policy*, 30(1): 107–26.

Page, R. M. (2015, forthcoming) *Clear Blue Water? The Conservative Party and the Welfare State Since 1940*. Bristol: Policy.

Park, A., Clery, E., Curtice, J., Phillips, M. and Utting, D. (eds) (2012) *British Social Attitudes 28*. Sage: London.

Park, A., Bryson, C., Clery, E., Curtice, J. and Phillips, M. (eds) (2014) *British Social Attitudes 30*. London: Sage.

Piachaud, D. (2008) 'Poverty and inequality: Labour in the 1970s', *Journal of Poverty and Social Justice*, 16(2): 147–56.

Poinasmy, R. (2013) *The True Cost of Austerity and Inequality: UK Case Study*. Oxford: Oxfam.

Raison, T. (1980) *Tories and the Welfare State*. Basingstoke: Macmillan.

Ramesh, R. (2014) 'Up to 40% of council tax levied on low-income households unpaid', *The Guardian*, 27 August.

Royston, S. and Rodrigues, L. (2013) *Nowhere to Turn? Changes to Emergency Support*. London: Children's Society.

Social Mobility and Child Poverty Commission (2013) *Social Mobility and Child Poverty in Great Britain*. London: Social Mobility and Child Poverty Commission.

Social Mobility and Child Poverty Commission (2014) *Understanding the Parental Employment Scenarios Necessary to Meet the 2020 Child Poverty Targets*. London: Social Mobility and Child Poverty Commission.

Social Security Advisory Committee (2014) *The Cumulative Impact of Welfare Reform: A Study by the Social Security Advisory Committee*, Occasional Paper No. 12. London: SSAC.

Syal, R. (2014) 'Benefit mismanagement hurting sick and disabled, watchdog says', *The Guardian*, 27 February. http://www.theguardian.com/society/2014/feb/27/ benefit-mismanagement-hurting-sick-and-disabled-atos-capita (last accessed 4 October 2014).

Taylor-Gooby, P. (2014) 'Commentary: What were the lasting effects of Thatcher's legacy for social security?', in S. Farrall and C. Hay (eds), *The Legacy of Thatcherism*. Oxford: Oxford University Press, pp. 100–07.

The Times (2012) 'Jimmy Carr tax arrangements "morally wrong" says Cameron', http://www.thetimes.co.uk/tto/money/tax/article3451438.ece (accessed 4 November 2014).

Thornton, S. (2009) *Richard Crossman and the Welfare State: Pioneer of Welfare Progress and Labour Policies in Post-War Britain*. London: IB Tauris.

Toynbee, P. and Walker, D. (2013) *Dogma and Disarray*. London: Granta.

Watt, N. (2014) 'The Workers' party? That's us say Conservatives in bid to rebrand', *The Guardian*, 25 February.

Wintour, P. (2014) 'Child poverty abolition plan stranded as George Osborne blocks new targets', *The Guardian*, 26 February.

6
The Coalition: How Green was My Tally?

James Connelly

Introduction

In a gloriously backhanded compliment, Roger Helmer, UKIP Energy spokesman, remarked on whether David Cameron had lived up to his pledge to lead the 'greenest government ever'. Helmer stated: 'they clearly haven't been the greenest ever government. But they have been sufficiently green to do huge damage' (Bawden, 2014). Have they? A notable feature of David Cameron's early leadership of the Conservative Party was the prominence he gave to the environment (Connelly, 2009, 2011). Shortly after the formation of the Coalition government in 2010, he pledged that 'this will be the greenest government ever' which will 'support sustainable growth and enterprise ... and promote the green industries that are so essential for our future (HM Government, 2010: 7). However, the environment has never been an easy issue for the Conservative Party, with one of the main problems being that the environment cuts across some of its key ideological fault lines. Thus, there has been willingness to embrace market-based solutions, but green taxes were regarded less favourably. The desire to avoid non-market, regulatory solutions sets a limit to how far a Conservative-led government can genuinely pursue environmental goals.

It is always difficult to push strong environmental policy during a recession, especially within a government committed to deficit reduction through cuts in public expenditure. Much depends on whether cuts are motivated by ideology or necessity. Those committed to green concerns find themselves uncomfortably caught between neo-liberal ideology and the Coalition's professed environmentalism. Again, although the

Coalition argued in its own policy documents that many environmental policies lead to green growth and employment, its commitment has, in practice, been weak. Very few any longer seriously claim that the Coalition is the 'greenest ever government'. On the contrary, the UK seems to have reverted to 'politics as usual'.

'Politics as usual'[1]

'Politics as usual', in this context, refers to an entrenched approach to the economy, economic growth, and economic and political interests, together with scepticism concerning environmental policy, especially where it is felt to be a brake on growth.[2] This does not necessarily imply active hostility to the environment, but it does imply relative indifference. The structure of 'politics as usual' comprises a set of deep presuppositions with a lexical ordering between levels of presuppositions and commitments, the structuring effects of power and influence, and the limits of bureaucratic rationality. On this view, the actions of government are an expression of underlying structures of power and influence, basic beliefs and administrative stasis. Mid-way between observable action and deep presuppositions lie approaches to tactics and strategy, manipulation and structuring of choices, and the shaping of the political opportunity structure.

An important dimension is power: at its deepest level lies the power of action-guiding presuppositions which are unquestioned and rarely challenged. At the next level there is the ability to shape and manipulate public debate through reputational power, or the implicit threat arising from the belief that political actors can access other forms of power if they wish. Finally, there is explicit observable power. Power operates on all these dimensions: they are not mutually exclusive but overlap, and differ in efficiency. For instance, it is more efficient to employ reputational power to manipulate the political agenda than to rely on explicit threats or physical force; and where the political agenda is founded on deep presuppositions ensuring prior agreement on fundamental ends, that is more efficient still (Lukes, 2005).

Thus a political actor can rely on reputation and implicit threat to achieve success in agenda manipulation. This is supplemented by the underlying constellation of presuppositions which absolves them of the need to argue their case explicitly because it is always already the default position. Only challengers to the *status quo* have to seriously argue their case, whereas its defenders are rarely required to provide more than a minimal level of argument. Thus defenders of the political and economic status quo possess an inbuilt advantage either because no one questions the desirability of economic growth (as an end), or of roads, planes, trade and industry (as means); or, if these are questioned, questioning is superficial. In this world, to be real is to be measurable, whatever is not measurable is not real, and the approved medium of measurement is GDP. In such 'debates' a conclusion is swiftly reached that, although hypothetical cases might exist where economic considerations are not paramount, in practice unlimited economic growth is an unqualified good. At this point all that then remains of policy debate is discussion of means, location or timing: when or where, rather than whether; more or less, rather than not at all; and hence opportunities for manipulation of decisions through pre-constrained choices open up nicely.

'Politics as usual', then, concerns a set of presuppositions within which deep presuppositions (taken for granted in political/economic argument) can be distinguished from surface presuppositions (relatively open to question). Surface presuppositions typically concern means not ends; deep presuppositions tend to concern ends, not means. Relations between these presuppositions are governed by a 'lexical' ordering in which certain conditions have to be satisfied before others can come into play. For 'politics as usual', once the conditions for ensuring economic growth are satisfied, environmental considerations can be considered, but not *vice versa*. Therefore, if environmental protection is at the expense of economic growth, it *should not* be pursued; if it promotes economic growth it *should* be pursued; if it has no palpable effect on economic growth it *might* be pursued if desired.

Debates surrounding climate change, energy, rail, roads and aviation policy take place within this framework, where two of the presuppositions of 'politics as usual' are the desirability of economic growth and belief that the relationship between environment and economy is typically a zero sum trade-off. The second presupposition is slightly more subtle than this, in that environment and economy are not taken *necessarily* to clash, but where they do (and they usually will), the economy should be prioritised. Both might co-exist in a green economy pursuing sustainable green development, but the implicit proviso is that this is so *only while there is no opposition between them*. It is revealing that 'green growth', the 'green economy' and so on are typically promoted not as green *qua green*, but as good for the *economy*: again, environmental values are subordinated to economic values.

'Politics as usual' rests on other presuppositions too, including attitudes to the scope and limits of governmental action, taxation and property rights. Consider attitudes to the scope and limits of governmental action: for some Conservatives the greatest heresy is the notion of taxation being construed as anything other than an unfortunate necessity. The positive use of taxation to promote social or environmental purposes is, on this view, anathema; hence many Conservatives would rule green taxation out as illegitimate on the grounds that the proper role of government does not include behaviour modification through taxation. This presupposition concerns legitimacy of means; where such presuppositions operate, certain means are regarded as impermissible, irrespective of ends.[3]

Policy making tends to be conducted incrementally. Incrementalism both describes how things happen and prescribes a model for rational decision making. Environmental issues wax and wane in public and political consciousness; when they return to active policy consideration, they already have an institutionalised footing. They become institutionally embedded and operate within the bounds of the structural presuppositions of bureaucracies. Institutionalisation, in the form of appropriate agencies and departments, possesses the advantage of providing a ready-made structure within which policy responses can be channelled. However, along with inherited techniques for dealing with issues, problems tend to be defined in ways that only allow solutions in accord with prevailing political and administrative arrangements. There are limits to the 'administrative mind' (Torgerson, 2005): policy makers typically pay attention only to problems amenable to technological and administrative solutions. Modern 'rational' administration presupposes a view of progress within which some approaches are regarded as reasonable and others are not; and within this frame, responses to environmental problems are often piecemeal rather than holistic, because the latter would challenge our views of economic and industrial development. Environmentalism challenges this because it implies that 'development' and 'progress' could, themselves, be the problem, not the solution.

The administrative mind thus denigrates those who articulate a different vision. Problems cannot be admitted to be systemic crises but have to be presented in a way that presents manageable, soluble and more or less separable problems packaged in ways that match the 'functional differentiation of the administrative apparatus' (Torgerson, 2005: 106). Doubtless, there is something to be said for reframing problems to admit of practicable solutions: it would be absurd to dismiss the importance of incrementalism, bounded rationality, and the constraints of the administrative mind. But taking environmentalism seriously presents a serious challenge to those limits and the presuppositions that sustain them.[4]

Environment, energy and climate change: going cold on climate change?

From his appointment as Secretary of State for Energy and Climate Change in 2010, Chris Huhne was seen as pivotal to the success of the government's environmental policy. He was a sufficiently powerful *virtuoso*[5] to harry the Chancellor and the Treasury in discussions leading to the formation of the Green Investment Bank (Connelly, 2011). He did not fully succeed, but success is relative. He was also a forceful negotiator in international climate change negotiations. However, he had to resign in February 2012 and his successor, Edward Davey (another Liberal Democrat) was regarded as both less green and less *virtuoso*. Liberal Democrats generally had not led the large and powerful departments and therefore had to be possessed of extraordinary *virtù* to be able to challenge the Treasury and other powerful ministries. They would have to achieve greatness; they would rarely have it thrust upon them. However, events showed that Davey was willing to fight hard for this corner.

The clearest symbol of Cameron's dissociation from the green agenda was the replacement (in September 2012) of Caroline Spelman as Secretary of State for the Environment by Owen Paterson (Carrington, 2012; Monbiot, 2012). He was in favour of exempting micro businesses from red tape, ending energy subsidies, rapid exploitation of shale gas, and 'urgent review of airport policy to ensure Britain gets its full share of global trade' (ConservativeHome, 2012). Paterson is a climate change 'sceptic' who failed, in office, to hold frequent and regular meetings with his chief scientific advisor, Ian Boyd. His predecessors met monthly; in over a year Paterson met twice, and both meetings were cursory. He relied on climate sceptics for advice.[6] Paterson's move to the Department for Environment, Food and Rural Affairs (Defra), in conjunction with Cameron's reported comments on 'green crap' and Osborne's increasingly outspoken opposition to green measures, all indicated the extent of the retreat from the green agenda and return to politics as usual. Green measures did not, of course, simply disappear, but the political will and drive to keep them at the centre of policy largely evaporated (Cusick, 2013).[7]

One notorious event, which showed either the extent of Cameron's abandonment of his green commitments (or the readiness of observers to believe that he had abandoned them), occurred in November 2013 when it was reported that he had ordered aides to 'get rid of all the green crap' that he believed was responsible for pushing up families' energy costs. This was denied, but given that he wanted to blame the rise in household energy bills on so-called 'green levies', it was certainly plausible (Bloodworth, 2014). Again, a proposal to include a target to decarbonise the UK's electricity generation by 2030 was defeated in the House of Commons in 2013 after the Coalition whipped its MPs to vote against it. Although he had originally supported the proposal, Cameron faced opposition from George Osborne (who opposed carbon targets) and backed down. The Chancellor also stated that he did not want Britain to be a world leader in fighting climate change because of the implications for competitiveness in international energy markets. At the height of Cameron's green period, he had previously argued that 'greening our economy can be a win-win solution'. The Chancellor had also cut taxes for the oil and gas industry to incentivise offshore drilling while at the same time cutting the budget for onshore wind farms by 10 per cent, removing the power of the Green Investment Bank to borrow and lend, and supporting airport expansion in the south-east (Bloodworth, 2014).

Osborne's lack of commitment to environmental leadership was paralleled by the reduction in the Foreign and Commonwealth Office's budget on its core climate change activities by 39 per cent between 2011 and 2014. This reduced the UK's ability to influence other countries' positions on climate action in the run-up to the United Nations Climate Change conference to be held in Paris in December 2015. Philip Hammond, appointed as Foreign Secretary in 2014, was less interested in climate change than his predecessor William Hague, which suggested there would be no reinstatement of funding. When taking office, Hammond stated that his priorities were 'security, economy and Europe': no mention of climate change (Darby, 2014).

However, the Chancellor does not always get his own way. On the occasion in July 2014 when Osborne tried to weaken the UK's carbon budget for the next decade, Edward Davey, Energy Secretary, insisted that the target would not be changed. The target – a cut of 50 per cent across 2023–27 against 1990 levels – was agreed in 2011 following a political battle between the Conservatives and Liberal Democrats: on that occasion Cameron intervened on Davey's side (Vaughan and Carrington, 2014). It should be remembered that this battle came only a few months after the Liberal Democrat leader had said that senior members of the Conservative Party were both ignoring the threat of climate change in the face of scientific evidence and also attacking environmental policies as anti-growth. Clegg went on to claim that the green agenda would be a priority for the Liberal Democrats in the forthcoming election, and that their commitment to the green agenda was 'as strong as it ever was'. Developing the theme, in a bid to highlight the differences between the two Coalition partners, he stated that 'conventional wisdom tells us that the environment must now go on the backburner while we prioritise our economic recovery – but I believe the opposite is true. If there was ever a time to sharpen our focus on our green commitments, it's now', and that there was 'a perfect symmetry between the nature of our economic recovery and our environmental responsibilities' (Choudhury, 2014).

In July 2014, Owen Paterson was replaced at Defra by Liz Truss, whose appointment was welcomed by some, although a popular view was that it did not take much to be greener than Paterson (Tickell, 2014). Paterson was angered by the decision, claiming that he was sacked as minister to appease the 'green blob', and has since started to campaign openly to scrap the 2008 Climate Change Act, among other things (Vaughan, 2014).

In his 2014 Autumn Statement, Osborne did not mention climate change or carbon emission targets, and his only direct reference to the environment was more money for flood defences. This shocked many environmentalists. Greenpeace UK's chief scientist, Doug Parr, said: 'In what looks like the warmest year on record, George Osborne has strikingly failed to shield the UK economy from climate change and grasp the opportunities of a modern cleantech economy … Instead, we get a 1980s style roadbuilding programme and subsidies/tax breaks for fossil fuel giants' (Merrick, 2014).

Tensions within the Coalition on environmental issues, and climate change in particular, can be seen not only within the leadership but also in the rank and file. A 2014 poll showed that 51 per cent of MPs agreed that it is a fact that global warming is largely man made. Sixty-seven per cent of Liberal Democrats and 73 per cent of Labour MPs agreed that man-made global warming is a scientific fact, but only 30 per cent of Conservative MPs accepted that climate change was caused by human activity, with 18 per cent agreeing that '*man-made climate change is environmentalist propaganda*'. Perhaps most telling was that half of MPs thought that climate change had fallen down the political agenda in the past five years: this was not a vote of confidence in the 'greenest government ever' (Benady and Owens, 2014; PRWeek, 2014).

From Heathrow to Boris Island and back again

The issue of increased runway capacity, whether it is required, and where it should be built if required, is an excellent case study of tensions both within the Coalition government, and within the Conservative Party. Before 2010, the Conservative MP Justine Greening was an eloquent opponent of a third runway at Heathrow Airport. Although her opposition might be for predominantly local reasons (her constituency lies under the flight path), her stance dovetailed with the Conservative Party's objections to Labour's plans for airport expansion. Hence the symbolism of her becoming Secretary of State for Transport in October 2010 was important; equally, her removal in September 2012 was seen as that symbolism's mirror image. Her replacement was Patrick McLoughlin, who was in favour of airport expansion. Greening's deputy at the Department for Transport, Theresa Villiers, was opposed to expansion of Heathrow and to Boris Johnson's proposal for a new airport on the Isle of Grain in the Thames estuary ('Boris Island'), and in favour both of High Speed 2 (HS2) and freeing capacity at Heathrow through increased use of Manchester and other northern airports.

Leadership is a complex topic: key variables include power or its lack and scope of action or its lack. Powerful actors, such as the Treasury, can dominate without needing to persuade; the relatively powerless, on the other hand, can (and have to) lead through skill in negotiating or facilitating agreements, or in redefining and conceptualising the terms of debate. Transport or environment ministers are likely to be relatively powerless and hence need to rely on entrepreneurial or cognitive leadership. How far they can succeed depends largely on a confluence of circumstances, although their leadership style is likely to be humdrum rather than heroic, or transactional rather than transformational (Wurzel and Connelly, 2011: 13). In the longer term, cognitive leadership can lead to significant change and to that extent 'politics as usual' can be subverted; but in the short term, the hegemony of powerful actors will tend to dominate.

When Greening left the Department for Transport, it was reported that there was rejoicing in the aviation industry, while elsewhere there was condemnation and suspicion. Boris Johnson stated:

[T]here can be only one reason to move her – and that is to expand Heathrow'. He continued: 'we will fight this all the way ... If we are to remain Europe's premier business hub we need a new four-runway airport, preferably to the east of London, that addresses the problem of aviation capacity before it is too late, and business is driven into the arms of our European competitors. (BBC News, 2012)

Although Johnson was opposed to Heathrow expansion he was not opposed to airport expansion as such. For Goldsmith, Greening's original appointment to Transport had shown the Prime Minister's position on Heathrow to be solid, and yielding so easily to pressure for her replacement indicated 'panic, not principle', while *Friends of the Earth* claimed that she had been 'shunted out' and was a 'victim of intense aviation lobbying over airport expansion' (BBC News, 2012).

Since 2010, chance and circumstance had combined in a move towards a third Heathrow runway. The argument, essentially, had been that airport expansion was bound to happen and 'Boris Island' was essentially a decoy, whose value lay in its deflecting attention from *whether* expansion was desirable to *where* it should be. Once Boris Island was rejected, the only serious remaining option would be expansion of Heathrow. In 2012, government officials had indicated that the prospect of building a third runway at Heathrow was 'dead and buried' and that they would consider 'all ideas bar a third runway'; but as one commentator observed: 'then we also had a Transport Secretary ... who lived under the flight path and had campaigned against the plan. What a difference to today, when a third runway at the UK's biggest and busiest airport is very much back on the table' (Westcott, 2013).

By the time of the 7 May 2015 general election, final decisions had yet to be taken, but it appeared to be a perfect example of the reassertion of 'politics as usual', with growth to the fore, the tactic of a constrained choice between an evil and a slightly lesser evil, and some ersatz environmental concern. Boris Island would be environmentally destructive and was therefore opposed by environmental groups. *Voila!* Heathrow would become, by default, the least worst environmental option. This political manoeuvring demonstrated the power and *virtù* of the Chancellor and his allies. Osborne had progressively revealed his support for more runway capacity in the south-east and for Heathrow as the only practicable solution, although still claiming that all options should be open. That is, all options (*except not increasing capacity*) were open; and although all options were 'open', *some remained more open than others*. What was most obviously absent was any systematic discussion of aviation in relation to transport or environmental policy as a whole.

The Coalition was nearing the end game. Although the government claimed that its position against airport expansion remained unchanged, the appointment of the Airports Commission, under Sir Howard Davies, suggested otherwise. In November 2012, the Secretary of State for Transport, Patrick McLoughlin, announced its terms of reference (McLoughlin, 2012). It was required to report by the end of 2013 on the nature, scale and timing of the steps needed to maintain the UK's global hub status, its recommendation for actions to improve the use of existing runway capacity in the next five years; and to report no later than summer 2015 on options for the UK's international connectivity needs (including economic, social and environmental impact). McLoughlin remarked that '[a]viation is vital to the UK economy and we need to have a long term aviation policy which meets the challenges of the future'. The presupposition was that there would be an increase in airport capacity and debate had been reduced to the future location and expansion of aviation. Given that the next general election would be in May 2015, the timescale was politically expedient, allowing the government to uphold the letter of the Coalition agreement which ruled out airport expansion in the current parliament.[8]

The Airports Commission issued its interim report in December 2013 and recommended that London would need another runway by 2030. It shortlisted only Heathrow and Gatwick for expansion. Surprisingly, it included a proposal to extend Heathrow's existing northerly runway westwards to allow takeoffs and landings from the same runway at the same time. Patrick McLoughlin did not comment on the shortlisted options, nor guarantee that the Conservatives would support the Commission's final verdict. The Commission was charged with examining these proposals and to recommend one in 2015; further studies were also to be made of a Thames Estuary airport (Boris Island): however, the logistical challenges of the latter were said to be 'very severe'. The London Mayor's alternative of expanding Stansted, was rejected along with more than 50 other schemes (Calder, 2013a).

In his analysis, Nigel Calder commented that 'Sir Howard Davies has tight-rope walked the line between Cameron and Boris over airport expansion'. Furthermore, although one purpose of the Commission was to elevate the debate among party political squabbles, 'airport expansion has become a proxy for the rivalry at the heart of the Conservative Party between the Prime Minister and the Mayor of London'. Ruling out all Thames Estuary options at this stage would have fuelled that political battle rather than allowing the Airports Commission diligently to evaluate each of the three shortlisted options. Sir Howard had bought some time by looking at the theoretical consequences for the environment and economic geography of an Isle of Grain development, while simultaneously focusing on his three preferred options (Calder, 2013b).

In September 2014 time ran out for Boris Johnson as the Commission announced that the Inner Thames estuary airport proposal had not been shortlisted (GOV.UK, 2014). Overall, the appointment and deliberations of the Airports Commission indicated the extent to which the Coalition had ceased asking serious questions about environmental policy in the round. Instead the debate has been reduced to one about timing and location (where, not whether) complicated by factional politics within the Conservative Party.

On the road again

Although the Chancellor's Autumn Statement at the beginning of December 2014 did not mention the environment directly, it announced measures that would have profound consequences for the environment. Among them were 'plans for the biggest road building programme for a generation', and 'billions of pounds to other road and rail improvements across the whole of the North of England'; this is all part of the Infrastructure Bill currently passing through parliament (Osborne, 2014). Since the demise of Mrs Thatcher's road-building programme in the early 1990s, little had been heard of major expansion of the road network: Osborne's proposals signified a considerable commitment to investment in the road network, with its attendant environmental and pollution issues. The £15 billion programme was designed to triple levels of spending by 2021 and invest in over 100 road schemes. Patrick McLoughlin, Transport Secretary, stated that: 'It will dramatically improve our road network and unlock Britain's economic potential' (Lean, 2014a). Cameron was quoted as saying, 'This will be nothing less than a roads revolution – one which will lead to quicker journey times, more jobs, and businesses boosted' (Chapman, 2014; McLoughlin, 2014).

Railways

In the summer of 2014, the East Coast mainline (ECML) franchise was returned to the private sector, despite its generating £1bn in surpluses and paying £235m back to the Treasury in its final years as a state-owned company (Moulds, 2014). Given that there was considerable public support for renationalisation of the railways and that most people oppose the re-privatisation of the ECML, this decision flew in the face of public opinion as well as the Opposition parties and the rail unions.

Meanwhile, HS2 had continued on its way and had recently been supplemented by a call for HS3 designed to connect northern cities in a so-called 'Northern Powerhouse' (Osborne, 2014). Responses to this initiative had been somewhat mixed. There were many who argued that the money would be far better spent on investing in the existing transport infrastructure and that the new scheme would, in effect, crowd out other transport investment. With 1.6 billion passengers per year, rail was now moving more people than in the 1920s when the network was twice its current size (Broadbent, 2014: 16–17). Given this, many argued that although there was a clear requirement for extra capacity, this required an examination of the infrastructure as a whole and could not be met by prestige high-speed schemes. Although there had been some reopening of lines and investment in rail infrastructure, there had been no systematic commitment to improving the rail network as a network, or to redress the regional imbalances in quality of service. The commitment had been to large-scale (not necessarily environmentally friendly) projects such as HS2 and HS3, justified on the grounds of providing conditions for enhanced economic growth.

Conclusion: Green chap or green crap?

The Prime Minister stated in 2013: '[F]racking has become a national debate in Britain – and it's one that I'm determined to win. If we don't back this technology, we will miss a massive opportunity to help families with their bills and make our country more competitive' (Cameron, 2013). The same Prime Minister also reportedly told aides to 'get rid of all the green crap', and had led a movement away from onshore wind farms. Despite this, David Cameron still appeared to believe that the Coalition government has been the 'greenest ever' (Lean, 2014b). Many close observers, however, found it hard to take this self-evaluation at face value. The Environmental Audit Committee (EAC) claimed that the government was failing to reduce air pollution, protect biodiversity and to prevent flooding. On another seven issues their verdict was that progress was unsatisfactory (EAC, 2014).

Emissions of airborne pollutants rose in 2013 after previously being steady for several years and the UK had failed to meet EU standards in two-thirds of the country's zones. The European Commission took legal action to force quicker action, but a Defra assessment concluded that London and two other regions would not meet the legal limits until 2030 (McGrath, 2014a, 2014b). On biodiversity, indicators showed a decline in three of the four key bird populations. On flooding, the committee stated that 2.4 million properties remained at risk from flooding from rivers or the sea and 3 million at risk from surface water. The committee proposed the formation of a new Office for Environmental Responsibility (as a parallel to the Office for Budgetary Responsibility) to advise on appropriate targets and monitor and publish performance.

Since 2010, the Coalition government had moved away from its loudly proclaimed green commitments, through a phase of relative silence, to a reassertion of traditional values: to 'politics as usual'. One indication was Cameron's speech discussing the need to challenge the EU's powers to dictate areas of environmental policy. He claimed that there were areas, including environmental legislation, 'where Europe has gone far too far'. He was not specific on details, but close observers thought that the Conservative Party would, while continuing to accept the EU carbon emissions reduction target, oppose the setting of a separate renewables target; that they would act on Osborne's long-established complaints about the 'ridiculous cost' the Habitats and Birds Directives placed on UK businesses (despite a Defra investigation showing the falsity of this claim); and that they would seek to make changes to the Air Quality Directive (ENDS, 2013).

Despite appearances, 'politics as usual' never really ceased to operate. And certainly, for its advocates, 'politics as usual' was neatly in its rightful place. The Treasury reigned supreme; radical, green and powerful ministers prepared or able to challenge the Treasury had resigned or been sidelined and replaced with weaker or hostile ministers; public opinion was indifferent and believed the claims of green government to be bogus; the deep lying assumption that economic growth was paramount was triumphant. Gestures had been made to green growth, sustainable development, and to the politics of ecological modernisation, but in any clash with the prevailing economic view they had been put firmly in their place.

Notes

1. This analysis is developed at greater length in Connelly (2013).
2. Economic neo-liberalism is an example of 'politics as usual', but it covers assumptions made by many who would not consider themselves neo-liberals.
3. Some might regard the *ends* as undesirable too; thus certain means are impermissible both because they are means to *improper* ends, and also because they are *improper* means to *any* ends.
4. For more on 'framing', see Matthews and Matthews (2014) and Connelly (2015).
5. Used in Machiavelli's sense: see Connelly (2013).

6. For example, Nigel Lawson's Global Warming Policy Foundation and his coal-field-owning, climate-sceptic brother in law, Matt Ridley.
7. Green Tory MP Zac Goldsmith saw the appointment was 'odd'; a year later he noted that Paterson had recently said there could be advantages to climate change which he said was 'a huge step forward ... he previously didn't think global warming was happening'.
8. Decision making on airport expansion is an example of Lukes' second dimension of power.

References

Bawden, T. (2014) UKIP green policy: climate change 'open to question' says energy spokesman Roger Helmer. *The Independent*, 30 December.

BBC News (2012) Boris Johnson's Heathrow warning after Justine Greening's move. 4 September. www.bbc.co.uk/news/uk-politics-19475249 (accessed 10 February 2013).

Benady, A. and Owens, J. (2014) Tory MPs: 'Climate change is not man made'. *The Ecologist*, 15 September. www.theecologist.org/News/news_round_up/2556680/tory_mps_climate_change_is_not_man_made.html (accessed 20 December 2014).

Bloodworth, J. (2014) 5 things the coalition did on climate change which it has suddenly shutup about. www.leftfootforward.org/2014/02/5-things-the-coalition-did-on-climate-change-which-theyve-suddenly-shutup-about (accessed 20 December 2014).

Broadbent, S. (2014) Rail passenger numbers reach post-First World War record. *Rail*, 764 (accessed 24 December 2014).

Calder, N. (2013a) Airports Commission: new runways considered at Heathrow and Gatwick. *The Independent*, 17 December. www.independent.co.uk/news/uk/home-news/airports-commission-report-third-runway-at-heathrow-and-second-at-gatwick-are-option--but-boris-island-left-off-shortlist-9009536.html (accessed 1 January 2014).

Calder, N. (2013b) Sir Howard Davies has tight-rope walked the line between Cameron and Boris over airport expansion. *The Independent*, 17 December. www.independent.co.uk/travel/simon-calder/simon-calder-sir-howard-davies-has-tightrope-walked-the-line-between-cameron-and-boris-over-airport-expansion-9009695.html (accessed 1 January 2014).

Cameron, D. (2013) We cannot afford to miss out on shale gas. *Daily Telegraph*, 11 August.

Carrington, D. (2012) Owen Paterson's climate change problem: cock-up or conspiracy? *The Guardian*, 7 September. www.guardian.co.uk/environment/damian-carrington-blog/2012/sep/07/owen-paterson-climate-change-sceptic (accessed 10 February 2013).

Chapman, J. (2014) The £15bn roads revolution: PM embraces Margaret Thatcher's 'great car economy' and promises biggest building blitz for 50 years'. *Daily Mail*, 10 November.

Choudhury, N. (2014) Nick Clegg: senior Tories are blocking UK climate policy. *RTCC: Responding to Climate Change*, 7 November. www.rtcc.org/2013/11/07/

nick-clegg-senior-tories-are-blocking-uk-climate-policy/ (accessed 10 January 2015).

Connelly, J. (2009) Voting Blue, Going Green? David Cameron and the Environment. In M. Beech and S. Lee (eds.), *Built to Last? The Conservatives under David Cameron* (London: Palgrave Macmillan).

Connelly, J. (2011) Vote Blue, Go Green, What's a Bit of Yellow in Between? In M. Beech and S. Lee (eds), *The Cameron–Clegg Coalition Government: Coalition Politics in an Age of Austerity* (London: Palgrave Macmillan).

Connelly, J. (2013) Coalition, Aviation and the Descent to 'Politics as Usual'. In L. Budd, S. Griggs and D. Howarth (eds), *Sustainable Aviation Futures* (Bingley: Emerald).

Connelly, J. (2015) Review of Matthews, L. and Matthews, A., *Framespotting: Changing how you look at things changes how you see them. Global Policy.* 13 January. www.globalpolicyjournal.com/blog/13/01/2015/book-review-framespotting-changing-how-you-look-things-changes-how-you-see-them (accessed 28 January 2015).

ConservativeHome (2012) Unemployment is down, exports are booming. 16 May. www.conservativehome.blogs.com/thetorydiary/2012/05/unemployment-is-down-exports-are-booming-but-paterson-hague-and-fox-all-urge-chancellor-to-do-more.html (accessed 1 January 2014).

Cusick, J. (2013) Owen Paterson, his sceptic brother-in-law, and how Defra went cold on climate change. *The Independent*, 29 November.

Darby, M. (2014) UK slashes climate diplomacy budget. *RTCC: Responding to Climate Change*, 31 July. www.rtcc.org/2014/07/31/uk-slashes-climate-diplomacy-budget/ (accessed 9 January 2015).

ENDS Europe (2013) UK PM calls for roll-back of EU green laws. 24 January. www.endseurope.com/30419/uk-pm-calls-for-rollback-of-eu-green-laws?referrer=bulletin&DCMP=EMC-ENDS-EUROPE-DAILY (accessed 10 February 2015).

Environmental Audit Committee (2014) *An environmental scorecard.* Fifth Report of Session 2014–15, HC.215 (London: The Stationery Office). www.publications.parliament.uk/pa/cm201415/cmselect/cmenvaud/215/215.pdf (accessed 5 January 2015).

GOV.UK (2014) Airports Commission announces inner Thames estuary decision. Press Release, 2 September. www.gov.uk/government/news/airports-commission-announces-inner-thames-estuary-decision (accessed 10 January 2015).

HM Government (2010) *The Coalition: Our Programme for Government* (London: The Cabinet Office).

Lean, G. (2014a) Will the Government's new road-building programme hit a dead end? *Daily Telegraph*, 3 December.

Lean, G. (2014b) Cameron still believes his is the 'greenest government'. *Daily Telegraph*, 18 December.

Lukes, S. (2005) *Power: A Radical View*, second edition (Basingstoke: Palgrave Macmillan).

McGrath, M. (2014a) EU Commission launches legal action over UK air quality. *BBC News*, 20 February (accessed 21 December 2014).

McGrath, M. (2014b) Red card on environment for 'greenest government ever'. *BBC News*, 15 September. www.bbc.co.uk/news/science-environment-29210467 (accessed 8 December 2014).

McLoughlin, P. (2012) Membership and terms of reference of Airports Commission. 2 November. www.gov.uk/government/speeches/membership-and-terms-of-reference-of-the-airports-commission (accessed 20 December 2014).

McLoughlin, P. (2014) Transport infrastructure: 'Road investment strategy'. 1 December. www.gov.uk/government/speeches/transport-infrastructure-road-investment-strategy (accessed 20 December 2014).

Matthews, L. and Matthews, A. (2014) *Framespotting: Changing How You Look at Things Changes How You See Them* (Alresford: Iff Books).

Merrick, J. (2014) Ed Miliband lambasts PM for 'ignoring advice on climate change'. *The Independent*, 7 December.

Monbiot, G. (2012) Declaring war on the environment. 6 September. www.monbiot.com/2012/09/06/declaring-war-on-the-environment/ (accessed 10 February 2012).

Moulds, J. (2014) East coast mainline pays taxpayers £1bn sparking fresh reprivatisation fury. *The Guardian*, 4 August.

Osborne, G. (2014) Autumn Statement 2014. 3 December. www.gov.uk/government/speeches/chancellor-george-osbornes-autumn-statement-2014-speech (accessed 24 December 2014).

PR Week (2014) Special report: climate change and communications. 10 September. www.prweek.com/uk/specialreportclimatechange (accessed 20 December 2014).

Tickell, O. (2014) Britain's new Environment Secretary is a breath of fresh air. *The Ecologist*, 15 July. www.theecologist.org/News/news_analysis/2478164/britains_new_environment_secretary_is_a_breath_of_fresh_air.html (accessed 5 January 2015).

Torgerson, D. (2005) The Ambivalence of Discourse: Beyond the Administrative Mind? In R. Paehlke and D. Torgerson (eds), *Managing Leviathan: Environmental Politics and the Administrative State*, second edition (Peterborough, Ontario: Broadview Press).

Vaughan, A. (2014) Owen Paterson proposal to scrap Climate Change Act is 'bonkers'. *The Guardian*, 13 October.

Vaughan, A. and Carrington, D. (2014) George Osborne defeated in attempt to weaken UK carbon budget. *The Guardian*, 22 July.

Westcott, R. (2013) Heathrow submits third runway options to Davies Commission. *BBC News*, 17 July. http://www.bbc.co.uk/news/uk-23337754 (accessed 17 July 2013).

Wurzel, R. and Connelly, J. (2011) *The European Union as a Leader in International Climate Change Politics* (London: Routledge).

7
Immigration and Housing
Rebecca Partos and Tim Bale

There are few policy areas in which the UK's current Coalition partners have more disparate views than immigration. The differences were apparent during the televised leaders' debates during the 2010 election campaign. Nick Clegg called for 'an immigration system which works', while David Cameron responded that 'Nick's ideas would ... make the situation worse' because the Liberal Democrats' policy of an amnesty for illegal immigrants would lead to higher immigration, and their regional work proposal 'sounds like they're going to put up border controls along the M5' (cited in BBC News, 2010). Clegg said 'we can't come up with promises like caps [on immigration, a central Conservative policy], which don't work' (ibid.). Coalition, one might have expected, would lead to some sort of compromise or *via media*. In practice, however, this is a policy area in which the Liberal Democrats have been able to exert very little constraining influence over the Conservatives; a party with a long tradition of tracking and occasionally exploiting public opinion on the issue in populist fashion (see Bale, 2012; Bale and Partos, 2014).

There was, in fact, little ambiguity in the Coalition Agreement of 2010: there would be an emphasis on tightening up immigration policy across the board (HM Government, 2010). Immigration levels would be controlled on the grounds that managed flows would ensure better community cohesion and lessen the strain on public services. The policies detailed an annual limit on the number of non-EU economic migrants admitted to the UK; the establishment of a Border Police Force and an 'e-borders' system; and the reintroduction of exit checks (the Tories had removed them in 1994). Notably, there would be a new emphasis on abuse within the immigration system and measures would be put in place to expedite the processing of asylum claims. In light of the much higher than expected flows of migrants from A8 countries from 2004 onwards, citizens from any new EU member states would be subject to transitional controls. The only evidence of Liberal Democrat influence was a line which promised an end to the detention of minors for immigration purposes (see Hampshire and Bale (2015) for a detailed study of inter-party, intra-coalitional and interdepartmental differences on the issues).

The road not taken

The hard line spun in the Coalition Agreement was notable in part because there had been some signs before the election that immigration policy under a Tory government might be marked by a more moderate and evidence-based approach. First, the Conservatives' 2010 manifesto filed immigration under the heading 'business' and a commitment to 'attract the brightest and best to our country', rather than, say, crime or security (Bale and Partos, 2014). Second, Cameron appointed Damian Green, widely viewed as a left-of-centre Tory and a moderate, as immigration minister, an important portfolio by most accounts. Within months of his appointment, Green made it clear that he would not bow to unreasonable and exaggerated demands, declaring that 'whatever your stance on immigration, if you are not basing policy on decent evidence you will be likely to fail' (Green, 2010).

In practice, however, immigration policy has not simply been restrictive but often hyperbolic and hyperactive, driven it seems more by the Conservatives' concerns about losing voters, and even members, to UKIP than by anything else (see Partos and Bale 2015, forthcoming). It has also, according to the Conservatives' declared ambition to reduce the net migration figure to the tens rather than the hundreds of thousands, been deemed something of a failure after it was announced in November 2014 that net migration had by then exceeded the last figure recorded for the Labour government which left office in 2010 (ONS, 2014) and this despite the fact that the Coalition has actually managed to make serious reductions in some sources of immigration.

Despite those successes – effectively hidden by a net total driven both by the level of emigration and by the number of migrants attracted to the UK by its relatively healthy economy (*Economist*, 2010) – it is hardly surprising, perhaps, that policy which proudly purports to be responsive to public opinion has not always resembled evidence-based policy (Partos, 2014). Indeed, it sometimes seemed that under the Coalition, counterfactual policies abounded. For instance, 2012 began with fresh attempts by the government to link the issue of economic immigration with state benefits and tax revenue. And yet, at the same time, a government-commissioned study estimated that foreign-born workers are probably *less* likely to claim benefits than UK nationals (BBC News, 2012). Later on, in March 2014, a report on the impact of immigration was said to have been 'withheld' because it claimed that the negative economic impact of immigration was smaller than previously thought (Cook, 2014). Government sources initially said that the report was incomplete, but a day after the story became headline news, the report was promptly released.

Tough policies for tough times

The Coalition government has made great efforts to bring in hard-line policies on immigration to match the public's mood on the issue and to show it cares deeply about it. There have, for example, been ministerial visits to new wings of detention centres for foreign criminals and very public suspensions of universities' and colleges' licences to recruit students from overseas. The Prime Minister and his Home Secretary, Theresa May were even pictured in the immediate aftermath of immigration raids, posing in the domestic surroundings of suspects with police officers and border staff (Mason, 2014b). More generally, immigration policy under the Coalition government tightened controls and curtailed the rights of immigrants.

Economic migrants have been subject to stricter regulations in the hope of bringing down numbers and their rights to settlement and citizenship have been restricted. On the other hand, some economic migrants are encouraged to enter the UK with special promotional campaigns (such as 'Britain is GREAT') and new incentive schemes. Favoured visitors from China now have access to an unprecedented online 24-hour visa scheme (Home Office, 2014). There has been an increase in legislation that has passed border guards' responsibilities on to the public, such as the landlord, or the employer, and the cost of penalties has multiplied for those failing to carry out such obligations (ibid.).

International students, sometimes regarded as bogus economic migrants and potential security risks, now have to be better educated, and endure more intensive bureaucratic procedures in order to gain visas. Furthermore, graduates of UK universities no longer have the Tier 1 (Post-study work) route open to them; instead they need a skilled job offer from a sponsoring employer to remain in the country (see Home Office, 2012b). The number of student visas issued 'collapsed'

from 314,305 Tier 4 visas issued in 2009 to 218,773 in 2013, a drop of 36 per cent (Bowman, 2014).

Policy for asylum seekers has remained largely unchanged, and although there is a new emphasis on locating and deporting failed asylum seekers and expediting the process, the backlog of cases remains. Targets for concluding asylum applications within a set period of time have gone; a series of 'performance indicators' which monitor outcomes have taken their place. Gay and lesbian asylum seekers at risk of persecution if they are returned to their country of origin have greater protection (see HM Government, 2011), but there are still cases that have fallen through the cracks.

Greater financial requirements have been introduced for those who wish to bring a non-EU relative to the UK, which has decreased the number of British citizens and residents who can act as sponsors (see Commons Library Standard Note, 2014). More rigorous English-language tests and checks on marriages have been introduced. Appeal rights for those refused family visas to visit relatives in the UK have been severely reduced. Even those who do meet the requirements can only bring their partner into the UK after a 'probationary period' of several years to test how genuine the relationship is. In 2012, changes to family immigration policy were, according to government documents, primarily about 'stop[ping] family criminals hiding behind human rights law to dodge deportation' (a reference to Article 8) and 'ensur[ing] only migrants who can pay their way are allowed' to enter the UK (Home Office, 2012a).

An emphasis on illegal immigrants and trouble with Europe in the Coalition

The Coalition government has devoted an extraordinary amount of attention to the issue of illegal immigration. The Immigration Act of 2014 is explicit in its determination to make the UK a more 'hostile' place for illegal immigrants and allows for foreign criminals to be deported first and allowed to appeal later (HM Government, 2014). The Act also makes it more difficult for irregular migrants to open a bank account, apply for a driving licence or rent accommodation privately (ibid.). It makes sense to expend efforts on illegal immigration as illegal immigrants are the target of much negative, even hostile, public opinion and they may also operate outside the tax system. This made it all the more embarrassing for the government when the then immigration minister, Mark Harper, had to resign in early 2014 after he realised that his housekeeper had no right to work in the country. This was the same Mark Harper on whose watch the Home Office piloted 'go home' billboard vans directed at illegal immigrants. Whether or not they worked or enjoyed public support (Barrett, 2013), they proved to be too much for some of the Conservatives' Liberal Democrat partners. Business Secretary Vince Cable alleged that the adverts had been designed 'to create a sense of fear in the British population' (Swinford, 2013). He maintained that the Liberal Democrat ministers within the government had not been consulted, and that the 'stupid and offensive' campaign should be stopped (ibid.).

This was by no means the first time that Cable had been critical of his Conservative colleagues' words and actions on immigration. Cable's contrary stance had been driven both by ideological differences and the fact that his ministry, Business, Innovation and Skills (BIS), had very different priorities (mainly revolving around economic growth) to the lead department on the issue, the Home Office, whose main preoccupation was control, howsoever achieved (see Hampshire and Bale, 2015). Immigration has also proved a bone of contention between the two Coalition partners because it feeds into another, possibly even more profound difference between them, namely their respective positions on the European Union.

In the last few years, immigration control has become conflated with that of EU 'interference' with national issues. The parliamentary term has been dominated by fears that the lifting of transitional controls on Romanians and Bulgarians would lead to an influx of migrants to the UK. Tabloid headlines stoked fears by reporting on extra planes being booked to deal with demand from Romania and Bulgaria, yet independent investigations found no evidence for this (Andreou, 2014). Nonetheless, the government had difficulty with the issue and in January 2014 had to stave off a backbench rebellion (Mason, 2014a). Cameron acknowledged the limitations of being a member state within the EU: 'We've done the extent of what we can do within the rules' (ibid.).

The Conservative-led government might have acknowledged that the current rules limit its scope for action, but that does not mean that it has not attempted to revise the rules. Theresa May began talking about curbs on EU migration, such as access to the UK for dependants of EU citizens and, access to benefits for EU citizens in 2012. Although free movement of EU workers is a central part of the EU's single market, May was said to be considering 'revers[ing] previous European court of justice judgements that have in effect redefined free movement as available to *citizens* rather than merely *workers*' (Wintour, 2012, our italics).

These efforts have not gone unnoticed by other EU countries, which has provoked more bad feeling between the UK and the EU. Cameron's proposal to apply an 'emergency brake' or even bring in a cap on low-skilled EU workers has been described by European Commission president José Manuel Barroso as an 'historic mistake' and contrary to EU law (Watt, 2014). It had been reported that the number of national insurance registrations issued to EU immigrants with low skills could be restricted in order to reduce immigration. Germany appeared to rule out Cameron's plan to limit EU migrants in the UK with Chancellor Angela Merkel dismissing this, saying there could be no 'tamper[ing]' with the EU principle of free movement (Pancevski and Shipman, 2014). This might explain why David Cameron's 'big speech' on immigration in late November 2014 made no mention of ideas which had been floated to impose quotas, or some sort of emergency brake on the right of European citizens to enter the UK without hindrance, but resorted instead to promising changes to the benefits system.

Immigration and housing policy

The 2010 Coalition Agreement contained few references to housing, and where it did, the focus was mainly on devolving power to the local level so as to, 'return decision-making powers on housing and planning to local councils' and removing restrictions on turning existing buildings into homes even including an attempt to, 'promote ... schemes that encourage farmers to convert existing buildings to affordable housing' (HM Government, 2010).

It is generally acknowledged that the housing problem is mostly the result of the decreasing social housing stock and insufficient house building programmes of the last 30 years. A government report predicted that by 2026, the number of households would increase annually by 223,000 a year in England with one-third of this growth due to net migration (Shelter, 2008). Certainly there is no denying that immigration increases pressures on the housing stock, but it is important to note that migrants demand less housing than UK-born people, in part because they are more likely to live in larger households and so require fewer homes. However, this difference becomes less evident when immigrants have been in the UK for a while; they are then more likely to prefer to live in smaller households. As one might expect, given that the foreign-born population includes new arrivals, the foreign-born population has much lower rates of ownership at 44 per cent than the UK-born at 70 per cent (Migration Observatory, 2014). It is no surprise then that the foreign-born are around three times as likely to be in the private rental sector compared to the UK-born (ibid.). During the course of its term in office, the Coalition government brought in the Localism Act of 2011. Councils continue to have a duty to give preference to some groups, such as the homeless and those living in difficult conditions, but apart from that, they now have the autonomy to decide whom to support, such as those with a long-standing link to the local area. Those individuals who are subject to immigration control cannot be supported by local councils. This parliament has also brought in the National Planning Policy Framework, but there have been concerns raised (by Conservatives as well as others) that the reforms are leading to 'planning by appeal', in which decisions are forced through. Incentives have been introduced to try to reconcile people opposed to planning in their local area.

Plans for new garden cities to attempt to keep up with the need for housing have been largely put to one side, allegedly to keep the Conservatives' 'natural supporters at least vaguely calm in the run-up to 2015' (Hardman, 2014: 71). The idea to make use of existing buildings by converting them into housing has been largely ignored after plans to turn empty shops into homes were thwarted by local officials who do not want to change the use of buildings or do not have the funds to bring in the necessary infrastructure to support such changes (e.g. healthcare, local schools, etc.).

The situation has certainly not been resolved. With rising rents and an increasing housing benefit bill, the costs of not building more housing are felt by most people, if indirectly. As one contributor to the modernising Conservative group Bright Blue has said, 'ordinary taxpayers ... are forced to foot the bill for the failure of politicians to get enough homes built' (Hardman, 2014: 69). The government's efforts to cut the housing benefit bill by imposing a cap on how much each family can receive and bringing in penalties for those judged to have a 'spare bedroom', have made few savings and caused much bitterness, as they are only dealing with the symptoms of the problem. In 2013, the Coalition government stated that it would commission 37,000 new affordable homes for poorer residents; a fifth of the number ministers had promised to build by the end of the parliament (Ramesh, 2013).

Schemes that encourage people with as little as a 5 per cent deposit to purchase, for example, by subsidising the mortgages of first-time buyers, have served to keep house prices rising. Cable – a thorn in his Coalition partner's side on this issue as well – has criticised the Help to Buy and Right to Buy schemes (which offer incentives and make it easier to buy private council house properties) for causing a deepening inequality between social classes and making the intergenerational divide worse (Mason, 2014c).

With research pointing to immigration pushing rents up in some areas (Home Office, 2013), and potentially pushing prices down through sales of lower quality houses (Migration Observatory, 2014), the results are mixed. Even in a zero-net migration scenario, the housing shortage would continue (see Barker, 2004). It should also be noted that while immigration might impact on the price of housing within a certain district, the price of housing also has an impact on the decision to migrate and, therefore, 'it is challenging to establish a causal relationship between the price of housing and the level of immigration' (Migration Observatory, 2014: 6).

Conclusion

There is no denying that the Coalition government have brought in a number of important changes to immigration policy in a relatively short time frame. Many, if not all, of these measures have been geared towards reducing levels of immigration to the UK, yet, while they are significant developments, they have not been effective. Net migration is not significantly lower than it was at the start of the Coalition's term in 2010; it has decreased from 252,000 to 243,000 in the year to March 2014. Efforts to reduce immigration can, on this superficial basis at least, be regarded as something of a failure and an understandable one given that the Coalition have little control over net migration. It is unclear, however, to what extent the government will be punished for this at the ballot box. Voters, after all, attach more meaning to their lived experiences and perceptions than to statistics.

There are signs that efforts to more clearly delineate between migrants (those we 'want' versus those we 'do not want') have in fact muddied the waters. Mixed messages on migration, a border control system in constant flux, and greater bureaucratic procedures to obtain a visa might well have discouraged potential highly skilled migrants from coming to the UK by in effect installing, in the words of the ultra-liberal *Economist*, 'a "keep out" sign over the white cliffs of Dover' and ratcheting up measures 'that would turn an entrepôt into a fortress' (*Economist*, 2012).

Frequent and high-profile amendments to immigration policy form part of Tory efforts both to paint Labour as a soft touch on the issue (see

Partos, 2014) and to prevent the loss of their supporters and potential Conservative voters to UKIP, both on immigration and on the linked issue of EU membership (Watt, 2014). Senior Liberal Democrats have openly remarked that their partner's tougher tone on immigration stems from electoral strategy rather than a pragmatic response to real-world developments or policies based on evidence. The Liberal Democrat Secretary for Energy and Climate Change, Ed Davey, for instance, put down Conservative Defence Secretary Michael Fallon's comments about immigration 'swamping' communities to, 'Conservative concerns of the UKIP threat in the Rochester by-election [more] than they are based on the facts' (Syal, 2014).

If Davey was correct, it is not a strategy that seems to have worked. A YouGov survey from October 2014 polled the public on which of the four main party leaders they trusted to take the right decisions on key issues. Cameron was most trusted on the economy, defence and tackling crime (again, traditional Conservative issues), Clegg on none of the issues, and Farage was in the lead on immigration and Europe (YouGov, 2014). Moreover, both Tory defectors to UKIP, Douglas Carswell in Clacton and Mark Reckless in Rochester and Strood, won their by-elections easily. The decision to give a peerage to the chair of right-wing pressure group MigrationWatch, Andrew Green – seen by many as yet another attempt to reclaim the issue and bring in votes from the anti-PC brigade (*Independent*, 2014) – looked no more likely to succeed. Indeed, UKIP could end up gaining most from such a strategy if the Conservative-led government continues to push the immigration issue up the agenda. It might even serve to highlight the failure of the Coalition to restrict levels of immigration. Furthermore, even when popular policies are legislated, the public has been unwilling, it seems, to credit either party in the Coalition for enacting them, and even when they notice it is happening, they do not seem to believe that legislation will be effective.

The public might well be justified in its lack of faith in the government's attempts to decrease immigration. It is difficult to see the missed target for net migration as anything other than a failure for the government. The inability to increase housing stocks has also been widely regarded as a failure. Coalition government plans to accommodate the population by building new garden cities and converting existing buildings previously used by businesses into domestic housing have amounted to very little. Attempts to reduce the growing housing benefit bill by, in part, penalising those judged to have a 'spare bedroom', have been more trouble for the government than they were worth.

Given voters' heightened focus on immigration, which is regarded as in the top two of public concerns (the other being the economy), it is unsurprising that the mainstream parties have all been jostling for tougher policies. Even the Liberal Democrats have been doing more than dipping a toe into the water. The party's draft manifesto was leaked in October 2014, and top of the list of policies was 'Bring back proper border checks so we know who's coming in and leaving the UK, allowing the government to identify and deport people who over-stay their visa' (Swinford, 2014). New claimants for Jobseeker's Allowance with a 'poor' level of English would have their benefits cut unless they took language lessons (ibid.). In this competitive climate, it is not surprising that the Conservatives are moving ever right-wards and trying to 'out-UKIP UKIP'. Sadly for both the Liberal Democrats and the Conservatives, Farage always seems to enjoy the last laugh. He was even able to condemn as 'nasty' and 'unpleasant' the Coalition government's billboard van campaign which urged illegal immigrants to 'go home or face arrest' (Dominiczak, 2013). Perhaps, he volunteered, the billboards should be replaced with the slogan, 'Please don't vote UKIP. We're doing something' (ibid.). He was not the only one making similarly waggish suggestions: as the Spectator's Alex Massie noted perhaps the Tory pitch could best be summarised as 'UKIP are right. Don't vote for them' (Massey, 2014).

References

Andreou, A. (2014) 'The immigration invasion that never was'. *The Guardian.* 2 January 2014. Available at http://bit.ly/1bBMogD (Accessed 17 November 2014).

Bale, T. (2012) *The Conservatives since 1945: The Drivers of Party Change.* Oxford University Press.

Bale, T. and Partos, R. (2014) 'Why mainstream parties change policy on migration: A UK case study – The Conservative Party, immigration and asylum, 1960–2010'. *Comparative European Politics* 12: 603–619.

Barker, K. (2004) 'Barker Review of Housing Supply – Final Report – Recommendations'. *HM Treasury.* 17 March 2004. Available at http://bit.ly/1yhJPxz (Accessed 17 November 2014).

Barrett, D. (2013) 'Illegal immigrants cost taxpayer more than £4,000 a head each year'. *The Telegraph.* 31 October 2013. Available at http://bit.ly/1Ha612G (Accessed 17 November 2014).

BBC News (2010) 'Second prime ministerial debate, 22 April 2010, transcript'. *BBC News.* 23 April 2010. Available at http://bbc.in/1zwpAx0 (Accessed 17 November 2014).

BBC News (2012) 'Migrants on work-related benefits study published'. *BBC News*. 20 January 2012. Available at http://bbc.in/1AcarnO (Accessed 17 November 2014).

Bowman, S. (2014) 'Small steps: immigration', in R. Shorthouse, K. Maltby and J. Brenton (eds), *The Modernisers' Manifesto*. 14 April 2014. Available at brightblue.org.uk/bbmanifesto.pdf (Accessed 4 June 2014).

Commons Library Standard Note. (2014) 'The financial (minimum income) requirement for partner visas'. *Commons Library*. 2 September 2014. Available at http://bit.ly/1nAO5AP (Accessed 23 January 2014).

Cook, C. (2014) 'Immigration impact report withheld by Downing Street'. *BBC News*. 5 March 2014. Available at http://bbc.in/1fFoEQl (Accessed 17 November 2014).

Dominiczak, P. (2013) 'Nigel Farage attacks "Big Brother" Government immigration campaign'. *The Telegraph*. 25 July 2013. Available at: http://bit.ly/1zw3tGW (Accessed 17 November 2014).

Economist, The (2010) 'Scrap the cap'. *The Economist*. 18 November 2010. Available at http://econ.st/1DFvvUp (Accessed 17 November 2014).

Economist, The (2012) 'The Tories' barmiest policy'. *The Economist*. 20 October 2012. Available at http://econ.st/1xIbIPY (Accessed 17 November 2014).

Green, D. (2010) 'Immigration: Damian Green's speech to the Royal Commonwealth Society'. *Home Office*. 7 September 2010. Available at http://bit.ly/1qjYhWO (Accessed 17 November 2014).

Hampshire, J. and Bale, T. (2015) 'New administration, new immigration regime: do parties matter after all? A UK case study'. *West European Politics* 38(1): 145–166.

Hardman, I. (2014) 'Humble homes: Housing'. *The Modernisers' Manifesto*. Bright Blue. Available at http://bit.ly/1t7XkLO (Accessed 17 November 2014).

HM Government. (2010) 'The Coalition: our programme for government'. *HM Government*. May 2010. Available at http://bit.ly/1rKNswT (Accessed 17 November 2014).

HM Government. (2011) 'Sexual orientation in asylum claim: process'. *HM Government*. 13 June 2011. Available at http://bit.ly/1BkIkRO (Accessed 23 January 2015).

HM Government. (2014) 'Immigration Act 2014'. Chapter 22. *HM Government*. Available at http://bit.ly/1vNt0uN (Accessed 23 January 2014).

Home Office. (2012a) 'Radical immigration changes to reform family visas and prevent abuse of human rights'. *Home Office*. 11 June 2012. Available at http://bit.ly/1xIqlmg (Accessed 4 June 2014).

Home Office. (2012b) 'Statement of Intent: Changes affecting study, post-study work and maintenance requirements for students and workers'. *Home Office*. February 2012. Available at http://bit.ly/1wsdMIq (Accessed 23 January 2014).

Home Office. (2013) 'Social and public service impacts of international migration at the local levels'. July 2013. Available at http://bit.ly/1yhKY8v (Accessed 17 November 2014).

Home Office. (2014) 'Immigration Minister announces new improvements to the visa system in China'. *Home Office*. 28 July 2014. Available at http://bit.ly/1t3RJGi (Accessed 4 June 2014).

Independent, The (2014) 'Sir Andrew Green peerage: A highly misguided Lords appointment for the Migration Watch founder'. *The Independent*. 21 October 2014. Available at http://ind.pn/11jTQiE (Accessed 17 November 2014).

Mason, R. (2014a) 'David Cameron: Romania and Bulgaria immigration levels "reasonable"'. *The Guardian*. 27 January 2014. Available at http://bit.ly/1i44pKP (Accessed 17 November 2014).

Mason, R. (2014b) 'David Cameron criticised for PR stunt in home of suspected illegal immigrants'. *The Guardian*. 30 July 2014. Available at http://bit.ly/1qKQAbX (Accessed 17 November 2014).

Mason, R. (2014c) 'Vince Cable warns of inequalities caused by housing market crisis'. *The Guardian*. 6 October 2014. Available at http://bit.ly/1n9CrmW (Accessed 17 November 2014).

Massie, A. (2014) 'Tories reveal innovative new election strategy ...' *The Spectator*. 20 October 2014. Available at http://bit.ly/1sHM9fU (Accessed 23 January 2015).

Migration Observatory (2014) 'Migrants and housing in the UK: Experiences and impacts'. *Migration Observatory*. 2 October 2014. Available at http://bit.ly/1vlgllh (Accessed 17 November 2014).

ONS (2014) 'Migration Statistics Quarterly Report, August 2014'. *Office for National Statistics*. 28 August 2014. Available at http://bit.ly/1sZ92JI (Accessed 17 November 2014).

Pancevski, B. and Shipman, T. (2014) 'Merkel: I will block PM on immigrants.' *The Sunday Times*. 26 October 2014. Available at http://thetim.es/1tqW3oQ (Accessed 17 November 2014).

Partos, R. (2014) No immigrants, no evidence? The making of Conservative Party immigration policy. *Political Insight*. 5(3), 12–15.

Partos, R. and Bale, T. (2015) Immigration and asylum policy under Cameron's Conservatives. *British Politics*. Forthcoming.

Ramesh, R. (2013) 'Sharp drop in new affordable homes under coalition, council data shows.' *The Guardian*. Available at http://bit.ly/1xLkpcv (Accessed 17 November 2014).

Shelter (2008) 'Immigration and housing.' *Shelter*. Available at http://bit.ly/1qjFGu3 (Accessed 17 November 2014).

Swinford, S. (2013) 'Illegal immigrant poster campaign is "stupid and offensive", Vince Cable says'. *The Telegraph*. 28 July 2013. Available at http://bit.ly/1ulW4sk (Accessed 17 November 2014).

Swinford, S. (2014) 'Liberal Democrat manifesto leaked'. *The Telegraph*. 21 October 2014. Available at http://bit.ly/1xI3ZS0 (Accessed 17 November 2014).

Syal, R. (2014) 'Michael Fallon's "swamped by migrants" remark leaves Tories in disarray'. *The Guardian*. 27 October 2014. Available at http://bit.ly/1wBFMLK (Accessed 17 November 2014).

Watt, N. (2014) 'David Cameron making "historic" mistake over EU, says, José Manuel Barroso'. *The Guardian*. 20 October 2014. Available at http://bit.ly/ZLrwW1 (Accessed 17 November 2014).

Wintour, P. (2012) 'Theresa May considers curbs on EU migration'. *The Guardian*. 7 October 2012. Available at http://bit.ly/14DYpXk (Accessed 17 November 2014).

YouGov. (2014) 'Loyalty Index hands advantage to Cameron'. 6 October 2014. Available at http://bit.ly/11vx0FJ (Accessed 17 November 2014).

8
Justice, Home Affairs, Civil Liberties and Human Rights

Peter Munce

Introduction

In his well-known magnum opus, *On Liberty*, John Stuart Mill remarked that the 'struggle between Liberty and Authority is the most conspicuous feature in the portions of history' (Mill, 1859: 7–8). In British party politics, this pendulum between liberty and authority has swung back and forth over the years, often depending on whether a party was in government or Opposition. Reflecting on the state of liberty in Britain during the Thatcher years Ronald Dworkin declared famously that 'Liberty is ill in Britain' (Dworkin, 1988: 7). Similarly, Keith Ewing accused New Labour of having a 'bonfire of the liberties' (Ewing, 2010) during their time in office. This ideational struggle between liberty and authority has been at the heart of many contemporary debates about the relationship between citizens and the state and speaks to some of the most profound tensions at the heart of the Coalition in many areas from secret courts to penal policy and human rights. The purpose of this chapter is to explore the extent to which the liberal Conservatism of the Prime Minister and his supporters has succeeded in shaping this policy area. It explores this question by doing two things. First, it considers the context in which the Prime Minister's liberal Conservatism must be judged. To that end, it explores how civil liberties and law and order issues featured in the early part of Cameron's strategy of Conservative modernisation. Second, it then moves on to examine the extent to which Cameron's liberal Conservatism has shaped different policy areas. It does this, first, through the lens of civil liberties, including secret courts and gay marriage; second, through Coalition policy on the European Convention of Human Rights (ECHR) and the Human Rights Act (HRA); before, third, considering what is argued to be an authentic expression, in policy terms, of what liberal Conservatism might look like: the introduction of directly elected Police and Crime Commissioners (PCCs) and the impact of austerity on public expenditure on law and order.

This chapter's central argument is that when it comes to the broad area of criminal justice, human rights and civil liberties, the extent to which the liberal Conservatism of the Prime Minister and his supporters has influenced the development of policy in this area has been somewhat mixed. On the one hand, it is possible to point to the liberal Conservatism of Cameron's support of gay marriage, the introduction of PCCs and early Cameron pronouncements on rolling back the creeping authoritarianism of, what Conservatives argued was, New Labour's attack on civil liberties. However, on the other hand, a more traditional Conservatism is evidenced in Cameron's response to broader human rights questions around the UK's relationship with the ECHR and in the various counter-terrorism measures introduced by the Coalition. In sum, the ambiguities and tensions at the heart of what liberal Conservatism means in practice are reflected in how this particular policy agenda has been shaped and developed.

Hugging hoodies in broken Britain: Conservative modernisation in practice

One of the defining characteristics of the Conservative Party in the modern era of British politics has been its profound desire to be perceived as the party of law and order reflecting, in part, the importance of respect for the rule of law and authority, which is central to the Conservative political tradition. Therefore, establishing 'governing competency' in crime and related law and order matters was an essential element of the Conservative's statecraft strategy during the Thatcher years (Bulpitt, 1986). Margaret Thatcher stands accused of politicising law and order in the 1979 Conservative general election manifesto, which 'built on stirrings of penal populism stretching back throughout the 1970s' (Farrall and Hay, 2010: 552). The 1979 manifesto made fighting crime and restoring law and order a central priority (Riddell, 1983). Riddell notes the inherent conflicts between 'instinct and pragmatism' (ibid.: 192), which underlined Thatcher's approach to law and order. The social authoritarianism associated with Thatcherism perfectly illustrates the 'free economy and the strong state thesis' of Andrew Gamble. He argues that at the same time that Thatcher was rolling back the frontiers of the state in monetary and fiscal policy, she was strengthening the state in other ways, particularly when it came to law and order (Gamble, 1988: 126). During Thatcher's time in office, the police received more powers (Police and Criminal Evidence Act [PACE], 1984) and 'substantial increases in policy pay, manpower and equipment were made' (Gamble, 1988: 134). Thatcher's tough approach to sentencing and punishment found continued expression during the Major years.

Mindful of this inherited governing agenda of the Conservatives, it is worth reflecting on how civil liberties and law and order issues fitted within the wider modernisation strategy pursued by the Conservative leadership after the election of David Cameron as leader in December 2005. Conservative modernisation, rooted in the realisation that the party must change after three successive election defeats, involved 'dissociation with the recent past as continued association carries with it negative electoral consequences. To modernize is to attempt to change the narrative and/or image of the party leader, the policy agenda or the organizational structures of the party' (Hayton and Heppell, 2010: 436). It involved emphasising the party's support for public services, especially the NHS, civil liberties, environmental protection and social liberalism and de-emphasised what the Conservatives viewed as politically 'toxic themes' such as immigration, crime and Europe.

There are two dimensions worth exploring further. First, explanations of Cameron's modernisation agenda do not usually tend to focus on the shifts that took place on law and order and, in particular, the repositioning on civil liberties that were both an important part of the Conservatives' wider modernisation strategy in Opposition. This was partly driven by Cameron's own social liberalism but also as a way of demonstrating the ways in which the party had changed since he became leader. This repositioning saw the Conservative Party campaign against the further erosion of liberty that they argued had been accelerated under Labour. As a result of this, Conservatives opposed the government over identity cards and 42-day detention, resulting in Cameron's opponent in the 2005 leadership election, David Davis, resigning his Westminster seat in protest at the Labour government's proposals for the latter. As David Erdos argues, the idea of creating a British Bill of Rights 'fits alongside initiatives within the Conservative Party aimed at reaching out to new constituencies and developing a more socially liberal policy approach' (Erdos, 2010: 39). However, it is debatable the extent to which this position of strong support for civil liberties went beyond Cameron and the group of modernisers around his leadership.

Second, in July 2006 Cameron delivered a speech at the Centre for Social Justice, which in the tabloid press was presented, as his 'hug a hoodie' speech where Cameron argued that:

So when you see a child walking down the road, hoodie up, head down, moody, swaggering, dominating the pavement – think what has brought that child to that moment. If the first thing we have to do is understand what's gone wrong, the second thing is to realize that putting things right is not just about law enforcement. It's about the quality of the work we do with young people. It's about relationships. It's about trust. Above all, it's about emotion and emotional development. (Cameron, 2006b)

This change in the rhetorical emphasis of the Conservatives' crime policy sought to emphasise the new, modern, compassionate Conservative Party that Cameron was trying to build. However, the extent to which this represented a new direction in penal policy for the Conservatives is questionable. Within a year Cameron had sought to distance himself from the comments describing 'hug a hoodie' as 'three words I never said' arguing that:

Aggressive hoodies who threaten the rest of us must be punished. They need to know the difference between right and wrong, and it's our job to tell them. But what do we really want, a society where more and more kids are out of control, a rising tide of crime and punishment? Or do we want those kids to behave properly in the first place? If we do, we've got to stop the problems before they start, and that means making sure every child grows up in a stable loving home. (Cameron, 2007)

By 2008, Cameron's crime policy had been subsumed in the wider 'Broken Britain' narrative, which argued that in the economic and social sphere Britain was broken after 10 years of Labour government. As Cameron argued: 'Our mission is to repair our broken society – to heal the wounds of poverty, crime, social disorder and deprivation that are steadily making this country a grim and joyless place to live for far too many people' (Cameron, 2008).

In other words, Cameron's 'hug a hoodie' speech represented a high-water mark for a liberal Conservative crime policy that soon receded and which saw, 'the reassertion of classic tenets of New Right thinking' (Bennett, 2008: 464).

Civil liberties: from secret courts to gay marriage

In the aftermath of the election and the subsequent negotiations that led to the formation of the Coalition, it was clear that differences between the Conservatives and Liberal Democrats over the HRA, both as a constitutional issue and as a matter of principle, would not be insurmountable in the process of Coalition formation. Indeed, leaving the HRA and the divergences between the two Coalition partners on the Act aside, significant areas of policy convergence on civil liberties issues were found between the Coalition partners. Both Coalition partners shared a critique of New Labour's authoritarianism and its consequences for civil liberties. According to insider accounts, it would appear that in the early stages of the Coalition negotiations there was significant consensus between the Conservatives and Liberal Democrats on civil liberties (Laws, 2010: 70) evidenced in a speech by Cameron delivered on the afternoon of Friday 7 May, the day before formal negotiations with the Liberal Democrats began. Cameron's 'big, open offer' to the Liberal Democrats highlighted that the two parties shared a, 'common commitment to civil liberties and to getting rid, immediately, of Labour's ID cards scheme' (Cameron, 2010). For one of the Liberal Democrat negotiators this proved important because while the speech set out the Conservative's red lines on a range of policy areas, it also 'contained a detailed description of the scope for delivering key Liberal Democrat manifesto commitments on schools funding, a low-carbon economy, taxation, civil liberties and political reform' (Laws, 2010: 50). The Coalition Agreement stated:

> The Government believes that the British state has become too authoritarian, and that over the past decade it has abused and eroded fundamental human freedoms and historic civil liberties. We need to restore the rights of individuals in the face of encroaching state power, in keeping with Britain's tradition of freedom and fairness. (HM Government, 2010: 11)

This section of the Coalition Agreement contained 13 specific pledges on civil liberty issues that included rolling back some of the legislation put on the statute books by Labour as part of their counter-terrorism efforts. This meant scrapping the identity card scheme, the National Identity Register, halting the next generation of biometric passports and the introduction of a Freedom Bill. In a highly symbolic act, the first piece of legislation passed by the Coalition was an Act to scrap the ID card scheme.

The issue of why the Conservatives and Liberal Democrats found significant agreement on civil liberties is important to address, not least because it reveals the extent to which Cameron's social liberalism was dominant in the earlier phases of Conservative modernisation. In many ways this agreement on specific matters relating to civil liberties was a reflection of a wider ideological convergence between the Orange Book Liberal Democrats and the modernisers within the Conservatives who shared a similar outlook about the protection of civil liberties, localism and the size and role of the state. For Conservatives, support for civil liberties fitted within a broader critique of the growth of state power in Britain which, they argued, was the legacy of a bloated bureaucratic state that had grown unsustainably during New Labour's time in office. This argument, in turn, came to be framed within the broader Big Society narrative of the Conservatives' 2010 election campaign. The Big Society themes of decentralisation, localism and a critique of the growth of state power were ones to which Orange Book Liberal Democrats could subscribe. Indeed, the civil liberties section of the Coalition Agreement should be viewed not as a compromise but as genuine agreement between partners. Liberal Democrats have a long tradition in British politics of support for civil liberties and were the earliest advocates of constitutional reforms that would formally protect liberties either through a domestic UK Bill of Rights or through incorporation of the ECHR. On the other hand, the issue has historically been much more difficult for Conservatives. However, under Cameron's leadership, and as part of his modernisation project, the Conservatives became much more supportive of civil liberties insofar as it fitted within their broader Big Society narrative and critique of the growth of state power in Britain under Labour.

Despite the early agreement between the Coalition partners on civil liberties it did not take long for cracks in the consensus to appear. After a difficult legislative process, the Justice and Security Act (JSA) received Royal Assent on 25 April 2013. By far the most controversial aspect of the Act was contained in Part 2 of the legislation, which provided for Closed Material Procedure (CMP) or secret courts, which came into effect in July 2013. The genesis of the legislation containing secret courts can be found in litigation that arose against the government post-9/11 on matters such as extraordinary rendition, allegations of torture and detention without trial. The JSA has been criticised by human rights organisations such as Liberty as offending ancient liberties contained in the common law of the right to a fair trial and as the latest piece in a long line of repressive and excessively authoritarian counter-terrorist legislation that has been introduced by the government in the wake of the 9/11 and 7/7 terrorist attacks (Liberty, 2012). In essence, the CMP provides for certain civil court proceedings to be held in secret where the government is of the opinion that the evidence is too sensitive on the grounds of national security to be disclosed in normal court procedures. The CMP was already available in the Special Immigration and Appeals Commission (SIAC) but is now extended to the main civil courts so that the government can now, where suitable, introduce secret intelligence in certain civil proceedings to defend itself in cases for damages arising from allegations of torture and extraordinary rendition.

The leaderships of both the Conservatives and Liberal Democrats supported the introduction of secret courts. This enabled the Coalition to present a united front, despite the significant internal opposition within the Liberal Democrats to the policy and the profound opposition that Nick Clegg faced. A motion introduced at the Liberal Democrats' 2012 annual conference called for the withdrawal of Part 2 of the Justice and Security Bill, which contained the provisions on secret courts, and criticised the leadership for supporting their introduction. Party activists overwhelmingly backed the motion opposing secret courts but in the final parliamentary vote on the Bill, only seven Liberal Democrat MPs voted against the Bill at third reading. As a consequence of Nick Clegg's support for secret courts the party suffered a number of high-profile resignations, including the former parliamentary candidate, Jo Shaw, and leading human rights academic and lawyer, Philippe Sands QC.

As this chapter has noted, support for civil liberties, a promise to halt the creeping authoritarianism of the Labour governments and roll back legislation, which the Coalition partners argued was an affront to historic British freedoms, was part of the formational glue that brought the Coalition together. One of the problems the Liberal Democrats were always going to face was how genuine the Conservatives' long-term commitment to a robust civil liberties agenda would be during the lifetime of the Coalition. As proved to be the case, once the initial commitments contained in the Coalition Agreement – among other things, to repeal ID cards – were fulfilled, the Conservatives retreated to a more authoritarian and less liberal position on counter-terrorist legislation. It is possible to argue that Cameron's support for civil liberties in the early part of his modernisation agenda was an exemplification of his liberal Conservatism. Opposition to 42-day detention coupled with the strong civil liberty measures of the Coalition Agreement show this was also more than just a rhetorical commitment by Cameron. Similarly, insofar as gay marriage can be conceived as a rights and liberty issue, it can be argued that Cameron's support for this policy, both in Opposition and in government, at significant risk to his own internal political position, is further evidence of his liberal Conservatism manifesting itself as a civil liberties issue. However, when it comes to civil liberties, the story of the Coalition is one of the retrenchment of liberal Conservatism and a return to a more traditional Conservatism, as the introduction of secret courts and the desire of the Home Secretary to introduce the so-called 'snoopers charter' demonstrate.

European Convention on Human Rights (ECHR) and the British Bill of Rights (BBoR) Debate

The Conservative Party and Liberal Democrats entered the 2010 general election with very different policies towards the HRA. Since the HRA was passed in 1998, the Conservative Party have expressed profound concern with the legislation. This opposition manifested itself in June 2006 when Cameron delivered a speech to the Centre for Policy Studies where he committed the Conservative Party to seek an alternative mechanism for the protection of rights in Britain by proposing that the HRA be replaced with a new BBoR (Cameron, 2006a). The outworking of this debate within the Conservative Party was a commitment contained within the 2010 manifesto that a future Conservative government would replace the HRA with a BBoR. While the Conservatives were committed to replacing the HRA, their Liberal Democrat Coalition partners were equally committed to protecting and defending its political legacy. It is clear for the Liberal Democrats that any move by the Conservatives to withdraw from UK commitments under the Convention would cause them to resign from the Coalition. In the early stages of the Coalition, from May 2010 until February 2011 there was a truce over the ECHR issue insofar as the Conservatives signed up to a paragraph in the Coalition Agreement establishing a Bill of Rights Commission to investigate the creation of a BBoR that, 'incorporates and builds on all our obligations under the European Convention on Human Rights and ensures that these rights continue to be enshrined in British law' (HM Government, 2010: 8).

The Bill of Rights Commission established by the government in March 2011 was, according to its Chair, the retired senior civil servant Sir Leigh Lewis, 'the classic response to a political impasse' (Lewis, 2013).

Establishing the Commission was a clear example of the Coalition outsourcing this contentious policy area to the work of an external Commission. It was established on 18 March 2011 and consisted of eight part-time Commissioners. The clear intention of the Coalition partners in establishing the Commission was to put the issue of the HRA and Britain's relationship with the ECHR into cold storage until after the next general election and navigate a course of least resistance until both parties were at greater liberty to argue for their respective distinctive positions on the HRA and the protection of human rights in the UK. The Commission was, arguably, destined for stalemate from its inception, as its composition 'merely reflected the dividing lines within the coalition on the HRA with its membership equally divided between those who wanted to keep it and those who wanted to repeal it' (Munce, 2012: 62).

The Liberal Democrats appointed four members and the Conservatives appointed four members. The Liberal Democrat appointees (Anthony Lester QC, Helena Kennedy QC, Philippe Sands QC and Professor Sir David Edward QC) all supported the ECHR and the idea of incorporation of Convention rights into UK domestic law while the four Conservative appointees (Jonathan Fisher QC, Martin Howe QC, Michael Pinto-Duschinsky (later replaced by Lord Faulks) and Anthony Spaight QC) were broadly sympathetic to the argument of withdrawing from the ECHR and enacting a UK Bill of Rights to replace the HRA. For Liberal Democrats the fact that a Commission was established to build upon the foundations of the ECHR should be considered a significant victory. For some Conservative MPs, however, the fact that Britain's relationship with the Convention was not within the remit of the Convention was problematic.

However, from late 2012 onwards, it became increasingly clear that the Conservatives' goal when it came to the HRA and ECHR was to develop as distinctive a policy on these matters as they could within the context of Coalition government. This transition to a more openly hostile Conservative position on the ECHR and HRA was made easier when Ken Clarke was replaced as Justice Secretary by the more right-wing Chris Grayling in September 2012, and when the Attorney General, Dominic Grieve QC, was sacked from the government in July 2014.

The articulation of this distinctive policy position on the HRA and ECHR culminated in October 2014 with the publication of proposals for changing Britain's human rights laws (Conservatives, 2014). The document outlined familiar criticisms of the HRA and Strasbourg institutions, namely that the HRA undermines parliamentary sovereignty and the European Court of Human Rights (ECtHR) has engaged in 'mission creep' by interpreting the Convention as a 'living instrument' and involving itself in debates about rights that were never envisaged by those who drafted it (ibid.). The proposals commit a future Conservative government to repeal the HRA and replace it with a BBoR and to placing strict limitations on the influence of the ECtHR so that it 'is no longer able to order a change in UK law and becomes an advisory body only' (ibid.: 5). In many ways, the toughening of the Conservatives' position on the HRA and ECHR, in particular, must be viewed within the context of UKIP and the electoral threat it poses to the Conservatives.

When it comes to assessing the Coalition's record on the HRA and the ECHR, it is the liberalism of the Liberal Democrats that has triumphed. The HRA remains on the statute books and the UK remains a signatory to the ECHR. If the Conservatives had the luxury of governing alone for the past five years, it is questionable whether this would have been the case. However, as the years of Coalition government have passed by, Conservative opposition to the HRA and to the UK's continued adherence to the Strasbourg regime for rights protection has grown stronger. The centre of gravity within the Conservative ranks has moved to such an extent that ECHR withdrawal is no longer a pariah position within the Parliamentary Party but is a mainstream position. Cameron's liberal Conservatism, in foreign policy terms, has been strong in its commitment to uphold and protect individual rights. A tension at the heart of their liberal Conservatism, when it comes to human rights, however, is the dissonance between scepticism of the HRA and the ECtHR and enthusiasm for international human rights (Munce and Beech, 2014). Abroad, Conservatives espouse liberalism to defend the human rights of non-British citizens when it comes to human rights. However, at home, Conservatives are often the sharpest critics of human rights and of the 'liberal-legalist' (Gray, 2007) rights project of realising the constitutional entrenchment of rights, interpreted by a judiciary and placed outside the confines of political deliberation.

Liberal Conservatism in practice – PCCs and Justice and Home Affairs in a cold climate

When it comes to Home Affairs issues, as John Benyon has argued, the 'theme of a smaller state and greater local involvement and influence is evident in the Coalition's policies and approach to home affairs' (Benyon, 2011: 134). For example, the idea of localism is foundational in the creation of locally, democratically elected PCCs. In the wider pursuit of austerity, with significant expenditure cuts on Home Affairs and Justice, it is possible to discern the emergence of a distinctive liberal Conservative agenda that combines the predilection of the Big Society idea of localism with the commitment to a smaller state through significant reductions in public spending.

First, in terms of both central and local government expenditure on criminal justice across the UK, the Coalition, as a headline figure, has overseen a 15 per cent reduction in public spending on public order and safety, including police services, prisons, immigration law courts and fire safety, since it took office (Centre for Crime and Justice Studies, 2014: 22). In England and Wales, alone, central government spending has reduced by 13 per cent; law courts and 'Offender Management (prisons, probation and the National Offender Management Service) have experienced the greatest cuts since 2010/11, declining by 29 and 18 per cent respectively' (ibid.). Significant reductions in public expenditure have had a knock-on effect on the numbers of police and prison officers, with a 9.2 per cent reduction in police officer levels and an 11.4 per cent reduction in prison staffing since the Coalition came to office (ibid.: 24). The Coalition has not been afraid to see police officer and prison staffing numbers fall in the pursuit of the greater economic and political goal of deficit reduction. This stands in stark contrast to the Thatcher years, which witnessed increased numbers of police and prison officers and increases in public spending on criminal justice. Cameron's pursuit, on the other hand, of a neo-liberal policy of austerity, has left vulnerable every aspect of the strong state that Thatcher sought to construct, including law and order and the criminal justice system. Indeed, in juxtaposition to the Thatcher revolution, the Home Secretary, Theresa May, has argued that the Coalition's pursuit of austerity coupled with police reforms means, 'you don't have to be the party of big spending to be the party of law and order' (May, 2013a).

Second, the introduction of directly elected PCCs to bring greater accountability and transparency to scrutiny of the police forces in England and Wales 'represents arguably the most significant constitutional change in the governance of the police in the past 50 years' (Lister, 2013: 239). In many ways, PCCs are viewed as the 'flagship policing and criminal justice policy of the Coalition Government' (ibid.). Building on commitments contained in both the Conservative and Liberal Democrat manifestos to bring greater accountability to, and enhanced local involvement in, oversight of the police, the Coalition Agreement committed the Coalition to: 'Introduce measures to make the police more accountable through oversight by a directly elected individual, who will be subject to strict checks and balances by locally elected representatives' (HM Government, 2010: 13).

The elections for 41 posts in England and Wales, excluding London, took place in November 2012. Despite the significant changes in police governance that the election of PCCs ushered in by replacing the existing Police Authority structure, voter apathy was the big story of PCC Election Day with a turnout of only 15 per cent. PCCs have significant powers in holding a police force's Chief Constable to account and have the authority under the Police Reform and Social Responsibility Act 2011 'to hire and, if they deem it to be necessary, fire the Chief Constable, but also to determine the force's budget and priorities' (Lister, 2013: 239). In many ways it is still too early to judge whether PCCs will lead to better police governance and a more authentic form of localised decision-making but some initial academic assessments have expressed concern that much wider changes in the culture of decision-making at central and local level are required before the full potential of PCCs can be realised (Lister and Rowe, 2014). Notwithstanding the concerns expressed, the government remains committed to their implementation as the practical outworking of what a liberal Conservative approach in this area might look like. As May argues:

> When I took office three years ago, it was clear to me that the police had become disconnected from the public they serve. Central government had taken power and responsibility away from local forces; instead imposing targets and bureaucratic procedures on them. Officers spent too much time filling in forms rather than fighting crime. Targets prevented officers from using their judgement and stifled innovation. And that had an impact on their effectiveness. That is why giving back responsibility to local police forces has been at the heart of my reforms. (May, 2013b: 5)

In sum, through a combination of the localism of the PCCs and the austerity measures, which have seen a reduction in spending on Justice and Home Affairs, the clearest example of the Coalition's liberal Conservatism can be seen.

Conclusion

Liberal Conservatism might be a central part of Cameron's narrative of self-understanding but, in practice, the record of liberal Conservatism in human rights, civil liberties and law and order is somewhat mixed. It reached its high-water mark in the 2006–2009 period with Cameron's 'hug a hoodie' speech and repositioning on civil liberties. On civil liberties Cameron's support in Opposition was abandoned once the pledges in the Coalition Agreement were fulfilled, in favour of a more authoritarian approach. The Conservatives' approach to the ECHR and HRA is also Janus-faced, promoting and defending civil and political rights abroad but, at home, pursuing a full-scale assault on the 'liberal-legalist' project of the entrenchment of constitutional rights. If one understands liberal Conservatism as combining support for a smaller state with localism, then PCCs and the cuts in public expenditure at the Home Office and Ministry of Justice represent quintessential liberal Conservative policies.

However, the inherent tensions and paradoxes at the heart of liberal Conservatism are reflected in Cameron's approach to this policy area. At the same time Cameron has simultaneously pursued gay marriage, ECHR withdrawal and greater authoritarianism in civil liberty issues when it comes to counter-terrorism when, in reality, these positions taken together could hardly be described as liberal Conservatism. Liberal Conservatism might have more credibility as an ideologically coherent set of ideas in other policy areas, such as foreign affairs, but when it comes to human rights, civil liberties and other matters of crime policy it is difficult to argue that the Coalition's policy in these areas has displayed any real ideological coherence.

References

Bennett, J. (2008) 'They hug hoodies, don't they? Responsibility, irresponsibility and responsibilisation in Conservative crime policy', *The Howard Journal of Criminal Justice*, 47(5), 451–469.

Benyon, J. (2011) 'The Con-Lib Agenda for Home Affairs', in M. Beech and S. Lee (eds), *The Cameron–Clegg Government: Coalition Politics in an Age of Austerity*, Basingstoke: Palgrave Macmillan, 134–152.

Bulpitt, J. (1986) 'The discipline of the new democracy: Mrs Thatcher's domestic statecraft', *Political Studies*, 34(1), 19–39.

Cameron, D. (2006a) 'Balancing Freedom and Security: A Modern British Bill of Rights', London: The Conservative Party.

Cameron, D. (2006b) 'Speech to the Centre for Social Justice', London: The Conservative Party.

Cameron, D. (2007) 'Speech to the Police Federation', London: The Conservative Party.

Cameron, D. (2008) 'Fixing Broken Politics', London: The Conservative Party.

Cameron, D. (2010) 'David Cameron: National Interest First', London: The Conservative Party.

Cameron, D. (2012) 'Speech on the European Court of Human Rights', London: Cabinet Office.

Cameron, D. (2013) Interview on *The Andrew Marr Show*, 28 September.

Centre for Crime and Justice Studies (2014) *UK Justice Policy Review*, Vol. 3, 17 March. Available at: http://www.crimeandjustice.org.uk/publications/uk-justice-policy-review-volume-3 (last accessed, 22 December 2014).

Conservatives (2014) *Protecting Human Rights in the UK: The Conservatives' Proposals for Changing Britain's Human Rights Laws*, London: The Conservative Party.

Dworkin, R. (1988) 'Devaluing liberty', *Index on Censorship*, 17(8), 7–8.

Erdos, D. (2010) 'Smoke but no fire? The politics of a "British" Bill of Rights', *Political Quarterly*, 81(2), 188–198.

Ewing, K. (2010) *Bonfire of the Liberties: New Labour, Human Rights, and the Rule of Law*, Oxford University Press: Oxford.

Farrall, S. and Hay, C. (2010) 'Not so tough on crime? Why weren't the Thatcher governments more radical in reforming the criminal justice system?', *British Journal of Criminology*, 50(3), 550–569.

Gamble, A. (1988) *The Free Economy and the Strong State: The Politics of Thatcherism*, Basingstoke: Palgrave Macmillan.

Gray, J. (2007) *Enlightenment's Wake: Politics and Culture at the Close of the Modern Age*, London: Routledge.

Hayton, R. and Heppell, T. (2010) 'The quiet man of British politics: the rise, fall and significance of Iain Duncan Smith', *Parliamentary Affairs*, 63(2), 425–445.

HM Government (2010) *The Coalition: Our Programme for Government*, London: Cabinet Office.

Laws, D. (2010) *22 days in May: The Birth of the Lib-Dem Conservative Coalition*, Biteback: London.

Lewis, L. (2013) 'Speech to UCL Constitution Unit', 25 January. Available at: http://www.ucl.ac.uk/constitution-unit/constitution-unit-news/leighlewis (last accessed 24 January 2015).

Liberty (2012) 'Liberty's response to the Ministry of Justice's Green Paper – Justice and Security', London: Liberty. Available at: https://www.liberty-human-rights.org.uk/sites/default/files/liberty-s-response-to-the-ministry-of-justice-consultati.pdf (last accessed 24 January 2015).

Lister, S. C. (2013) 'The new politics of the police: Police and Crime Commissioners and the "operational independence' of the police", *Policing*, 7(3), 239–247.

Lister, S. and Rowe, M. (2014) 'Electing Police and Crime Commissioners in England and Wales: prospecting for the democratisation of policing', *Policing and Society: An International Journal of Research and Policy*, http://dx.doi.org/10.1080/10439463.2013.868461.

May, T. (2013a) 'We Will Win by Being the Party for All', Speech to Conservative Home Conference, 9 March, London: Conservative Home. Available at: http://www.conservativehome.com/thetorydiary/2013/03/full-text-of-theresa-mays-speech-we-will-win-by-being-the-party-for-all.html (last accessed 22 December 2014).

May, T. (2013b) 'Foreword', in *The Pioneers: Police and Crime Commissioners, One Year On*, London: Policy Exchange. Available at: http://www.policyexchange.org.uk/images/publications/the%20pioneers.pdf (last accessed 22 December 2014).

Mill, J. S. (1859) *On Liberty*, London: John W. Parker & Son.

Munce, P. (2012) 'Profoundly un-Conservative? David Cameron and the UK Bill of Rights debate', *Political Quarterly*, 83(1), 60–68.

Munce, P. and Beech, M. (2014) 'The place of human rights in Conservative foreign policy: sceptics or enthusiasts?' APSA 2014 Annual Meeting. Available at *SSRN*: http://ssrn.com/abstract=2454853 (last accessed 22 January 2015).

Riddell, P. (1983) *The Thatcher Government*, Oxford: Martin Robertson.

9
Parliament and the Constitution: The Coalition in Conflict

Philip Norton and Louise Thompson

Introduction

The provisions of the Coalition's agenda covering constitutional issues were embodied in section 24 of *The Coalition: Our Programme for Government*, entitled 'Political Reform' (HM Government, 2010: 26–7). The 27 bullet points included fixed-term five-year parliaments, a referendum on the introduction of the Alternative Vote (AV), reform of the House of Lords, legislation to provide for recall of MPs, and implementation of the Wright Committee recommendations for reform of the House of Commons.

The section created inherent problems when it came to implementation. In part, these were practical. However, the most substantial problem derived from competing ideologies. There were also problems in carrying out changes not envisaged in the agreement. Governments have mandates that are permissive and not just prescriptive. The Coalition had to deal with the unplanned. Among the changes not included in the agreement were press regulation and strengthening parliament in waging war. There were also two issues that were essentially designed to be sidelined through the use of commissions – one on English votes for English laws and the other on a British Bill of Rights. However, the referendum in Scotland in 2014 gave fresh impetus to the former and pressure from Conservative MPs, responding to some judgments from the European Court of Human Rights, reawakened demands for the latter.

The practical problems could be seen as the result of negotiations being rushed and of the negotiators not necessarily being well-versed in constitutional issues. This was illustrated by the commitment on fixed-term parliaments. There was no reference to an early general election being triggered by a vote of no confidence (Norton, 2014: 211). This had to be included when the Fixed-term Parliaments Bill was brought before parliament. The Coalition's Programme for Government did state: 'We will put a binding motion before the House of Commons stating that the next general election will be held on the first Thursday of May 2015' (Conservative Party/Liberal Democrats, 2010: 3). No such motion was ever forthcoming because the government realised there was no one to be bound by such a 'binding' motion (Norton, 2014: 210). Practical difficulties also presented themselves in seeking to render in legislative form the commitment for electors to recall MPs. The rushed nature of the agreement was also reflected in the fact that it did not commit the government to introduce a Bill to provide for a largely elected second chamber. It committed the Coalition to setting up a committee to bring forward proposals for such a largely elected chamber, based on proportional representation, and for the committee to bring forward 'a draft motion' by December 2010 (Conservative Party/ Liberal Democrats, 2010: 3). The presumption is that it meant to refer to a draft Bill. In the text of the *Conservative–Lib Dem deal*, it stated, 'it is likely that this bill will …' (Conservative Party/Liberal Democrats, 2010: 3), whereas the full Coalition Programme for Government omitted the word 'Bill' (HM Government, 2010: 27). In any event, no motion or Bill was brought forward on such a rushed timetable.

The ideological differences were more profound. The section of the agreement opened with: 'The Government believes that our political system is broken. We urgently need fundamental political reform' (HM Government, 2010: 26). That was a Liberal Democrat view of the constitution, deriving from the liberal approach to constitutional change (Norton, 1982: 275–9). It was not a Conservative view. Conservative MPs generally adhere to the Westminster, or traditional, view of the constitution (Norton, 1982: 279–87). They do not regard the political system as broken and, if there is to be change, it should be incremental, tackling proven ills, not radical change fundamentally challenging the basics of the nation's constitutional underpinnings.

Conflict within the Coalition could arguably be expected to be greatest where negotiators had agreed compromises rather than when one side had made a concession. In the former case, one could envisage inter-party conflict, whereas in the latter case it would be intra-party dissent. The most obvious example of compromise was that on a referendum on AV, the subject that almost prevented the Coalition coming into being (Norton, 2011a: 155–6). For the Conservatives, wedded to the first-past-the-post electoral system, it went too far. For Liberal Democrats, favouring a system of proportional representation in the form of the Single Transferable Vote, it did not go far enough. The obvious example of a concession was that on fixed-term parliaments, which had been in the Liberal Democrat (and Labour) manifesto, but not the Conservative. The proposal on House of Lords reform could also be seen as a concession. Though the Conservative election manifesto committed the party to the principle of a largely elected chamber, it was on the basis of reaching consensus on the issue. No consensus was likely, certainly not within Conservative ranks, and David Cameron had made it clear that he regarded it as a 'third-term issue', in other words, not for this parliament. There were also some issues where there was no need for compromise or concessions, both parties being in agreement, and therefore the measures giving effect to these were not likely to give rise to intra-party or inter-party dissent. These included implementing reforms to the House of Commons, not least the Wright Committee recommendations, petitions with 100,000 signatures triggering debate, and individual voter registration.

In this chapter, we treat the key issues giving rise to conflict, within or across the Coalition partners. We do so under the headings of compromises, concessions and unplanned reforms. The first of these focuses on the referendum on AV and boundary reforms. The second addresses primarily House of Lords reform and fixed-term parliaments, and the third the issue of press regulation, English votes for English laws (the English question) and a British Bill of Rights. There is also one constitutional issue which, during the period of Coalition, has formed a fault-line for the Conservatives, that of European integration.

Compromises

The future of the electoral system was the issue that came closest to derailing the negotiations between the Conservatives and the Liberal Democrats. For the Liberal Democrats, achieving a system of proportional representation (PR) was their long-standing and most treasured goal in terms of constitutional change. Any agreement had to include a commitment to change. The Conservatives were wedded to retaining the first-past-the-post system of election. They had fought a successful campaign against the recommendations of the Jenkins Commission, for the introduction of a hybrid system, the Alternative Vote Plus (AV+), in 1998 and were in no mood to concede the case for any form of PR system. Conflict was predictable (Boulton and Jones, 2010: 183) and the issue came close to ending the negotiations (Wilson, 2010: 162; Laws, 2010: 104). It was only resolved by the two party leaders, David Cameron and Nick Clegg, talking to one another and agreeing to a referendum on the introduction of AV for parliamentary elections. Cameron was keen to reach agreement – he saw himself as in competition with Labour to complete a deal – and due to some lack of clarity as to what was being offered by Labour, Cameron told his MPs that he believed that Labour was offering to introduce AV without a referendum, though Clegg said that no such offer was made (see Norton, 2011b: 256; Stuart, 2011: 49–50). For the Conservatives, the pill was sweetened by the fact that the parties would be free to campaign on different sides and that the Liberal Democrats had agreed to a measure providing for more equal constituency electorates.

The provisions for the referendum and the changes to constituency boundaries were embodied in the Parliamentary Voting System and Constituencies Bill. Getting the Bill through was far from problem free, but the biggest challenge in terms of the relationship between the Coalition partners came during and after the referendum campaign.

The Bill proved problematic for the government's business managers in two respects. One was ensuring that Coalition members supported the Bill. The other was staving off an attempt to derail the Bill by Labour peers in the House of Lords. In the Lords, unlike in the Commons, there is no formal programming of Bills. Also, again unlike in the Commons, there is no selection of amendments for debate. All amendments that are tabled are considered. The need to get the Bill enacted in time for a referendum in May 2011 gave the peers exceptional opportunities to talk at length on amendments to the Bill and prevent it getting through by the necessary date.

In the event, the Bill encountered opposition from a number of Tory MPs, but not enough to deny the government a majority in any division. In the first six months of Coalition, the Bill accounted for almost half (26 out of 59) of all the votes witnessing dissenting votes by Coalition MPs. In the Lords, the challenge came from Labour peers talking on amendments – at one point resulting in all-night sitting – and on occasion from cross-bench peers joining with Labour in divisions. However, the stance taken by the Opposition may have served to bolster Conservative and Liberal Democrat peers in supporting the Bill. Tory peers voted for the referendum – as one put it, 'through gritted teeth' (Tory peer to Lord Norton) – but voted for it nonetheless.

Getting the Bill through represented a success for the Coalition, and reflected the emphasis of the Prime Minister in delivering on the Coalition agreement in the face of some backbench dissent. However, the focus changed in the referendum. Cameron had not intended to take a notable lead in the campaign, leaving it to the initiative of others to create and run the 'no' campaign. However, when initial surveys suggested a victory for the 'yes' campaign and there were problems raising funds, Conservative MPs put pressure on the leadership for a more robust stance. Party co-chairman, Baroness Warsi, faced hostile questioning at a meeting of the party's 1922 Committee. The executive of the 1922 Committee conveyed the sense of backbenchers to Cameron (Norton, 2013: 62). As a result, the Prime Minister played a prominent role in the campaign, one that was seen as being notably hostile to the Liberal Democrats and in particular Nick Clegg.

The need for party unity thus trumped Cameron's desire to keep the relationship sweet between the two Coalition partners. Whereas the first year of Coalition had witnessed some backbench dissent, the emphasis had been on keeping the Coalition together on a fairly harmonious basis. The referendum campaign and outcome changed that the relationship. If there had been a honeymoon period between the two partners, it ended in May 2011.

Concessions

There were two notable concessions on constitutional issues. One left Conservative MPs perplexed as much as angry, whereas the other aroused strong opposition from a large number of backbenchers (and, less overtly, some ministers). The first was the provision for fixed-term parliaments and the latter reform of the House of Lords.

The Liberal Democrat manifesto committed the party to support fixed-term parliaments. The Labour manifesto had a similar commitment. The Conservative manifesto was silent on the issue. The party had previously set its face against any move from the existing constitutional arrangements (Norton, 2000: 122–3, 126). However, in the negotiations the Conservatives had conceded the case for reform; indeed, Cameron was reported to be a willing adherent to the proposal (D'Ancona, 2013: 16). For Cameron, it was a price worth paying to tie the Liberal Democrats into the Coalition. The imperative was tackling the deficit and anything that facilitated Liberal Democrat support in the task was to be embraced. While many Tory MPs could understand why a commitment to a five-year parliament made sense for the purpose of the

Coalition, they queried why it was necessary to enshrine it in legislation – a commitment from the PM would have tied him to an election in May 2015 – and why it was to apply in perpetuity. The constitution was being changed for the purpose of a short-term fix.

Conservative MPs were prepared to give the Prime Minister the benefit of the doubt and, despite some opposition, the Bill emerged unscathed from the Commons. It ran into more sustained criticism in the Lords, and as a result underwent significant amendment, primarily in respect of the triggers for an early general election (Norton, 2014) and a post-legislative review in 2020. Some MPs and peers made clear their disquiet about the provision for a five-year fixed term – the Liberal Democrat manifesto had supported four years – but the government got the provision through. However, Tory disquiet swelled after the measure was enacted, especially in the final session of the parliament. In October 2014, Tory MP Sir Edward Leigh initiated a backbench debate calling for the repeal of the Act, supported by a number of other Tories and Labour MP Austin Mitchell (*HC Debates*, 23 October 2014: cc.1069–1113), and he pushed his motion to a vote. It was defeated by 68 votes to 21, the majority lobby comprising Labour and Liberal Democrat MPs. Though the Coalition had got the measure onto the statute book, MPs in the two parties appeared more divided than before on its merits.

If the honeymoon between the two Coalition partners had been ended by the AV referendum, the relationship moved to one of coldness, indeed hostility, the following year. Replacing an appointed House of Lords with an elected chamber was second only to electoral reform in the constitutional priorities of the Liberal Democrats. David Cameron's Conservative predecessors as Prime Minister – Margaret Thatcher and John Major – were not supporters of an elected chamber. However, his predecessors in Opposition had expressed support for an elected House and Cameron continued their position. He had made clear that he regarded it as a 'third-term' issue – in other words, it was not going to happen in the foreseeable future – but the party manifesto nonetheless embraced the principle. Given that, and the composition of the party's negotiating team, agreement was reached quickly on the proposal for a committee to consider a Bill for 'a wholly or mainly elected upper chamber on the basis of proportional representation'.

Unlike the Bill providing for a referendum on AV, Conservative MPs could not hold fire for a later date. Many were opposed to an elected House. However, it was not until the second year of Coalition that it came before the House. In line with the Coalition agreement, a joint committee was appointed to consider a draft House of Lords Reform Bill.

The joint committee reflected the divisions on the issue. It produced a report recommending a referendum on the issue (Joint Committee on the Draft House of Lords Reform Bill, 2012). Of the 26 members, 12 were opposed to election and published an alternative report (Campaign for an Effective Second Chamber, 2012).

This presaged the problems encountered by the government when it introduced the Bill. There was substantial opposition from Conservative MPs. The executive of the 1922 Committee had for some time taken a different view to that of the leader (Norton, 2013: 51). Backbenchers opposed to the measure formed a group, 'the Sensibles', to lobby colleagues and engaged in an effective whipping operation (see Norton, 2015). The two-day Second Reading debate in the Commons saw opponents on the Conservative benches prominent by presence and voice (see *HC Debates*, 9–10 July 2012: cc.24–132, 188–274). When the House divided, the government won easily with Opposition support. However, 91 Tory MPs voted against and 19 abstained. The Opposition had made clear they would not support a programme motion to limit debate. Their votes combined with those of Conservative rebels meant that such a motion would be defeated. The government decided not to move the motion. Facing endless debate on the Bill, it bowed to the inevitable and on 6 August 2012 Nick Clegg announced that the government was not proceeding with the Bill.

The loss of the Bill infuriated Liberal Democrats and Clegg decided to punish his Coalition partners by withdrawing support for the boundary changes enshrined in the Parliamentary Voting System and Constituencies Act. An amendment to delay the changes until after the next election was carried in the Lords by 300 votes to 231. It was then upheld in the Commons by 334 votes to 292. Liberal Democrat ministers were among those voting for the delay. This enraged Tory MPs. The Deputy Prime Minister claimed Conservatives had reneged on a deal on constitutional reform, but Tory MPs argued that the deal had been the referendum on AV in return for constituency boundary changes – hence their inclusion in a single Bill. The House of Lords Reform Bill was not part of any deal. After the events of 2012, neither side fully trusted the other, fuelling doubts on the part of some Conservative MPs as to the utility of maintaining the Coalition.

Unplanned reforms

The issues of compromise and concession thus saw both Coalition partners having to navigate a bumpy road through parliament.

The reforms required as a result of the Leveson Inquiry in particular constituted a detour without even a roadmap for guidance. The issues of a British Bill of Rights and of English votes for English laws may have been a low priority for the Coalition in 2010, but unanticipated events would bring them firmly into the spotlight and cause considerable friction within the Coalition in the latter half of the parliament.

Although the reforms to the press were themselves unplanned, problems in the area of press regulation were apparent well before the 2010 general election. Andy Coulson, David Cameron's Director of Communications, had appeared before the House of Commons Culture, Media and Sport Select Committee in July 2009, as part of its inquiry into press standards, privacy and libel. Coulson resigned when the Coalition was just seven months old and, in the wake of further revelations of press intrusion and phone hacking, his former employer the *News of the World* closed in July 2010. Following cross-party discussions, the Prime Minister announced an official inquiry, to be led by Lord Justice Leveson. The inquiry was to have two parts. A review of press regulation would be carried out within 12 months and would be followed by an inquiry into the improper conduct of the *News of the World* and other newspapers. It was established under the 2005 Inquiries Act and so had the power to summon witnesses to give evidence under oath.

Although the formal process of the inquiry was not kind to either Coalition party (both David Cameron and Nick Clegg were called to give oral evidence which was widely reported in the press), internal parliamentary pressure on the Coalition did not appear until November 2012, when Lord Leveson published his report. There were fundamental differences between the Conservative and Labour party positions on the Leveson recommendations for regulation of the press. The primary dividing line was over the issue of statutory regulation. In his statement to the House on the day of its publication, the Prime Minister expressed his 'serious concerns and misgivings' about Leveson's proposals for the creation of a new regulatory body through statute (*HC Debates*, 29 November 2012: c.449). In contrast, Ed Miliband stated that Leveson's recommendations 'should be accepted in their entirety' (*HC Debates*, 29 November 2012: c.451). The problem for the Coalition was that Nick Clegg and the Liberal Democrats also favoured tackling the issue through legislation. In an unusual move, the Deputy Prime Minister also gave a statement to the House, noting that 'it is right that Parliament is clear on the initial views of the whole coalition' (*HC Debates*, 29 November 2012: c.470), and supporting the creation of a new regulator by statute. Once again clear ideological divisions became apparent between the two parties. As a result of the differences, all parties entered into a series of talks which would extend into the New Year and beyond.

The Conservatives favoured the use of a Royal Charter to establish an independent press regulator and published their proposals formally in February 2013. These were published through the Department for Culture, Media and Sport (DCMS), appearing on its website to show how a Royal Charter 'might be created without using an Act of Parliament' (DCMS, 2013). It did not reflect Coalition policy, as the document itself – and the Liberal Democrats – made clear. The proposals would permit the creation of an independent self-regulatory body which would be overseen by a Recognition Panel established under Royal Charter and protected from amendment. The following month revised proposals were published by the Conservatives, with Labour and the Liberal Democrats publishing an alternative.

Progress of the cross-party talks was made more complicated and more urgent by the behaviour of the parliamentary parties. Frustrated by the events going on around them, Labour peers began to move Leveson-inspired amendments to government Bills, including the Defamation Bill. Here, the government was defeated on an amendment by Lord Puttnam to establish a Defamation Recognition Commission and was forced to accept a later amendment by Conservative peer Lord Fowler to tone down the change. Although the Puttnam amendment was later reversed by the Commons, it put further pressure on the Coalition partners, highlighting their lack of coordination. As discussions became more heated, there was a clear threat to the Coalition's legislative programme, with Labour MPs threatening to table similar amendments to other key government Bills including the Enterprise and Regulatory Reform Bill and the Crime and Courts Bill. *The Times* reported that they had the support of some Liberal Democrat MPs in this endeavour and the Prime Minister spoke of Bills being 'hijacked' and 'contaminated' (Cameron, 2013).

The threat to some of the Coalition's flagship proposals prompted drastic action by the Prime Minister, who pulled out of the cross-party talks in favour of putting the Royal Charter proposal to parliament just a few days later in order to '[unblock] the logjam' (*HC Debates*, 18 March 2013: c.635). Putting the proposal before the Commons, the Prime Minister chose his language very carefully, stating that legislation was needed to 'protect' rather than to 'recognise' the Royal Charter (*HC Debates*, 18 March 2013: c.633), preventing its amendment without a two-thirds majority in both Houses of Parliament. Although it did include an element of legislative underpinning, the proposal was described as simply a series of 'relatively small legislative changes' (*HC Debates*, 18 March 2013: c.633). It was a clear compromise on the part of the Coalition partners.

Although the proposal had the support of the three main party leaders, the assent of parliament was not guaranteed. It was clear from the language used by the Prime Minister in the days leading up to the vote that the result was on a knife edge. Most notably, he began to talk of a 'hung parliament' – something that had previously been absent from Coalition language and a sign of the imperfect nature of the Coalition. As *The Daily Telegraph* reported, 'the ties that bind the Coalition are fraying' (Kirkup, 2013). There were fears that the Coalition might lose the vote. The change was finally enacted through amendments to two existing government Bills, the Enterprise and Regulatory Reform Bill and the Crime and Courts Bill. This unplanned reform, therefore, ushered in five months of inter-party conflict, which was played out prominently in the parliamentary arena.

If the stresses and strains of the government's response to the Leveson Inquiry showed the cracks in the Coalition, the problems posed by the English question and a British Bill of Rights demonstrated how the management and containment of ideological differences within a coalition can be complicated by events. Both issues had appeared in some respects in the two parties' election manifestos and were included in the *Programme for Government*. They fall within the category of unplanned reforms as, had events in the latter half of the parliament not prompted immediate action by the government, it is unlikely that any reform would have been made.

Both parties had made reference to citizens' rights in their respective 2010 election manifestos, though only the Conservative Party explicitly referred to a Bill of Rights. There was a fundamental difference between the two. While the Liberal Democrat manifesto emphasised that the party would preserve people's freedom by 'protecting the Human Rights Act' (Liberal Democrats, 2010: 94), the Conservative manifesto stated that the party would 'replace the Human Rights Act' with a Bill of Rights (Conservative Party, 2010: 79). Similarly, although the Liberal Democrat manifesto included a commitment to a 'federal Britain' (Liberal Democrats, 2010: 92), it did not specifically address the issue of English votes directly. The Conservative Party manifesto, however, committed the party to 'introduce new rules so that legislation referring specifically to England … cannot be enacted without the consent of MPs representing constituencies of those countries' (Conservative Party, 2010: 84). A cautionary approach was thus taken when including these issues in the Coalition's legislative programme. The *Programme for Government* committed the two parties only to establish commissions to 'investigate' (HM Government, 2010: 11) and 'consider' the two issues (ibid.: 27). However, in what has been described as a 'clear victory' for the Liberal Democrats (Hazell and Yong, 2012: 167), the Programme for Government emphasised the need to ensure that a Bill of Rights would incorporate existing obligations under the European Convention on Human Rights.

The creation of commissions reflected the fact that 'serious differences' existed between the two Coalition parties (Hazell and Yong, 2012: 39). It was a practical move to ensure that these differences could be ironed out far away from parliament. Given the strong differences of opinion between (and within) the two Coalition parties, it is no surprise that establishing these commissions was not a priority. It would have perhaps remained this way, had a series of events surrounding voting rights for prisoners and the rights of sex offenders which were raised in parliament in early 2011 not prompted David Cameron to push for a commission to finally be formed to consider a Bill of Rights. Speaking at Prime Minister's Questions, he confirmed that a commission would be 'established imminently' (*HC Debates*, 16 February 2011: c.955). The nine-member commission was chaired by retired civil servant Sir Leigh Lewis, with four Conservative and four Liberal Democrat nominees. The formation of a commission to consider the English question took even longer and was only announced in January 2012. Chaired by former Clerk of the House of Commons, Sir William McKay, it was to take evidence across the UK and report in the following session.

Progress within the Bill of Rights Commission was by no means consensual. Its disagreements reflected the wider fractures within the Coalition on the issue. Inter-party divisions on the Human Rights Act in particular would run throughout the parliament, though expressions of difference by party frontbenchers tended to be made away from the parliamentary arena, through party conferences and the press.

In its final report, published in December 2012, the Commission readily acknowledged that it was a 'politically disparate' group of people, each with 'long-standing convictions' on the issues (Commission on a Bill of Rights, 2012: 6). Although no member rejected the notion of a Bill of Rights outright, its conclusions were divided into majority and minority conclusions. One of the few areas of consensus was the decision that no action should be taken right away. Rather, the Commission recommended that changes should be avoided until the Scottish independence referendum had been held in September 2014 and that it should be discussed further through a constitutional convention.

In a written answer the following month it was revealed that the government would make 'no formal response' to the Commission's report (*HC Debates*, 22 January 2013: c.215W) and during a parliamentary debate on the issue in March, Government Minister Damien Green confirmed that the government did not believe that 'now is the right time' to make any changes (*HC Debates*, 1 March 2013: c.627). Progress seemed to be hinging on the outcome of the Scottish referendum.

Just as the Coalition seemed to have put the issue of a Bill of Rights firmly on the back burner, the McKay Commission delivered its report on the English question. It recommended that a new constitutional principle be established for legislation being considered by parliament which had 'a separate and distinct effect for England (or for England-and-Wales)' whereby the assent of a majority of MPs from the corresponding constituencies was obtained (McKay Commission, 2013). A series of options were put forward. In its response, the government adopted a very similar strategy to that adopted following the report of the Commission on a Bill of Rights, describing it as being a 'positive step forward' and announcing a government response 'in due course' (Chloe Smith, *HC Debates*, 25 March 2013: c.65WS). Twenty months later, this response had not yet been published.

If the Coalition's strategy had been simply to sideline the issues of English votes for English laws, the impending referendum on Scottish independence presented a huge obstacle. Activity by parliament on the one hand, and by the Coalition itself on the other, forced the English question back onto the agenda before the first referendum vote had even been cast. As part of its inquiry into the consequences of Scottish independence, the House of Lords Constitution Committee began to consider the position of Scottish MPs following a yes-vote. This, combined with the pledge by the three main party leaders shortly before election day to transfer extensive additional powers to Holyrood in the event of a no-vote (Clegg, 2014), gave fresh impetus to address the position of English MPs. With the announcement of a no-vote on 19 September 2014, it could be sidelined no longer.

Addressing the issue in his post-referendum statement, the Prime Minister announced the creation of a Cabinet Committee chaired by William Hague to produce a 'definitive answer' to the English question (Cameron, 2014). Coalition activity was therefore forced to step up a gear, with all of the main parties invited to participate in the committee's discussions.

Yet strong tensions within the Coalition remained and this was noted by the Deputy Prime Minister on several occasions on the floor of the House (see, for example, *HC Debates*, 18 November 2013: c.124). In particular, the Liberal Democrats had hoped for a constitutional convention to discuss the proposals, something also put forward by the Labour Party. In addition, they cautioned against creating two tiers of MP and wanted any arrangement in the House to take account of each party's share of the vote rather than simply on their number of MPs.

By the late autumn of 2014, no consensus had been reached between the Coalition partners on proposals for a Bill of Rights or for English Votes on English Laws. On the former, the Coalition was very quiet, though David Cameron announced at the Conservative Party Conference that a Conservative government would introduce a Bill of Rights. More progress could be seen on the latter, with a full set of proposals being published by the government by the end of the year (Cabinet Office, 2014).

The other issue – essentially the traditional elephant in the room for the Conservatives – was that of European integration. The Coalition had come together to ensure passage of the European Union Act 2011, providing for a referendum on any proposal to transfer further national powers to the European Union. However, the two parties were divided on whether to claw back powers and, more fundamentally, on the UK's continued membership of the EU. A number of Eurosceptic Tory MPs championed the cause of a referendum on Britain's withdrawal. The Liberal Democrats were seen as the essential block on any Bill to provide for such a referendum.

The Prime Minister initially conceded to Liberal Democrat demands and made no attempt to pursue such a measure. When Tory backbencher David Nuttall initiated a debate on holding a referendum, a three-line whip was imposed, but 81 Tory MPs defied the whip to vote for a referendum. The scale of backbench dissent appeared to unnerve No. 10 and David Cameron pursued the cause of negotiating reform within the EU and then putting the renegotiated terms to the British people in a referendum. Tory backbenchers continued to press him to deliver on his new policy. In May 2013, two Tory MPs moved an amendment to the Queen's Speech regretting the absence of any mention of a Referendum Bill. The amendment was defeated, by 277 votes to 130, but the fact that 114 Tory MPs voted for it demonstrated the distance between the Coalition and a large section of the parliamentary Conservative Party.

In response to the continued pressure, Downing Street produced a draft Bill, providing that a referendum must be held before 31 December

2017. The Bill had Conservative, but not Liberal Democrat, support. It was introduced as a Private Member's Bill by Tory MP James Wharton, who topped the ballot for Private Members' Bills. Although the Labour and Liberal Democrat parties did not support it, they did not vote against it in the Commons, instead mobilising their supporters in the Lords to kill it off (*HL Debates*, 31 January 2014: cc.1545–7). The Bill was reintroduced the following session by another Tory backbencher, Bob Neill. This time, it was killed off in the Commons. Although given a Second Reading on 17 October 2014 by 283 votes to 0 (*HC Debates*, 17 October 2014: cc.629–32), it made no further progress following a row between the Coalition partners. Neill decided not to proceed with the Bill, claiming that the Liberal Democrats had demanded support for a Bill reforming the so-called 'bedroom tax' as a condition of support. The Liberal Democrats denied it, though they conceded they were opposed to Neill's Bill being given government time in order to make progress. The two sides engaged in a bitter war of words (Lusher, 2014). The difference between the two sides was especially stark.

Conclusion

The Coalition held together, not so much because of the Coalition programme for constitutional change, but rather despite it. The two parties started from diametrically opposite positions on constitutional change. The Coalition almost failed at the first hurdle, that of formation, because of the parties' stances on the electoral system. It almost ended near the close of the parliament because of their stance on European integration. Along the way, Coalition unity was severely tested by a range of measures, not least on House of Lords reform. A combination of the bitter AV referendum campaign in 2011 and the failure of the House of Lords Reform Bill the following year cheered Tory backbenchers, but meant that the relationship between the two parties to the Coalition was less than harmonious and, at times, tense. The parties stayed together for the sake of tackling the economic crisis. They would doubtless have happily gone their own ways in dealing with the constitution of the United Kingdom.

References

Boulton, A. and Jones, J. (2010) *Hung Together* (London: Simon & Schuster).
Cabinet Office (2014) *The Implications of Devolution for England*, Cm.8969 (London: The Cabinet Office).

Cameron, D. (2013) Press Conference, Brussels, 15 March 2013. www.gov.uk/government/speeches/transcript-of-brussels-press-conference (accessed 14 November 2013).

Cameron, D. (2014) *Statement, Scottish Independence Referendum*, Downing Street, 19 September 2014. www.gov.uk/government/news/scottish-independence-referendum-statement-by-the-prime-minister (accessed 4 December 2014).

Campaign for an Effective Second Chamber (2012) *House of Lords Reform: An Alternative Way Forward* (London: Campaign for an Effective Second Chamber).

Clegg, D. (2014) 'David Cameron, Ed Miliband and Nick Clegg sign joint historic promise which guarantees more devolved powers for Scotland and protection of NHS if we vote No', *The Daily Record*, 15 September 2014.

Commission on a Bill of Rights (2012) *A UK Bill of Rights? The Choice Before Us, Vol. 1*. (London: Ministry of Justice). webarchive.nationalarchives.gov.uk/20130128112038/http://www.justice.gov.uk/downloads/about/cbr/uk-bill-rights-vol-1.pdf (accessed 26 November 2014).

Conservative Party (2010) *Invitation to Join The Government of Britain: The Conservative Manifesto 2010* (London: The Conservative Party).

Conservative Party/Liberal Democrats (2010) *Conservative Liberal Democrat Coalition Agreement Negotiations: Agreements Reached 11 May 2010* (London: The Conservative Party/Liberal Democrats).

D'Ancona, M. (2013) *In It Together: The Inside Story of the Coalition Government* (London: Viking).

DCMS (2013) 'Lord Justice Leveson Report – regulatory system for the press'. Policy Report (London: Department for Culture, Media and Sport), 12 February. https://www.gov.uk/government/publications/lord-justice-leveson-report-regulatory-system-for-the-press (accessed 14 November 2014).

Hazell, R. and Yong, B. (2012) *The Politics of Coalition: How the Conservative-Liberal Democrat Government Works* (Oxford: Hart).

HM Government (2010) *The Coalition: Our Programme for Government* (London: The Cabinet Office).

Joint Committee on the Draft House of Lords Reform Bill (2012) *Draft House of Lords Reform Bill: Report*, Session 2010-12, HL Paper 284-I, HC 1313-I (London: The Stationery Office).

Kirkup, J. (2013) 'David Cameron and Britain's hung parliament: the ties that bind the coalition are fraying', 14 March 2013. http://blogs.telegraph.co.uk/news/jameskirkup/100207052/david-cameron-and-britains-hung-parliament-the-ties-that-bind-the-coalition-are-fraying/ (accessed 14 November 2014).

Laws, D. (2010) *22 Days in May* (London: Biteback).

Liberal Democrats (2010) *Liberal Democrat Manifesto 2010* (London: Liberal Democrats).

Lusher, A. (2014) 'Plan for EU referendum Bill collapses amid bitter Coalition row', *The Independent*, 28 October. www.independent.co.uk/news/uk/politics/plans-for-eu-referendum-bill-collapses-amid-bitter-coalition-row-9824413.html (accessed 13 December 2014).

McKay Commission (2013) *Report of the Commission on the Consequences of Devolution for the House of Commons*, Executive Summary, March 2013 (London: The McKay Commission).

Norton, P. (1982) *The Constitution in Flux* (Oxford: Martin Robertson).

Norton, P. (2000) 'Would Fixed-Term Parliaments Enhance Democracy?' In L. Robins and B. Jones (eds), *Debates in British Politics Today* (Manchester: Manchester University Press).

Norton, P. (2011a) 'The Con-Lib Agenda for the 'New Politics' and Constitutional Reform'. In S. Lee and M. Beech (eds), *The Cameron–Clegg Government* (Basingstoke: Palgrave Macmillan).

Norton, P. (2011b) 'The Politics of Coalition'. In N. Allen and J. Bartle (eds), *Britain at the Polls 2010* (London: Sage).

Norton, P. (2013) *The Voice of the Backbenchers* (London: Conservative History Group).

Norton, P. (2014) 'From flexible to semi-fixed: The Fixed-term Parliaments Act', *The Journal of International and Comparative Law*, 1(2): 203–20.

Norton, P. (2015) 'The Conservatives and the Coalition'. In A. Seldon and M. Finn (eds), *The Coalition Effect, 2010–2015* (Cambridge: Cambridge University Press).

Stuart, M. (2011) 'The Formation of the Coalition'. In S. Lee and M. Beech (eds), *The Cameron–Clegg Government* (Basingstoke: Palgrave Macmillan).

Wilson, R. (2010) *5 Days to Power* (London: Biteback).

10
The Condition of England under the Coalition

Simon Lee

Introduction

This chapter explores the profound impact the Coalition's policies have had upon the condition of England, arguably far greater than in the other constituent nations and territories of the United Kingdom because of the absence in England of devolved, directly elected institutions, which elsewhere have acted as veto points on Westminster and Whitehall, and led to a different political settlement for schools, hospitals, housing, universities and social care from that experienced in England. The chapter also highlights how the Coalition's Programme for Government was quintessentially a programme for England, because of the consequences of the devolution implemented by the Blair and Brown governments. Many of the key elements of the Coalition's programme, such as David Cameron's vision of the 'Big Society' and the top-down reform of the National Health Service (NHS), have applied to England alone, even though they have been framed within a political narrative of British rather than English modernisation. In this important regard, Coalition ministers have continued the long-standing British tradition of conflating the identity, interests and institutions of England with those of the centralised British state.

The developmental state and developmental market

Following the political, institutional and policy precedent set by all four British Ways of modernisation implemented since May 1945 (Lee, 2015), the Coalition's Fifth Way of British modernisation – its June

2010 Programme for Government – did not incorporate a strategic vision for the future of England. However, the urgent need to reform the governance of England was to remain a constant theme throughout the Coalition's tenure. For example, the House of Commons Political and Constitutional Reform Committee produced a series of reports identifying England as 'the most centralised country in the Union', where 'Strong control by the central state means that our localities underachieve on their massive potential'. Ruling out a revival of English regional government, on the grounds that '[t]here is neither the political nor public appetite for this', the Committee recommended that 'Local government should be the vehicle for devolution in England, and that 'the English Question needs to be addressed swiftly', by supporting 'the principle of fiscal devolution in England' (House of Commons Political and Constitutional Reform Committee, 2013a: 3, 2013b: 3, 2014a: 3).

In the event, the Coalition opted not to act upon any of these recommendations for political or fiscal devolution, or the codification of the relationship between central and local government in England, as part of a broader constitutional settlement which would not just mark the 800th anniversary of the signing of the Magna Carta, but actually provide England with a new Magna Carta (House of Commons Political and Constitutional Reform Committee, 2014b). Instead, there was to be significant continuity with, as well as important departure from, the pattern of governance of England that had been established under previous British modernisation programmes and their accompanying British models of political economy.

First, the overriding importance attached to austerity and deficit reduction served to further entrench, rather than challenge, the central role of the Treasury in enforcing fiscal discipline over public spending bodies in England. This had been a definitive element in English governance since the September 1976 financial crisis, and the Callaghan government's resort to a loan from the International Monetary Fund, allied to the introduction of cash limits in public expenditure planning. Under both the Blair and the Brown governments, the centrality of the Treasury had been strengthened by both Blair's 'earned autonomy' and Brown's 'constrained discretion', as the basis of their respective statecraft (Lee, 2009). In both instances, these principles dictated that public spending bodies in England would only be allowed autonomy and discretion in accordance with the degree of their compliance with central government's prescriptions over resource allocation and policy design. That Treasury dominance was maintained during George Osborne's tenure as Chancellor of the Exchequer. Despite a Coalition political narrative which repeatedly emphasised its commitment to decentralisation of power in England, the pattern of governance after May 2010 continued to reflect a series of top-down, centrally prescribed reforms.

Second, in previous British models of political economy, the Treasury had fulfilled the role of being the pilot agency of the British developmental state, using its administrative guidance to nurture the interests and development of the financial and commercial interests of the City of London, and the military manufacturers of the UK's defence industries, in sharp contrast to the later industrialising Asian developmental states' proclivity for picking winners in civilian manufacturing industries (Lee, 2015). Under the Coalition, the Treasury's priority remained enhancement of the competitive advantage of London as a global financial centre. The rescue of major UK banks in 2008, following on from the succession of debt-, consumer- and property-led economic booms and busts of the previous 40 years, had left the Coalition with rapidly deteriorating public finances, and the people of England with an accumulated trillion pounds of private mortgage and credit card debt. The austerity imposed upon public spending programmes in England reflected the primacy in the Coalition's British model of political economy of the City's interests, and the opportunism of David Cameron and George Osborne in exploiting the financial crisis to engineer a wholesale redefinition of the role of the state in England (see Chapter 2 in this volume).

Third, the Coalition maintained the 'developmental market' agenda for the reform of England's major public services. Power would continue to be devolved both to corporations and to individuals, empowered as consumers and entrepreneurs, via market choice and competition, rather than as citizens, via directly elected devolved institutions. This substitute for technocratic expertise, as the prime agency of modernisation, had been adopted by successive British governments since the mid-1970s. Then, the implementation of the Heath government's reorganisation of local government in England, on 1 April 1974, had marked the final major contribution by a Conservative government to the long-standing British tradition of technocratic pragmatism (Lee, 2015). It had witnessed the entrusting of key elements of constitutional, economic and social modernisation to a succession of Royal Commissions and expert bodies, purportedly guided by technical expertise and experience, rather than ideology or party political dogma. However, under the developmental market agenda of liberalisation, deregulation and privatisation, policy design and resource allocation had not only increasingly become the preserve of central government, but had also become separated from the administration and delivery of services by local government and allied public spending bodies. That trend, which under the Blair and Brown governments had been strengthened and deepened by the introduction of centrally prescribed Public Service Agreements, output measures and other performance indicators between the Treasury and public spending bodies to gauge their performance, continued under the Coalition (as documented in this volume, in the chapters on health and education policy).

Therefore, under the Coalition, as under every United Kingdom government elected since October 1974, the governance arrangements for England would take two principal forms. First, an extensive patronage state of unelected public bodies, lacking the legitimacy, public accountability and transparency derived from competitive elections, and whose institutions would continue to cast a bewildering network of acronyms across the landscape of English governance. These would frequently prove impossible to join up or coordinate in a strategic manner, as a succession of reports from the National Audit Office and parliamentary select committees would attest. Second, an array of private market and non-governmental organisations would be actively encouraged to tender for and deliver public services. The fragmentation and complexity which had arisen from the greater choice and competition among service providers fostered by the Coalition's devolution of power via the developmental market would complicate the task of coordination and integration. The absence of strategic national political leadership for England, combined with the impact of austerity, left the financial viability of many of England's major institutions in question, particularly in health, social care, education and local government.

Conflation and confusion: England in the Programme for Government

From the very outset, because of the legacy of the process of devolution to Scotland, Wales and Northern Ireland initiated by the Blair government, and then continued by the Brown government, the Coalition's capacity to implement many of the most controversial policy reforms in its Programme for Government, e.g. in healthcare, housing, education and higher education, would be confined to England. Indeed, the devolved institutions elsewhere in the United Kingdom would appear to take a particular interest, if not tangible pride, in devising their own initiatives, as departures from Westminster's legislative programme, to symbolise their own democratic and policy-making autonomy.

David Cameron and Nick Clegg's joint identification of the Coalition's 'potential for era-changing, convention-challenging, radical reform'; their shared conviction that 'the days of big government are over; that centralisation and top-down control have proved a failure'; and joint determination and ambition 'to oversee a radical redistribution of power away from Westminster and Whitehall to councils, communities and homes across the nation', would ostensibly be focused upon England (HM Government, 2010: 7). However, like their immediate New Labour predecessors, the Coalition's predominantly English programme of government would be articulated within a British political narrative that studiously avoided any attempt to provide England with its own separate national political and institutional identity.

The Programme for Government detailed plans to create Local Enterprise Partnerships, to replace the Regional Development Agencies; the abolition of Regional Spatial Strategies; the radical devolution of power and greater financial autonomy to local government and community groups; the commitment 'to stop the top-down reorganisations of the NHS'; the significant cutting of the number of health quangos; the direct election of individuals on to the boards of Primary Care Trusts; the giving to local communities of greater control over public health budgets; the reform of 'our school system' to ensure that 'new providers can enter the state school system in response to parental demand'; the return of Sure Start to its original purpose of early intervention; the creation of a 'Big Society Bank' and introduction of National Citizen Service; the establishment of a commission on long-term care; and, in due course, judgement of Lord Browne's final report into higher education funding (HM Government, 2010: 10–31). Paradoxically, all of these policies applied to England alone, but in each of these cases England was not mentioned. Moreover, while the Coalition acknowledged its own belief that 'our political system is broken', and the urgent need for 'fundamental political reform', that urgent and necessary repair job did not embrace any proposals for devolution in England. Indeed, there was merely mention of the commitment to establish 'a commission to consider the "West Lothian question"' (HM Government, 2010: 27).

In the event, this commitment was only belatedly implemented in January 2012 with the formation of the McKay Commission. It reported on 25 March 2013. However, although the Coalition promised an official response to the Commission's recommendations in the autumn of 2013, it was not until December 2014 that a Command Paper was published outlining the implications of devolution for England, but without any commitment to specific proposals (HM Government, 2014). Even then, the Command Paper only appeared in the aftermath, and as a consequence of, the 18 September 2014 Scottish independence referendum and the subsequent creation of, and recommendations from, the Smith Commission, for further devolution to the Scottish Parliament. There could hardly have been a greater contrast between the urgency and sustained political commitment demonstrated by the Coalition towards further devolution to Scotland, Wales and Northern Ireland, and the indifference shown towards the parallel development of a fair and just settlement for the people of England.

The problems that devolution would create for British modernisers' traditional conflation of the political agenda, institutional identity and interests of England with those of Britain and the centralised institutions of the British state, would be demonstrated in relation to the Coalition's flagship 'open' public services initiative. When the *Open Public Services White Paper* was published in July 2011, its content and extensive referencing was to policy schemes and initiatives confined to England. Nevertheless, the White Paper opened with a section entitled 'Scope'. In it, the Coalition stated its belief that open public services could benefit 'everybody in the UK', and that the scope of the paper was 'UK wide', but in devolved areas of policy it would be for the devolved administrations to determine their own approach to public service reform, including in relation to health, education and local government – all under 'devolved control' (HM Government, 2011: 2). In short, the Coalition was conceding that its 'open' public services agenda would be confined to England, but, despite this, England itself would not be acknowledged or given a national political, institutional or policy identity of its own.

The Coalition's approach to governing England

During its tenure, the Cameron–Clegg Coalition enacted a series of pieces of legislation that significantly reformed the local, regional and urban governance of England, and the manner in which major services were to be delivered and funded. Some of the most controversial reforms applied to England's schools, health service and higher education institutions. These included the raising of the cap on tuition fees at England's universities to £9,000, following a 46 per cent cut in real-terms funding for higher education (excluding research), and the

Coalition's biggest single infrastructure project in England: the £42.6 billion HS2 high speed railway. The latter had originally been justified in the Programme for Government as a means to 'the creation of a low carbon economy' (HM Government, 2010: 31). However, as more details emerged of its soaring cost, and the rationale for, and economic benefits of, its construction changed with an alarming regularity, HS2 increasingly appeared to be an expensive and taxpayer-funded means of solving London's housing shortage for affluent commuters, while spreading inflationary property prices from London and the South East to the North of England (Lee, 2015).

The overriding context for such reforms has been the austerity arising from the largest planned fiscal consolidation since 1945, set out in the June 2010 Emergency Budget, October 2010 Spending Review, and the June 2013 Spending Round. From the outset, the political rhetoric and language accompanying the Coalition's agenda for English governance was one of localism and decentralisation. In practice, all major reforms have been constrained by an overriding desire to enforce fiscal austerity and to set the political agenda, in terms of policy design (as opposed to service delivery and administration) from Westminster and Whitehall.

The first major legislation affecting the internal governance of England was the Localism Act 2011, which received Royal Assent on 15 November 2011. This single Act had a major impact not only upon the role of local government but also upon housing and planning policy within England. Local authorities were given a general power of competence, i.e. to do 'anything that individuals generally may do' (Sandford, 2014), permitted to return to the committee system of council governance, and the possibility in certain authorities of holding referendums for elected mayors. At the same time, local citizens were given the power both to initiate local referendums on any issue of concern, and to veto 'excessive' council tax increases. Communities were also given the right to challenge local authorities by expressing an interest in running any service currently commissioned or delivered by the authority; the right to bid for buildings and land considered to be of value to the community; and the right to build small-scale, site-specific, community-led developments. Statutory neighbourhood planning in England was also introduced by the Act. For their part, local authorities were given the power to place limits on who could apply for social housing within their locality, while also using private rented accommodation to discharge their duties to homeless people. In relation to planning policy, the Act also abolished the Regional Development Agencies and Regional Spatial Strategies in England, while giving additional housing and regeneration powers to the Greater London Authority.

However, the Coalition remained an advocate of administrative decentralisation through 'localism', i.e. the principle that services should be administered and delivered at the local level in England by a greater diversity of private and non-state actors, but not a champion of political devolution to local government per se. Therefore, the new general power of competence provided to local authorities did not extend to the right to raise taxes, to borrow, to set charges for mandatory services, or to impose fines, beyond those permitted by existing powers. Nothing would be sanctioned by central government in general, and the Treasury in particular, which would interfere with the centralised prescription over resource allocation (via the Spending Reviews) and policy design (via ministerial fiat) (Sandford, 2011: 7).

One English local authority also identified that, despite the rhetorical commitment to localism and decentralisation, the Localism Act 2011 had actually provided Eric Pickles, the Secretary of State, with around 140 additional reserve powers (House of Commons Political and Constitutional Reform Committee, 2013a: 9). Even before the Act had been passed, Greg Clarke, the then Minister for Decentralisation, had admitted that there were 'at least 1293 duties imposed on each local authority' in England, vividly demonstrating the way in which the British state had sought to micromanage the governance of England. Furthermore, only 8 per cent of these 1,293 duties had existed prior to the election of the first Thatcher government in May 1979, and no fewer than 39 per cent had been introduced by the Thatcher and Major governments between 1979 and 1996, and a further 50 per cent brought in by the Blair and Brown governments between May 1997 and 2009 (House of Commons Political and Constitutional Reform Committee, 2013a: 8–9). Rather than rolling back the frontiers of the state, like its predecessors from Thatcher to Brown, the Coalition's agenda would entail a redefinition, and frequent rolling forward of the frontiers of the state, especially where those frontiers could be advanced by statutory instruments and unelected, appointed public bodies.

By utilising the powers of the Brown government's Local Democracy, Economic Development and Construction Act 2009, in April 2011 the Greater Manchester Combined Authority was created. In April 2014, further combined authorities were created in Liverpool, West Yorkshire, Sheffield and the North East. However, these were far from acts of genuine political devolution. On the contrary, they followed the pattern established by the Coalition's earlier City Deals, of political bargains being struck between the Treasury and English local authorities. Only the Secretary of State for Communities and Local Government possessed the power to create a combined authority, using a statutory instrument, and only then after the local authorities concerned had first undertaken and published a review of governance (Sandford, 2015). In effect, local authorities have been given limited powers, but only within the overarching constraints of the Treasury's fiscal austerity measures and central government's broader centralised prescription over policy design in England. Such limited measures were presented by Coalition ministers as radical moves towards devolution. Little or nothing had been instituted by the Coalition to dismantle the vast accumulation of statutory powers possessed by central government over local authorities and other public spending bodies in England.

In this regard, a landmark moment came in March 2013 with the publication of the joint Treasury/Department for Business Innovation and Skills' response to Lord Heseltine's October 2012 report for the Coalition, *No Stone Unturned*. The Heseltine Review's first and most controversial recommendation was that 'Central government should identify the budgets administered by different departments which support growth. These should be brought together into a single funding pot for local areas, without internal ring fences' (Heseltine, 2012: 202). Heseltine identified a Single Pot totalling £49.073 billion, combined, of funding for skills, local infrastructure, employment, housing, business support, and innovation and commercialisation programmes in England. Local partnerships should bid for funding from this Single Pot on a competitive basis. In the event, the Government's Regional Growth Fund would provide a Single Pot of only £3.2 billion spread over the five years from 2011–12 until 2016–17. Even in their final year before abolition, the nine English Regional Development Agencies had been allocated funding totalling £1.4 billion. Consequently, once more, a measure presented by the Coalition as an act of significant decentralisation delivered a thinly veiled major cut in public funding for growth and regeneration in England.

Heseltine's ambitions for strategic intervention, and in effect an industrial policy, had been dashed by the Treasury, just as they had been crushed twice before. First, in January 1986, Heseltine had resigned from the Cabinet, following the Thatcher government's decision to back an American-led takeover of Westland, England's sole helicopter manufacturer, rather than Heseltine's own preferred solution of rescue by a European consortium. Second, in June 1992, following his return to the Cabinet, Heseltine's plans to intervene 'before breakfast, dinner and tea' were stifled by the Major government's abolition of the National Economic Development Council, the institution around which Heseltine had planned to engineer his industrial policy agenda. On this third occasion, while the Coalition accepted 81 of Heseltine's 89 recommendations, the greatest political significance for the future governance of England lay in the recommendations it rejected, and its downsizing of the 'Single Pot' Heseltine had envisaged.

The impact of austerity upon England: the national and local settlements

By far the biggest single impact of Coalition policy upon the condition of England has arisen from the austerity in public finances imposed by the Coalition's 'unavoidable deficit reduction plan'. In its 2015 Green Budget, the Institute for Fiscal Studies (IFS) has calculated that the Coalition has implemented a fiscal consolidation from 2010–11 to 2014–15 of £110.1 billion, equivalent to 5.8 per cent of UK GDP, composed of £90.4 billion or 4.8 per cent of GDP of total net spending cuts and £19.7 billion, or 1.0 per cent of GDP, of total net tax rises (Emmerson and Tetlow, 2015: 24). Real departmental spending between 2010–11 and 2014–15 has been cut, in real terms, by 7.8 per cent, for resource (non-investment) spending, and by 13.6 per cent for capital spending (Crawford and Keynes, 2015: 151). However, the impact of this overall fiscal consolidation has impacted very unevenly upon individual departments and programmes in England.

The Coalition promised to protect and increase real spending on the NHS and non-investment expenditure on schools in England. However, because it was planning a real cut in overall departmental spending of 9.5 per cent between 2010–11 and 2015–16, this meant that 'unprotected' departments would face real cuts of 20.6 per cent during this period (Crawford and Keynes, 2015: 158). Furthermore, despite the Coalition's commitment to protect non-investment spending on schools in England, the budget for the Department for Education was still planned to be cut in real terms by 7.4 per cent between 2010–11 and 2015–16, principally because of a forecast 41.2 per cent cut in capital expenditure (Crawford and Keynes, 2015: 158).

Of all the departments governing England, the department that would experience the greatest real budget cuts would be the Department for Communities and Local Government (DCLG). Local government in England would also face a much greater degree of austerity under the Coalition than central government. The IFS has calculated that the

DCLG's Communities budget, which covers the department's principal programmes, including expenditure on social housing, would be cut by 52.5 per cent in real terms between 2010–11 and 2015–16. The DCLG's Local Government budget, which includes both general and specific grants to England's local authorities, was forecast to be cut by 45.5 per cent (Crawford and Keynes, 2015: 161). Although local authorities would be able to protect their spending power by drawing upon other sources of revenue, notably council tax receipts, business rates and user charges, Crawford and Keynes have noted the Office for Budget Responsibility's forecast that local authority spending in England would fall by between 15 and 20 per cent in real terms from 2010–11 to 2015–16 (Crawford and Keynes, 2015: 161).

In sharp contrast, the Department of Health has witnessed a 4.6 per cent real increase in its resource budget and a 4.0 per cent increase in its capital budget between 2010–11 and 2014–15, compared to a 5.5 per cent reduction for the Department for Education (incorporating a 1.4 per cent real-terms fall in its resource budget, and a 34.4 per cent real cut to its capital expenditure) (Crawford and Keynes, 2015: 162). Despite these real-terms increases, and a planned average annual real-terms increase of 1.2 per cent between 2010–11 and 2015–16, NHS England has estimated that it will require real future budget increases (or improvements in its productivity) amounting to around £30 billion per annum (at 2020–21 prices) by 2020–21 (Crawford and Stoye, 2015: 176). Crawford and Stoye have calculated that, even if NHS England succeeds in achieving an annual 2.4 per cent improvement in its productivity, it will still need an annual budget increase of £8 billion by 2020–21. This would entail an annual real-terms budget increase of 0.8 per cent after 2015–16, which would mean other departments in England would need to average annual cuts of 6.1 per cent for the next government to meet the targets specified in the Coalition's December 2014 Autumn Statement (Crawford and Stoye, 2015: 176). While it might be possible to imagine such further swingeing cuts to England's public policies in accounting terms, the consequences for social cohesion would appear to be unimaginable in political terms.

Under the Coalition, England has remained the antithesis of any form of fiscal devolution, decentralisation or federalism. A parliamentary select committee report had observed: 'All previous attempts to create a more equal partnership between central and local government in England have fallen short, despite good intentions' (House of Commons Political and Constitutional Reform Committee, 2013a: 5). The Coalition's Programme for Government promised to reverse this trend:

'we will end the era of top-down government by giving new powers to local councils, communities, neighbourhoods and individuals' (Her Majesty's Government, 2010: 11). In practice, no such powers were to be extended, at least in the area of taxation.

On the contrary, the British state used its extensive powers to impose a much greater degree of austerity on English local government than anything required of central government as a whole. The National Audit Office (NAO) calculated that there would be no less than a 37 per cent real-terms reduction in government funding to local authorities in England from 2010–11 to 2015–16. This would mean an estimated 25 per cent real-terms reduction in local authorities' income, once council tax was taken into account, but a 40 per cent reduction for the largest local authorities (National Audit Office, 2014: 4). To achieve the necessary cuts from their budgets, the NAO estimated that between 2013 and 2014, English local authorities had reduced their full-time equivalent posts by 16.6 per cent, and between 2013–14 and 2014–15, had achieved 40 per cent of their total savings from cuts to budgets for adult social care (ibid.). In the run-up to the May 2015 general election, one parliamentary select committee highlighted the potentially damaging impact of such cuts on services in English local government, by asserting:

> The Department for Communities and Local Government (the Department) does not have a good enough understanding of the impact of funding cuts, either on local authorities' finances or on services. It is unclear whether the Department is exercising a cross government leadership role with respect to local government. It relies on data on spending and has little information on service levels, service quality, and financial sustainability. (House of Commons Committee of Public Accounts, 2015: 3)

England as an afterthought: The New English Politics

During the tenure of the Coalition government, one of the most important trends discernible from opinion polls and surveys has been a growing sense of English national political identity, allied to a growing discontent with the governance arrangements of the United Kingdom and the allocation of public resources provided to England by that particular political settlement. Such trends have been illustrated in a series of The Future of England surveys. In the 2014 survey, evidence emerged that 'England has a distinctive politics that combines a politicisation of English national identity with an increasingly clear political prospectus, and an increasingly vocal advocate for that prospectus' (Jeffery *et al.*, 2014: 3). While the survey suggested that the rallying point for a growing English national political consciousness had been 'an English desire for self-government', it was evident that people in England were 'not just reacting against their "others" in Scotland and the EU'. On the contrary, they were also searching not only for an institutional recognition of England to 'express their concerns better than the current political system', but also political advocates to press their case (Jeffery *et al.*, 2014: 3).

The findings of The Future of England Survey 2014 pointed towards the importance of taking England seriously, and acknowledging the existence of 'The New English Politics' (Jeffery *et al.*, 2014: 2). The survey identified four 'pillars' underlying the identification by people in England of a democratic deficit in the way they were governed and their quest for a self-government project to redress that deficit. These four pillars were Scotland, 'compared to which people in England feel disadvantaged'; the European Union, 'over which there is a sense of lack of control in England'; immigration, also characterised by a sense of lack of control; and the institutional arrangements that might enable the democratic deficit to be redressed (Jeffery *et al.*, 2014: 6). In this latter regard, the survey noted: 'political attitudes in England are essentially *English*, and not regionalist or localist'. Consequently, 'If institutional reform is needed to give expression to English views, then that reform needs to be about England as a whole, not parts of it' (Jeffery *et al.*, 2014: 24). Moreover, in party political terms, the survey revealed that 50 per cent or more of the supporters of the Conservatives, Labour, the Liberal Democrats and the United Kingdom Independence Party (UKIP) took a hard line both on public expenditure and the role played by Scottish MPs at Westminster. David Cameron, Nick Clegg and Ed Miliband had used their pre-independence referendum 'Vow' to the people of Scotland to commit themselves to the maintenance of the Barnett Formula. However, 56 per cent of people surveyed in England had agreed that public expenditure in Scotland should be reduced to the UK average, with Labour (50 per cent), Liberal Democrat (54 per cent), Conservative (69 per cent) and UKIP supporters (70 per cent) all affirming that proposition. At the same time, 62 per cent of people surveyed in England had agreed that Scottish MPs should not vote on English laws, with Labour (52 per cent), Liberal Democrat (67 per cent), Conservative (73 per cent) and UKIP supporters (81 per cent) all endorsing English Votes for English Laws (Jeffery *et al.*, 2014: 28).

Despite the mounting evidence of a growing English national political consciousness, the Coalition demonstrated little inclination to develop a new politics for England. The proposals enshrined in 'the Vow' made by the leaders of the three major UK political parties in the final days of the Scottish independence referendum had left the Barnett Formula in place. During 2012–13, total identifiable expenditure on public services in England had averaged £8,676 per person, more than 19 per cent or £1,651 lower than the average of £10,327 for Scotland, and 3 per cent below the UK average of £8,940. Spending per person was also £1,301 or 14 per cent higher in Wales, and £2,388 or 27 per cent higher in Northern Ireland than in England (HM Treasury, 2014: Table 9.4: 117). Not a single administrative region of England was allocated expenditure per person as high as that allocated to Wales, Scotland or Northern Ireland.

Many of the most significant initiatives affecting the condition of England under the Coalition did not occur until its final year in office. In this regard, anything approaching strategic thinking in relation to the political economy or constitutional future of England appeared something of an afterthought. For example, it was not until 23 June 2014, less than a year before the 2015 general election, that George Osborne made a speech addressing the need to 're-balance' the economy by creating a 'Northern Powerhouse', to 'deliver a real improvement in the long term economic performance of the north of England' (Osborne, 2014). Furthermore, it was not until December 2014, and less than five months before the end of the Coalition's parliamentary term, that William Hague, the Leader of the House of Commons, presented to Parliament the Coalition's Command Paper, *The Implications of Devolution for England* (HM Government, 2014). Moreover, this paper was published more than 17 years after legislation had been passed to initiate plans for devolution for Scotland, Wales and Northern Ireland, and thereby to strengthen and deepen democratic citizenship, voice and accountability. In the interim, and in the absence of any significant initiatives beyond the creation of the Greater London Assembly and directly elected Mayor, devolution in England had been channelled via the developmental market agenda in England's schools, hospitals and universities, empowering individuals as consumers, rather than as citizens per se.

It was not until 3 February 2015, barely three months before the end of its parliamentary term, that William Hague, the Leader of the House of Commons, identified how procedures at Westminster might be amended to alter the way in which scrutiny and votes on legislation affecting England would be conducted (Hague, 2015). However, these proposals would not be enacted by the Coalition. They would instead be contingent upon the election of a future Conservative majority government at Westminster. Under Hague's proposals, at the Committee stage of legislation affecting England alone, MPs elected by and representing constituencies in England, or England and Wales in the case of legislation affecting both nations, would meet as a Grand Committee, and be the only ones to consider and vote on that particular legislation. MPs from elsewhere in the United Kingdom would be excluded from voting. However, such proposals would still mean that, at the final reading of legislation by the House of Commons, any laws affecting England would still require the approval of a majority of MPs from all parts of the United Kingdom. Consequently, the settled democratic will of the elected representatives of the people of England could yet be vetoed by the votes of those MPs without any democratic mandate from, or accountability to, the English demos.

Conclusion

When it published its Programme for Government in May 2010, David Cameron and Nick Clegg claimed the Coalition possessed the potential for 'era-changing, convention-challenging, radical reform', asserted 'centralisation and top-down control have provided a failure', and promised 'a radical redistribution of power away from Westminster and Whitehall to councils, communities and homes across the nation' (HM Government, 2010: 7). Subsequently, during the tenure of the Coalition, it was acknowledged that '[e]nding the overcentralisation of England is the unfinished business of devolution' (House of Commons Political and Constitutional Reform Committee, 2013b: 3). In practice, The Coalition's multitude of reforms to the governance and public services of England have not challenged the conventions of the British state, including its long-standing and preferred modus operandi via an overcentralised England. Within 60 days of taking office, Cameron and Clegg's pledge of 'an emphatic end to the bureaucracy, top-down control and centralisation that has so diminished our NHS' (HM Government, 2010: 9) had been broken with the launch of a hugely expensive and complex top-down reform of the NHS in England. One influential health policy think tank's evaluation has described the reform's effects as 'damaging and distracting' (Ham *et al.*, 2015: 4).

The business of devolution remains unfinished. The people of England continue to await a radical redistribution of power away from

Westminster and Whitehall. The new governance arrangements for England instituted by City 'Devolution' Deals, Combined Metropolitan Authorities, Local Enterprise Partnerships, Enterprise Zones, and the Regional Growth Fund have all been implemented within the overarching framework of the Treasury's centralised prescription over budgets, spending and policy design. It has amounted to sham devolution, when compared to the haste with which significant new devolved powers have been promised for Scotland and Wales.

The belated identification of and commitment to an English 'Northern Powerhouse' have appeared to owe more to an imminent general election and poor opinion polls ratings than a principled commitment to political decentralisation. The fact that the Coalition waited 20 months in office before establishing the McKay Commission on the West Lothian Question, and then waited a further 21 months before publishing a response, in the limited form of a Command Paper setting out an analysis of the implications of devolution for England, but not definitive proposals for addressing them, have been indicative of the Coalition's strategic priorities. Completing the 'unfinished business of devolution' by reforming the national governance of England has not been among them.

References

Crawford, R. and Keynes, S. (2015) Options for further departmental spending cuts. In Emmerson, C., Johnson, P. and Joyce, R. (eds) *The IFS Green Budget*, February 2015 (London: Institute for Fiscal Studies).

Crawford, R. and Stoye, G. (2015) Challenges for health spending. In Emmerson, C., Johnson, P. and Joyce, R. (eds) *The IFS Green Budget*, February 2015 (London: Institute for Fiscal Studies).

Emmerson, C. and Tetlow, G. (2015) Public finances under the coalition. In Emmerson, C., Johnson, P. and Joyce, R. (eds) *The IFS Green Budget*, February 2015 (London: Institute for Fiscal Studies).

Hague, W. (2015) Speech, Westminster, 3 February.

Ham, C., Baird, B., Gregory, S., Jabbal, J. and Alderwick, S. (2015) *The NHS Under the Coalition Government: Part one: NHS Reform* (London: The King's Fund).

Heseltine, M. (2012) *No Stone Unturned in Pursuit of Growth* (London: The Department for Business, Innovation and Skills).

HM Government (2010) *The Coalition: Our Programme for Government* (London: Cabinet Office).

HM Government (2011) *Open Public Services White Paper*, Cm.8145 (London: The Cabinet Office).

HM Government (2014) *The Implications of Devolution for England*, Cm.8969 (London: The Cabinet Office).

HM Treasury (2014) *Public Expenditure Statistical Analyses 2014*, Cm.8902 (London: The Stationery Office).

House of Commons Committee of Public Accounts (2015) *Financial Sustainability of Local Authorities 2014*, HC.833 (London: The Stationery Office).

House of Commons Political and Constitutional Reform Committee (2013a) *Prospects for Codifying the Relationship between Central and Local Government*, HC.656-I (London: The Stationery Office).

House of Commons Political and Constitutional Reform Committee (2013b) *Do We Need a Constitutional Convention for the UK?* HC.371 (London: The Stationery Office).

House of Commons Political and Constitutional Reform Committee (2014a) *A New Magna Carta?* HC.463 (London: The Stationery Office).

House of Commons Political and Constitutional Reform Committee (2014b) *Devolution in England: The Case for Local Government*, HC.503 (London: The Stationery Office).

Jeffery, C., Wyn Jones, R., Henderson, A., Scully, R. and Lodge, G. (2014) *Taking England Seriously: The New English Politics: The Future of England Survey 2014* (University of Edinburgh: Centre on Constitutional Change).

Lee, S. (2009) *Boom and Bust: The Politics and Legacy of Gordon Brown* (Oxford: Oneworld).

Lee, S. (2015) *The State of England: The Nation We're In* (London: Palgrave Macmillan).

National Audit Office (2014) *Financial Sustainability of Local Authorities 2014*, HC.783 (London: The Stationery Office).

Osborne, G. (2014) 'We need a Northern Powerhouse'. Speech, Museum of Science and Industry, Manchester, 23 June.

Sandford, M. (2011) *Local Authorities: The General Power of Competence*. House of Commons Standard Note: SN/PC/05687 (London: The Stationery Office).

Sandford, M. (2014) *Directly-elected Mayors*. House of Commons Library Standard Note: SN/PC/5000 (London: House of Commons Library).

Sandford, M. (2015) *Combined Authorities*. House of Commons Library Standard Note: SN/PC/06649 (London: House of Commons Library).

11
The Coalition's Impact on Scotland

Margaret Arnott

Introduction

This chapter explores how the shifting constitutional and political landscape influenced the governing approaches of the UK Cameron–Clegg Coalition government towards the future position of Scotland in the UK. On entering government in May 2010 David Cameron was aware that past approaches of Conservative governments in the 1980s and 1990s to the governance of Scotland would not suffice. Cameron signalled that the devolved nations would have an ongoing relationship with the Coalition government based on dialogue and 'respect' (Randall and Seawright, 2012). However, as Aughey has stated (2013: 171–2), for Cameron, principles of (Westminster) parliamentary sovereignty were significant in the post-devolution UK political settlement. In Scotland this would raise tensions between a Scottish National Party (SNP) devolved administration which had stressed popular sovereignty over the sovereignty of the Westminster Parliament.

A reminder that the governance of the UK had entered a new phase had come in the 2007 devolved elections. Following the May 2007 Scottish devolved election, the largest party in the Scottish Parliament, the SNP, formed a minority devolved government. Enhancing the powers of the Scottish Parliament, up to and including 'full powers', would be central to the SNP's approach in devolved government (Arnott and Ozga, 2010a). The challenge for the UK government would be how to respond to what appeared to be growing divergence between the respective Scottish government and UK government political and constitutional agendas. Constitutionally, there would be renewed interest in enhancing the powers to the Scottish Parliament; politically, public policy appeared to be diverging along increasingly heterogeneous lines between the Edinburgh and London governments following May 2010 (Keating *et al.*, 2012).

Prominent politicians in both parties in the Coalition government and the Scottish government conceptualised Scotland's relationship with the UK as an evolving one (Alexander, 2013; Commission on Home Rule and Community Rule, 2012; Davidson, 2013; Sturgeon, 2012, 2013). By September 2014, the three main UK unionist parties were faced with a political landscape where the future of the British Union had been seriously brought into question. The Coalition government experienced one of the most dynamic periods of political and constitutional debate in the contemporary governance of the UK. Not since the 1970s had the 'Scottish' constitutional issue featured so prominently. Then, and largely led by Westminster (responding to rising electoral support for the SNP), the Wilson and Callaghan Labour governments had proposed various 'home rule' legislation schemes culminating in the 1978 Scotland Act and the post legislative devolution referendum in Scotland in March 1979.

By May 2010 constitutional politics had taken a new turn. Political arguments about the future governance of Scotland were increasingly framed in terms of popular sovereignty, legitimacy, and the government of Scotland experiencing a 'democratic deficit' (Scottish Constitutional Convention, 1990). The devolution reforms following the election of the Labour government in May 1997 had changed the political and constitutional dynamics in relation to Scotland's position within the UK. The devolved administrations across the UK, and in Scotland in particular, offered an institutional focus to political expressions centred upon advancing territorial interests (Mitchell, 2009). Both unionist and nationalist parties would have to adjust to the changing dynamics of constitutional politics in the UK.

When the 'Yes' campaign for Scottish independence secured 44.7 per cent of the vote, in its defeat to the pro-Union 'No' vote of 55.3 per cent, the ramifications of the 18 September 2014 Scottish Independence Referendum result played out at both the British and Scottish levels. Key questions and issues about the post-devolution governing apparatus, which had been sidestepped by successive UK governments after 1997, especially the operation of political accountability and representation in a UK comprised of four 'national' territories – had been forced up the Westminster political agenda in a way that would have been hard to predict, following the defeat of the 'Yes' side on 18 September 2014.

How did a Conservative-led UK Coalition government find itself facing a political scenario where, in David Cameron's words, it had to defend the UK being 'torn apart' (*The Herald*, 2014)? A successful vote in favour of Scotland remaining part of the United Kingdom, rather than producing answers to questions about the future governance of the UK, has opened up constitutional debates in the Westminster Parliament and in Scotland. The post-referendum political scenario marked a new period for the campaign for further enhanced powers to the Scottish Parliament, one in which the UK Coalition government found itself responding to debates about the constitutional future of Scotland in a manner which was not predicted following the unsuccessful 'Yes' campaign. Rising expectations that further substantial devolution would be offered if Scotland voted to remain within the UK (Curtice, 2014) placed the UK Coalition in a difficult political situation. Trying to reconcile any further devolution offered to Scotland with an as yet largely unreformed UK Parliament would add to the pressures the UK Coalition faced.

This chapter now explores the period leading up to the Scottish Independence Referendum and its immediate aftermath. Rather than providing a comprehensive narrative of events, it analyses the significance of the 2011 Scottish Parliament devolved elections and the 2014 Scottish Independence Referendum for the UK Coalition government. Since the formation of the Coalition government in May 2010, the political context has shifted dramatically on constitutional issues. From the 2012 Scotland Act, the Edinburgh Agreement, the formation of the Smith Commission on enhanced devolution and legislative proposals published in January 2015, the UK government has revisited the constitutional future of Scotland repeatedly. Why this should be the case requires us to consider important changes to the political landscape in Scotland.

Scotland and the constitution: political earthquakes and tremors

Three related issues shaped the political landscape the UK Coalition government negotiated following its formation in 2010: the electoral context, the constitutional debate about reforming the governance of the devolved UK, and the Scottish government's approach to governing, particularly its approach to independence. First, changing electoral patterns both at Scottish and UK levels have had profound implications for the UK Coalition. The electoral success of the SNP in the devolved Scottish Parliament elections of 2007 and 2011, and the shifting nature of party competition at UK elections, including the challenge from

UKIP, presented a difficult electoral terrain for both parties forming the UK Coalition government. In the May 2011 Scottish Parliament elections the SNP secured an historic electoral victory, whose scale undoubtedly changed the political context of territorial politics and governance in the UK. The party won 69 of the parliament's 129 seats and made significant electoral gains across all regions of Scotland. A majority Nationalist government was formed in the Scottish Parliament; an event not expected under the electoral system designed for the Scottish Parliament. The most obvious indication of added legitimacy for the SNP administration was that in September 2014 a Scotland-wide referendum on independence was held (Arnott and Ozga, 2012).

In the 2010 UK general election the Conservative Party failed to reverse the image of a party dependent on support from the middle and south of England (Randall and Seawright, 2012). In Scotland the party improved its electoral position in marginal terms, with its share of the vote increasing to 16.7 per cent from 15.8 per cent. It had one elected representative in the Westminster Parliament, a situation unchanged since 2001. The Liberal Democrats had a stronger presence electorally in Scotland, at least in terms of elected representatives. In the May 2010 Westminster election, the party returned 11 MPs in Scotland, with an 18.9 per cent share of the vote. That meant only 12 MPs out of 364 of the newly formed UK Coalition government's representation at Westminster had been elected from Scottish constituencies. The image of diverging electorates between Scotland and England created the conditions for the SNP to present a governing narrative questioning the legitimacy of a UK Coalition which followed an agenda of reducing public expenditure alongside a social policy agenda that prioritised market-orientated principles, especially in terms of the delivery of public services, and questioned universalist principles of public service provision.

It was against this backdrop that the second issue, concerning the constitution and the future governance of the UK, was framed. The changing electoral context produced in part by devolution, but also in part by the longer term post-1955 decline in the electoral position of the Conservative Party in Scotland, has shifted what could be presented as theoretical constitutional challenges in the early days of the UK Coalition government to very real practical challenges (Arnott and Macdonald, 2012). Political narratives surrounding the constitutional future of the UK were evolving in the context of a devolved UK where its largest nation, England, with 84 per cent of the UK's population, had not seen power devolved to directly elected institutions (Kenny, 2015).

Constitutional politics in the UK Coalition government's agreement had a shared commitment to decentralisation and localism (Hazell, 2012). Broadly, these could be characterised as measures to improve the 'efficiency' of Westminster rather than attempts to redress political issues surrounding asymmetric devolution and wider governance of the UK. Reducing the size of the House of Commons; a Commission on the West Lothian Question (English Votes for English Laws); introducing a petition mechanism for the Westminster Parliament; implementing the Wright Committee reforms for the House of Commons; and the right of recall of MPs were all other constitutional measures supported by the Conservatives. By focusing upon the status and role of the Westminster Parliament, particularly of the Commons, constitutional reform was constructed within a framework – where the 'English Question' could be seen as part of reforming the Westminster Parliament rather than reform of the devolved UK as a whole. England had continued to be governed through the pre-1999 UK governing apparatus (Aughey, 2012). The challenges this would present later for the Coalition government had not been fully appreciated. Focusing upon reforms of the Westminster Parliament, without considering the wider governance of the devolved UK, would present very real practical challenges for the UK Coalition government in the immediate aftermath of both the May 2011 Scottish Parliament Election and the September 2014 Scottish Referendum result.

Liberal Democrat proposals for constitutional reforms to the Westminster Parliament featured prominently in the Coalition Partnership Agreement. A referendum on the Alternative Vote (AV) system for Westminster elections; fixed-term parliaments; and the right to recall MPs all featured. Further reforms to the devolved arrangements for both Wales and also Scotland were included in the UK Coalition's Programme for Government (Cabinet Office, 2010). Both Coalition partners were committed to further reforms based on the final report of the Calman Commission (Commission on Scottish Devolution, 2009).

It is here that the third issue, concerning the Scottish government's approach to governing, specifically its approach to independence, must be addressed. Following the 2007 Scottish Parliament election, Scotland's position in the UK had once more risen up the political agenda. The National Conversation (Scottish Executive, 2007) launched by the SNP administration in August 2008, set out constitutional options for Scotland and demonstrated an SNP vision firmly tied to political self-determination and independence (Arnott and Ozga, 2010a). At this stage the SNP remained committed to introducing legislation for a referendum on independence in 2010. Its minority status, however, meant this remained an aspiration during its first period of government. The response of the three unionist parties was not to join the SNP's National Conversation. They set up their own review under the chairmanship of Sir Kenneth Calman. The Calman Commission considered how legislative devolution might be developed further *within* the devolved UK (Commission on Scottish Devolution, 2009). Its remit excluded consideration of independence. Both Coalition partners had given an undertaking during the 2010 UK general election campaign that the Calman proposals would be the basis of further reforms to the governance of Scotland. The ensuing legislation, the 2012 Scotland Act, however, found itself overtaken by the pace of electoral and political change (HM Government, 2012).

The scale of the SNP's victory in May 2011, and the increased electoral divergence across the UK displayed in the general election of May 2010, created further divergence in the political context rather than less, as did the differences between the Scottish and UK governments in the presentation of the governing project in response to economic crisis (Scottish Government, 2011, 2013a). Furthermore, with the SNP having established its competence as a minority government from 2007–11, there was now heightened referencing of the 'journey to independence' and an increased emphasis on independence as a 'means to an end rather than an end' in itself (Arnott and Ozga, 2012; Sturgeon, 2012). A majority SNP government formed in 2011 could now make a renewed case for a Scottish Independence Referendum.

In First Minister Alex Salmond's words, the UK Coalition government should recognise the 'moral authority' of the Scottish government to hold a Scottish Independence Referendum (Salmond, 2011). The SNP Scottish Parliament election manifesto committed the party to holding a referendum towards the end of its term of office (SNP, 2011). David Cameron spoke of the 'emphatic victory' the SNP had secured. The comments of both the First Minister of Scotland and also the UK Prime Minister hint at a recognition that constitutional issues had not only become more politicised but also that *both* governments – Scottish and UK – would play a significant role in how the constitutional issue would be taken forward. The UK government was now facing a number of very practical constitutional challenges on the future governance of Scotland.

Under the Scotland Act 1998, constitutional matters lay outwith the competence of the devolved Scottish Parliament. While this had been a matter for debate during the early period of the SNP minority government, it was brought into sharper focus after 2011. The Conservative position that the Scotland Act 2012 would shape the UK Coalition government's response to Scottish devolution debates looked to be increasingly untenable. A referendum on Scottish independence looked inevitable following the May 2011 election result. The question for the UK government was how this process would be handled. In January 2012 David Cameron, having accepted the case for an Independence Referendum, stated: 'We owe the Scottish people something that is fair, legal and decisive' (BBC, 2012).

The UK government launched a consultation document, *Scotland's Constitutional Future*, on the Scottish Independence Referendum (Scotland Office, 2012). The focus was on establishing the processes of the referendum. In January 2012 the then Secretary of State for Scotland, Liberal Democrat Michael Moore MP, announced to the House of Commons that the UK Coalition government was willing to facilitate the transfer of powers necessary to ensure the Scottish Parliament's competence to proceed with a Scottish Independence Referendum. A Section 30 Order followed to establish the legitimacy of the devolved Scottish government to oversee a referendum on the future of Scotland.

In October 2012 the UK and the Scottish governments signed the Edinburgh Agreement. Through the Agreement, the UK government and the Scottish government acknowledged that the referendum result would be respected 'with the consent and consensus' of *both* governments (UK Government/Scottish Government, 2012). The acceptance of the legitimacy of the Scottish Parliament to hold the Scottish Independence Referendum was not just a symbolic act. It could be seen as part of the wider 'pragmatic approach' David Cameron had taken to territorial politics and governance (Randall and Seawright, 2012). For the UK Coalition government, the 2011 Scottish devolved election had signalled a need to be seen to be taking the constitutional debate beyond the Scotland Act 2012 (Commission on Home Rule and Community Rule, 2012; Davidson, 2013).

The failure of the Calman Commission and the Scottish government's National Conversation to engage with each other had a direct bearing on the political context the UK Coalition government found itself facing after 2011. Calman's failure to consider independence enabled the SNP government to reignite the politics of legitimacy and question the relevance of the 2012 Scotland Act to current Scottish political aspirations. As part of the Edinburgh Agreement it was agreed a single 'Yes'/'No' question should be asked in the referendum ballot paper. While the SNP government had been arguing for a multi option referendum, which included enhanced devolution as an option, the UK Coalition government position came from a desire to secure a successful 'No' vote as a way to avoid protracted political debate about the future constitutional position of Scotland.

The Edinburgh Agreement signed in October 2012 had brought the two governments into the shared discussions about one aspect of the constitutional debate, namely the *process* of holding a referendum. The legitimacy of the devolved Scottish Parliament to conduct the referendum was accepted. While the UK government had been largely focused on progressing the 2012 Scotland Act and establishing the processes of holding a Scottish Independence Referendum, the SNP government had, since 2007, been building the 'why' case for Scottish independence. The minority status of the SNP administration between 2007 and 2011, and also its concern to create a new 'imaginary' of an independent Scotland, had made it extremely attentive to the use of discourse and establishing a political narrative surrounding the case for independence (Arnott and Ozga, 2010b). In contrast, the unionist parties had yet to engage in a sustained debate about the future governance of a devolved UK and the future of the Union. As an alternative political narrative, the SNP sought instead to persuade the public that government would be safe in its hands, and that independence was a realistic and unthreatening possibility. Indeed, since coming to power the SNP administration had been highly focused on 'crafting the narrative' around the case for Scottish independence (Arnott and Ozga, 2010b).

The Scottish Independence Referendum Franchise Bill was introduced in the Scottish Parliament in March 2013 and received Royal Assent in August 2013 (Scottish Government, 2013b). The bill focused on process issues surrounding the referendum including the timing of the referendum, wording of the question, the role of the Electoral Commission, campaign rules and provision to allow voting rights to 16 and 17 year olds. In November 2013 the Scottish government published its White Paper on Independence, *Scotland's Future* (Scottish Government, 2013c). The 600-page document set out both the case for Scottish independence and how independence might be achieved. Each of the three unionist parties was to present its own proposals on further devolution. While the Liberal Democrats presented the argument for further devolution on the basis of their 2012 Commission on Home Rule and Community Rule, it would not be until 2014 that the Scottish Conservative Party and the Scottish Labour Party published their respective proposals. The Scottish Conservative Party established a Commission on Scottish Devolution in 2013 with its final report published in May 2014 (Scottish Conservative Party, 2014). Of the three unionist political parties, the Conservative report was seen to propose the most substantial reforms to devolution; recommending devolution of income tax and assigning a proportion of VAT proceeds. Further devolution of welfare policy was also recommended with specific mention of housing benefit and attendance allowance. These proposals received the support of David Cameron and the intention was they would be included in the Conservatives' 2015 UK election manifesto. However, the failure to present an agreed unionist response to the Scottish Government White Paper and the wider case for the Union would have significant repercussions during the Scottish Independence Referendum Campaign and its aftermath.

The Scottish Independence Referendum and its aftermath

Perhaps the most notable intervention made by the UK Coalition partners came just three days before the Scottish Independence Referendum was to be held. What has become known as the 'Vow' by the three UK unionist party leaders was published on the front page of the *Daily Record*. The 'Vow' promised 'extensive new powers' for the devolved Scottish Parliament and that work on delivering these new enhanced powers would begin the day after the referendum (Clegg, 2014). Concern that the 'Yes' side had been closing the gap in the latter stages of the referendum campaign had led the unionist parties to intensify arguments that a 'No' vote would not amount to a vote for no further devolution. The catalyst for the late intervention by the three unionist UK party leaders came following the publication of a YouGov opinion poll on 5 September placing the 'Yes' side marginally ahead of the 'No' side for the first time in the campaign (Jeffrey, 2014). The publication of the 'Vow' reiterated that, for the UK Coalition partners, the 2012 Scotland Act had been superseded and an acceptance that this legislation did not mark the end of constitutional reforms to the governance of Scotland. The harder question was did this now open up debates for wider constitutional reform *across* the devolved UK?

In the closing weeks of the referendum campaign the approach of the UK Coalition government had changed in response to both opinion poll evidence about growing support for Scottish independence and to the unprecedented level of public engagement in the campaign. The fact that the 'Better Together' campaign did not have an agreed set of devolution proposals had become one of the areas of contention during the campaign. While each of the three parties had published their own proposals (HM Government, 2014a) including the Scottish Conservative Party and the Scottish Liberal Democrats, the UK government found itself adopting a difficult balancing act between being conscious that direct interventions, especially from David Cameron and other Conservative members of the Cabinet, might be perceived negatively in Scotland, and concerns that standing back from direct debates could fuel the sense that the UK government was failing to respond to growing political engagement in Scotland around the question of Scotland's constitutional future. The tipping point would come in the week prior to the 18 September 2014 Referendum vote, culminating in the 'Vow'.

Following a speech given by former Prime Minister Gordon Brown in early September 2014, the UK government had now agreed to a timetable for further constitutional reform (BBC, 2014a). In broad terms a 'No' vote on 18 September would set off a chain of events to deliver further devolution. This process was to begin the day after a 'No' vote. A paper would also be published by the UK Coalition government in October 2014. The agreed powers would be set by November and legislation drafted for January 2015. If a successful 'No' vote was achieved on 18 September the nature of the 'Vow' and its associated timetable ensured that the focus of the debate would move to how the UK government would respond, and in particular to the timeline initially set by Gordon Brown.

Cameron's first public reaction to the Scottish Independence Referendum result triggered an immediate further reaction among both pro-independence and unionist political parties. On the morning of 19 September, in front of No. 10 Downing Street, Cameron repeated the commitment to move forward on Scottish devolution. This would, Cameron argued, happen in 'tandem' with reform of the Westminster Parliament on 'English votes for English laws'. The linking of enhanced powers for the devolved Scottish Parliament with the 'West Lothian' question had been a response to pressures within the Conservative Parliamentary Party. Wider issues about the governance of the UK, where asymmetric devolution had largely developed in an ad hoc manner, were sidestepped. Cameron also announced the formation of a commission to undertake cross-party discussions on the devolution process in Scotland. The Commission chaired by Lord Smith of Kelvin would consider 'powers over tax, spending and welfare all agreed by November and draft legislation published by January' (BBC, 2014b).

By establishing the Smith Commission, the UK Coalition government had not only responded to the Brown timetable but it had also intensified debates among Conservative backbenchers at Westminster about the

'West Lothian' question. In Scotland, the Smith Commission brought together all five parties represented in the Scottish Parliament. Each party was requested to submit its proposals for enhanced devolution by 10 October, and members of the public and organisations by the end of October. Over 18,000 submissions were received from the general public and some 407 responses from organisations. From these submissions across political and civic Scotland, representatives of the five major political parties in Scotland negotiated 'Heads of Agreement' to be published by 27 November. Key issues addressed in the Heads of Agreement covered taxation and welfare (Smith Commission, 2014). For the unionist parties the key focus on taxation centred around income tax. Enhanced taxation powers were part of a wider agenda advanced by all three unionist parties that the Scottish Parliament needed these additional powers to enhance political accountability and move away from a parliament where 'spending' rather than revenue-raising powers had featured. On welfare devolution the Smith Commission was responding to calls that the devolution settlement to date had failed to handle the interface and spill-over effects between devolved and reserved powers in welfare adequately. For the unionist parties, three specific welfare policy areas were highlighted for consideration in the Smith Commission negotiations, namely housing benefit, the Work Programme and Attendance Allowance.

While the publication of the Smith Commission Report brought agreement across the five parties represented in the Scottish Parliament about what additional taxation and welfare powers would be devolved, there was less consensus around the practicalities of implementing these proposals. The implications for the Scottish block grant, and the continued interconnectedness of welfare policy in a devolved Scotland with the UK government, remained two of the most contentious areas. The challenge for the UK government was that by highlighting a particular solution to the 'West Lothian Question' – English votes for English laws (HM Government, 2014b) – wider considerations about the interconnectedness of the devolved nations and UK government, in policy terms, alongside the UK's financial and taxation system, had been neglected following the September 2014 Scottish independence vote.

The UK government published further legislative proposals for devolved powers to the Scottish Parliament on 22 January 2015 (HM Government, 2015). For David Cameron, its publication met the promises contained in the 'Vow': 'The leaders of the other main political parties and I promised extensive new powers for the Scottish Parliament – a vow – with a clear process and timetable. And now, here we have it:

new powers for Scotland, built to last, securing our united future' (UK Government, 2015).

The Liberal Democrat Scottish Secretary, Alistair Carmichael, also spoke of the proposals in the Command Paper as 'an agreement which was built to last ... [and] struck the right balance of powers for Scotland as part of the UK' (UK Government, 2015). The pace for publication of the UK government's Command Paper following the Smith Commissions Report at the end of November 2014 had been set by the 'Vow'. Maintaining the commitment to additional powers beyond the 2012 Scotland Act as was set out in the Vow was critical for the UK Coalition government.

The Command Paper title, *Scotland in the UK: The Enduring Settlement*, indicated that the UK Coalition government regarded the legislation as a line in the sand for the devolution of further powers to Scotland. However, whether an 'enduring settlement' can be reached on the basis of the Command Paper is an open question. It seems unlikely that the proposals set out in the January 2015 UK government's Command Paper mark the culmination of the devolution process for Scotland. Scotland's position within the UK and the future of the UK are part of an ongoing and potentially increasingly politicised constitutional and political process. The proposals do not appear to provide a clear path to implementation or a sustainable constitutional position in the UK. One of the most significant areas to emerge from the Smith Commission was in relation to 'Principle five', namely that post-referendum constitutional change should 'not cause detriment to the UK as a whole nor to any of its constituent parts' (Smith Commission, 2014: 9). The Command Paper repeats this commitment. How this could be sustained is far from clear.

Cameron's commitment on 19 September 2014 to make further reforms to Scottish devolved powers, 'in tandem' with reform within the House of Commons on 'English votes for English laws', focused upon constitutional anomalies rather than a UK-wide vision of the future of the British Union. The extent to which the January 2015 UK government Command Paper has moved away from the Smith Commission Report has also been raised. Questions about whether the Scottish Parliament would have ability to put in place new welfare benefits have been posed.

Events since the 18 September referendum had moved quickly. The vote had failed to produce a majority 'Yes' vote, but the SNP-led administration responded quickly to the defeat. Alex Salmond resigned as First Minister and SNP Party Leader the day following the Scottish

Referendum vote. That Nicola Sturgeon, then Deputy First Minister and Deputy Party Leader, would be elected to both posts Salmond had relinquished had been widely expected by political commentators. However, another twist came in the unprecedented growth in SNP party membership following the 'No' vote. The Scottish Green Party – itself pro-independence – also gained party membership. Some four days after the Scottish Referendum vote the SNP membership had risen by 17,000 and the Scottish Greens' membership by 2,000. By 22 November 2014, SNP membership had risen from 25,000 at the time of the Scottish Referendum vote to 92,187 (SNP, 2014). SNP support in opinion polls on voting intentions for the 2015 UK general election also increased. One poll by Ipsos Mori placed the SNP ahead by 28 per cent over the Scottish Labour Party in Westminster election voting intention on the 21 January 2015 (Brookes, 2015). The SNP would, with this level of support secure 55 of 59 Scottish Westminster seats, with Scottish Labour winning only four seats. If this trend of rising support for the SNP was to be maintained in the 7 May 2015 UK general election, the implications would be considerable. Falling electoral representation from Scotland could have significant implications for the Labour Party in its ability to secure a majority government at the UK level.

Conclusion

The Scottish Independence Referendum result was a defining event for the UK Coalition government. On 19 September 2014, the focus of debates about the constitutional future of Scotland moved to the level of the UK Coalition government. Increasingly, what might have appeared to be theoretical concerns by the UK government about further constitutional reform extending beyond the 2012 Scotland Act have become very real practical constitutional concerns. Questions about funding mechanisms in the devolved UK, and intergovernmental relations and interdependencies between reserved and devolved policy areas, will all require careful consideration in the context of maintaining the Union. How the UK government responds to constitutional debates about the future of England and the devolved nations is now being conducted against a growing sense of English political consciousness. This will have important implications for the future of the UK (Jeffrey *et al.*, 2014). The challenge for the UK-wide parties, especially the three main unionist parties, in the 2015 UK general election is how to respond to the growing politics of identity and nationhood across the UK.

References

Alexander, D. (2013) Scotland's Constitutional Future. Speech, University of Edinburgh, 1 March. www.newstatesman.com/politics/2013/03/douglas-alexanders-speech-scotland-full-text (accessed 29 March 2013).

Arnott, M. A. and Macdonald, C. M. M. (2012) More Than a Name: The Union in Conservative Rhetoric and Policy. In D. Torrance (ed.), *The Scottish Conservative Party: From Unionist Scotland to Political Wilderness* (Edinburgh: Edinburgh University Press).

Arnott, M. A. and Ozga, J. (2010a) Nationalism, Governance and Policy Making: The SNP in Power, *Public Money and Management*, 30(2): 91–7.

Arnott, M. A. and Ozga, J. (2010b) Education and Nationalism: The Discourse of Education Policy in Scotland. *Discourse: Studies in the Cultural Politics of Education*, 31(3): 335–50.

Arnott, M. A. and Ozga, J. (2012) Education and Social Policy. In G. Mooney and G. Scott (eds), *Social Justice and Social Policy in Scotland* (Bristol: Policy Press).

Aughey, A. (2012) The Con-Lib Coalition Agenda for Scotland, Wales and Northern Ireland. In S. Lee and M. Beech (eds), *The Cameron–Clegg Coalition Government: Coalition Politics in an Age of Austerity* (Basingstoke: Palgrave Macmillan).

Aughey, A. (2013) *The British Question* (Manchester: Manchester University Press).

BBC (2012) David Cameron Pushes for Scottish Vote Clarity. 8 January. www.bbc. co.uk/news/uk-politics-16462539 (accessed 1 November 2014).

BBC (2014a) Brown Sets out More Powers Timetable. 8 September. www.bbc.co.uk/news/uk-scotland-scotland-politics-29115556 (accessed 10 September 2014).

BBC (2014b) David Cameron Statement on the Future of the UK. 19 September. www.bbc.co.uk/news/uk-politics-29271765 (accessed 20 September 2014).

Brookes, L. (2015) Poll Shows the SNP Could Win all But Four Scottish Seats in General Election. *The Guardian*, 21 January. www.theguardian.com/politics/2015/jan/21/poll-snp-labour-scottish-seats-election (accessed 21 January 2015).

Cabinet Office (2010) *The Coalition: Our Programme for Government* (London: The Cabinet Office).

Clegg, D. (2014) David Cameron, Ed Miliband and Nick Clegg Sign Joint Historic Promise Which Guarantees More Devolved Powers for Scotland and Protection of NHS if We Vote No. *The Daily Record*, 15 September. www.dailyrecord.co.uk/news/politics/david-cameron-ed-miliband-nick-4265992 (accessed 11 November 2014).

Commission on Home Rule and Community Rule (2012) *Federalism: The Best Future for Scotland* (Edinburgh: Scottish Liberal Democrats).

Commission on Scottish Devolution (2009) *Serving Scotland Better: Scotland and the UK in the 21st Century: Final Report* (Edinburgh: Commission on Scottish Devolution).

Curtice, J. (2014) Smith Commission: Will Voters Be Satisified? *Scotcen*, 28 November. www.scotcen.org.uk/blog/smith-commission-will-voters-be-satisfied (accessed 15 December 2014).

Davidson, R. (2013) 'Strengthening Devolution, Taking Devolution Forward'. Speech, Royal Society of Edinburgh, 26 March. www.scottishconservatives.com/2013/03/strengthening-devolution-taking-scotland-forward/ (accessed 27 March 2013).

Hazell, R. (2012) Case Study 1: Constitutional Reform. In R. Hazell and B. Yong (eds), *The Politics of Coalition: How the Conservative–Liberal Government Works* (Oxford: Hart Publishing).

Herald, The (2014) Cameron Urges Scots: 'Don't Rip Apart UK and Break my Heart', 10 September. www.heraldscotland.com/politics/referendum-news/cameron-urges-scots-dont-rip-apart-uk-with-a-leap-in-the-dark.1410332546 (accessed 11 September 2014).

HM Government (2012) *The Scotland Act* (London: The Stationery Office).

HM Government (2014a) *The Parties Published Proposals on Further Devolution for Scotland.* Cm. 8946 (London: The Cabinet Office).

HM Government (2014b) *The Implications of Devolution for England.* Cm. 8969 (London: The Cabinet Office).

HM Government (2015) *Scotland in the UK: An Enduring Settlement.* Cm. 8890 (London: The Cabinet Office).

Jeffrey, C. (2014) Constitution Making on the Hoof that Could End in Meltdown. *The Herald,* 27 December. www.heraldscotland.com/comment/columnists/charlie-jeffery-constitution-making-on-the-hoof-that-could-end-in-meltdown.115189171 (accessed 28 December 2014).

Jeffrey, C., Wyn Jones, R., Henderson, A., Scully, R. and Lodge, G. (2014) *Taking England Seriously: The New English Politics – The Future of England Survey 2014.* www.futureukandscotland.ac.uk/sites/default/files/news/Taking%20England%20Seriously_The%20New%20English%20Politics.pdf (accessed 31 November 2014).

Keating, M., Cairney, P. and Hepburn, E. (2012) Policy Convergence, Transfer and Learning in the UK Under Devolution. *Regional and Federal Studies,* 22(3): 289–307.

Kenny, M. (2015) Englishness Politicised? Unpacking Normative Implications of the McKay Commission. *British Journal of Politics and International Relations,* 17(1): 152–70.

Mitchell, J. (2009) *Devolution in the United Kingdom* (Manchester: Manchester University Press).

Randall, D. and Seawright, D. (2012) Territorial Politics. In D. Seawright and T. Heppell (eds), *Cameron and the Conservatives: The Transition to Coalition Government* (London: Palgrave Macmillan).

Salmond, A. (2011) Scotland will Join Family of Nations, 17 October (Edinburgh: The Scottish National Party). www.snp.org/blog/post/2011/oct/alex-salmond-scotland-will-join-family-nations (accessed 17 December 2014).

Scotland Office (2012) *Scotland's Constitutional Future.* Cm. 8203 (London: The Stationery Office).

Scottish Conservative Party (2014) *Commission on the Future Governance of Scotland* (Edinburgh: The Scottish Conservative and Unionist Party).

Scottish Constitutional Convention (1990) *Towards Scotland's Parliament: A Report to the Scottish People* (Edinburgh: The Convention).

Scottish Executive (2007) *Choosing Scotland's Future: A National Conversation: Independence and Responsibility in the Modern World* (Edinburgh: The Scottish Executive).

Scottish Government (2011) *The Government Economic Strategy* (Edinburgh: The Scottish Government).

Scottish Government (2013a) *Scotland's Future: From the Referendum to Independence and a Written Constitution* (Edinburgh: The Scottish Government).

Scottish Government (2013b) *Scottish Independence Referendum Act 2013* (Edinburgh: The Scottish Government).

Scottish Government (2013c) *Scotland's Future: Your Guide to an Independent Scotland* (Edinburgh: The Scottish Government).

Smith Commission (2014) *Report of the Smith Commission for Further Devolution of Powers to the Scottish Parliament* (Edinburgh: The Smith Commission).

SNP (2011) *Re-Elect: A Scottish Government Working for Scotland* (Edinburgh: The Scottish National Party).

SNP (2014) SNP Membership Now Exceeds Extraordinary 90,000. Press Release, 22 November. www.snp.org/media-centre/news/2014/nov/snp-membership-now-exceeds-extraordinary-90000 (accessed 1 December 2014).

Sturgeon, N. (2012) Building a Better Nation. Speech, University of Strathclyde, Glasgow. 2 December.

Sturgeon, N. (2013) Speech to SNP Spring Conference. 24 March. Inverness www.snp.org/blog/post/2013/mar/snp-spring-conference-address-nicola-sturgeon (accessed 2 April 2013).

UK Government/Scottish Government (2012) *Agreement between the United Kingdom Government and the Scottish Government on a Referendum on Independence for Scotland*, 15 October. www.scotland.gov.uk/Resource/0040/00404789.pdf (accessed 2 February 2013).

UK Government (2015) All Party Promise of New Powers for Scotland Delivered. 22 January. Press Release. www.gov.uk/government/news/all-party-promise-of-new-powers-for-scotland-delivered (accessed 22 January 2015).

12
The Coalition's Impact on Wales

Roger Scully

Introduction

Wales has experienced the Conservative–Liberal Democrat Coalition government rather differently from the other nations of the UK. While the macro-economic consequences of the Coalition government's austerity agenda have largely been common, as a poor part of the UK with a high public-sector dependency, the economic cost of austerity on Wales has been heavier than average. Austerity has also had direct consequences – via the magical workings of the Barnett Formula – on the resources that Wales and the other devolved nations have available to use within areas of policy that are otherwise under their own control. Devolution, and the existence of a Welsh Assembly and Welsh Government, has meant that many flagship policies of the UK government have not been implemented in Wales. Major elements of the Coalition's domestic agenda, such as the reforms to schooling and the NHS, have concerned only England. However, with its devolution dispensation being rather more limited than that of both Scotland and Northern Ireland, Wales has experienced the Coalition in a rather more 'full-on' manner than have the UK's other two minority nations.

In addition to its consequences for public policy and the daily lives of people in Wales, however, there have also been clear political consequences of the Coalition. In this chapter I will explore two key areas. First, I will examine the consequences of the Coalition for the party politics of Wales. Though heavily influenced by wider UK political developments, party politics in Wales has long taken a distinct and peculiar form: there is a lengthy history of one-party dominance, while since the 1960s Wales has had an additional significant party, Plaid Cymru. What impact has the Coalition had on the parties? Second, I will examine the constitutional politics of Wales. This is an issue that has been a matter of political debate for decades, and which the creation of the National Assembly for Wales (NAW) did not settle, largely due to the unsatisfactory nature of the various devolution 'settlements' offered to Wales. The Coalition government included one party that has traditionally been cautious about, if not downright hostile towards, devolution; and another with a long-standing history of support for Welsh home rule. How did the Coalition manage this potential tension, and what impact has the Coalition had on constitutional debates and reforms in Wales?

Party politics under the Coalition

As observed in the introduction, democratic politics in Wales has often taken a distinct, and rather unusual form. Throughout the democratic era, Wales has rarely had truly competitive party politics. Instead, we have experienced long periods of one-party dominance – under the Liberals between 1880 and 1914, and by Labour from 1945 onwards. The obverse of this dominance has been persisting Conservative weakness: since the mid-nineteenth century the Tories have always attracted much lower levels of electoral support than in England (Scully, 2014a). Labour has won at least a plurality of the votes, and a majority of the parliamentary seats, in Wales at every general election from 1945 onwards. Democratic politics in Wales has tended to have a very lopsided character.

In the years prior to the May 2010 general election, however, things seemed to be changing. Labour's dominance appeared to be under some threat. From the Blairite high-water mark of 1997, Labour's vote share fell more substantially in 2001 and 2005 in Wales than it did in either England or Scotland. In the 2007 devolved elections, while Labour remained the largest party in Wales, its vote share fell much further there than in the equivalent poll in Scotland. And in the 2009 European election, Labour failed to come first across Wales in an election for the first time since 1918.

The saving grace for Welsh Labour, however, was their opposition. Unlike in Scotland with the SNP, Labour in Wales did not face a single, clear and strong challenger. The Conservatives remained toxic to much of the Welsh electorate. Plaid Cymru, after an electoral *annus mirabilis* in 1999 when they twice (in devolved and European elections) came very close to beating Labour, floundered electorally after 2000 under a new leader, Ieuan Wyn Jones, who possessed many political qualities but was almost wholly lacking in one: voter appeal. The Liberal Democrats made some advances, but in Wales as elsewhere these were only in isolated pockets. Moreover, the seats that these parties were targeting often involved them fighting each other, rather than challenging Labour. Thus, Labour was saved from major electoral damage. The party lost lots of votes in the 2007 NAW election, but with no clear challenger emerging it remained by far the largest party in the Assembly (governing in coalition with Plaid Cymru in Wales from 2007–11). In the 2010 general election, Labour won their lowest Welsh vote share in a general election since 1918 (indeed, given that in 1918 Labour did not stand candidates in every seat it was, in reality, Labour's lowest general election vote share in Wales *ever*). Yet as Table 12.1 shows, Labour escaped major seat losses. There were advances in vote share for both the Conservatives and the Liberal Democrats, but even though the soon-to-be coalition partners collectively won many more votes than Labour in Wales, they had only 11 MPs to Labour's 26. Meanwhile, Plaid Cymru came fourth, and continued to tread water.

Table 12.1   2010 general election, Wales

Party	% Vote share (change)	Seats (change)
Labour	36.2 (–6.5)	26 (–3)
Conservatives	26.1 (+4.7)	8 (+5)
Liberal Democrats	20.1 (+1.7)	3 (–1)
Plaid Cymru	11.3 (–1.3)	3
Others	6.2 (+1.2)	0

Source: Cracknell *et al.*, 2011

Almost from the moment that the ink was dry on the Coalition Agreement, however, patterns of party support in Wales began to change. Perhaps surprisingly, these changes did not relate much to the senior partner in the UK Coalition. The Conservatives' poll ratings remained robust at what were, by their historic standards in Wales, quite respectable levels. They were not going forwards, and they remained heartily disliked by much of the Welsh electorate, but they were not going backwards either, and retained the stubborn support of between one-fifth and one-quarter of voters.

The major hit was taken, in Wales as elsewhere, by their Coalition partners. Many of the supporters that the Liberal Democrats had attracted in the years up to 2010 had been essentially disillusioned former Labour voters; once the party had joined up with the

Conservatives in government those people rapidly abandoned the Liberal Democrats, who saw their support levels fall by around half. Meanwhile, no longer tarnished by association with an unpopular UK government, Labour in Wales rapidly began to revive in popularity and resumed a commanding lead. These changes are shown in Figure 12.1, which charts voting intentions for the NAW constituency vote: from a poll conducted immediately after the May 2010 general election until the final pre-election poll for the Assembly election exactly 12 months later.

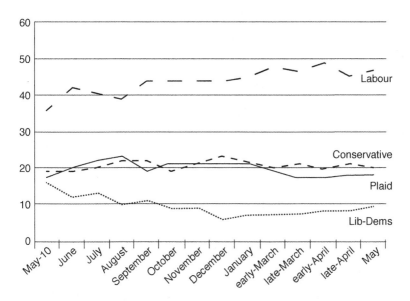

Figure 12.1 Opinion polls for NAW constituency vote, May 2010–May 2011

Source: http://blogs.cardiff.ac.uk/electionsinwales/

The 2011 devolved election in Wales was, in various respects, something of an oddity. It was unique in modern British experience in that all four of the main parties fighting the election were doing so as parties of government – being members of either the London or Cardiff coalitions. The election was also rather bizarre in that the party who had been in government in Wales continuously since 1999, Labour, largely fought the election as a party of Opposition. Rather than focusing on its own record in power in Wales, Labour sought to position itself as the best party to 'stand up for Wales' against the Conservative-led UK government. That they were able to pull off this rather implausible political trick with considerable success reflects, perhaps, the strong influence of UK-level politics within Wales (Scully, 2013).

The result of the 2011 NAW election (see Table 12.2) contrasted sharply with the simultaneous election to the Scottish Parliament. There the SNP had their best-ever outcome to a devolved election and Scottish Labour their worst. In Wales the exact opposite transpired: Welsh Labour did better than ever before in a devolved contest, while the SNP's sister party, Plaid Cymru, had their worst-ever outcome, finishing third in both seats and votes for the first time. Plaid, like the Liberal Democrats, was finding that there seem to be few votes in being a junior coalition partner. But they were hurt by two other factors as well. First, the closeness of the NAW election to the March 2011 referendum on more powers for the NAW (discussed below) had a particularly harmful effect on Plaid. They had supplied a large proportion of the ground troops for the successful Yes campaign; many of their activists had little time or energy left for an Assembly election merely nine weeks later. Labour's success in focusing the NAW election largely on UK-level politics also did nothing to help Plaid.

Table 12.2   2011 National Assembly for Wales election

Party	% Constituency vote (change)	% Regional list vote (change)	Seats (change)
Labour	42.3 (+10.1)	36.9 (+7.3)	30 (+4)
Conservatives	25.0 (+2.6)	22.5 (+1.1)	14 (+2)
Liberal Democrats	10.6 (–3.8)	8.0 (–3.7)	5 (–1)
Plaid Cymru	19.3 (–3.1)	17.9 (–3.1)	11 (–4)
Others	2.8 (–5.4)	14.7 (–1.6)	0

Source: http://blogs.cardiff.ac.uk/electionsinwales/

A further oddity of the 2011 election was that while Labour performed strongly on the basis of an essentially anti-Conservative campaign, the Tories also did well, becoming the second largest party in the NAW for the first time. Again it was the junior Coalition party that suffered. Aided by a strong campaign from their Welsh leader, Kirsty Williams, and winning two regional list seats by very small margins, the Liberal Democrats narrowly avoided the crushing defeat handed out to their Scottish counterparts. Still, this was by far their worst performance yet at a devolved election in Wales.

Since the NAW election, Labour in Wales – now governing in the Assembly alone – have continued to try to position themselves in opposition to the UK Coalition government. However, they have done so with steadily diminishing success. Labour's polls ratings remained very strong throughout 2012, but through 2013 and 2014 their popularity steadily eroded (as shown in Table 12.3). In part, the detailed survey evidence suggested, this was because of Labour's own lacklustre performance in government. Voters were not, in general, much impressed by Labour's performance in key policy areas in Wales (Scully, 2014b). Indeed, the apparent failure of Labour to manage the NHS in Wales effectively became a UK-wide political issue in 2014: the Conservatives, and newspapers sympathetic to them, sought to use the alleged failures of the Welsh NHS as exemplifying poor Labour performance in government.

Table 12.3   Average poll ratings for Westminster general election, Wales (%)

Party	2012	2013	2014
Labour	51.0	48.3	40.5
Conservatives	23.5	22.0	23.5
Liberal Democrats	6.0	8.3	6.1
Plaid Cymru	10.5	10.3	12.0
UKIP	5.7	8.3	13.4

Source: http://blogs.cardiff.ac.uk/electionsinwales/

Labour's decline did not mean that the UK Coalition parties were advancing. The Conservatives' poll ratings held steady: not advancing, but remaining broadly level at a respectable if not outstanding level of support. The Liberal Democrats continued to suffer. This was seen most dramatically in the May 2014 European Parliament election, where the party came sixth in Wales, behind even the Greens. However, with the Liberal Democrats struggling and Labour's poll rise on the slide, it was not, in the main, Plaid Cymru who took advantage. Under a new, and increasingly popular, leader in Leanne Wood from 2012, Plaid began to make modest ground in the polls in 2014, but the big change in the Welsh party system during 2013 and 2014 was the rise of UKIP. Hitherto, Wales had seemed relatively immune to the charms of Nigel Farage's party. Wales had been UKIP's second or third worst 'region' in the 1999, 2004 and 2009 European elections, and the party had also repeatedly failed to win any seats in the NAW. But from 2013 onwards, UKIP started to figure significantly in the Welsh polls. And in May 2014, it caused a sensation by coming within 0.6 per cent of beating Labour for first place in Wales in the European election. With the polls during the remainder of the year showing it maintaining a significant level of support, it seemed that UKIP had arrived as a serious player in Welsh party politics (see Table 12.4).

Table 12.4   2014 European Parliament election, Wales

Party	% Share (change from 2009)	MEPs
Labour	28.15 (+7.86)	1
UKIP	27.55 (+14.76)	1
Conservatives	17.43 (–3.79)	1
Plaid Cymru	15.26 (–3.25)	1
Greens	4.52 (–1.04)	0
Liberal Democrats	3.95 (–6.73)	0
Others	3.10 (–7.90)	0

Source: Hawkins and Miller, 2014

Overall, the Conservative–Liberal Democrat Coalition has not fundamentally changed party politics in Wales. Indeed, for the first half of the Coalition's life, it appeared to have reinforced the long-term pattern of party politics here – Labour dominance. But the ability of Labour in Wales to successfully position itself in opposition to the London Coalition has steadily diminished over time. Wales approached the 2015 general election with Labour's dominance here once more looking shaky. And Labour now faced a new threat, in the shape of UKIP, which had made a major breakthrough in Wales during 2014.

Constitutional politics and the Coalition

The National Assembly was created after Welsh devolution had received a very narrow public endorsement in the September 1997 referendum. But the path for Welsh devolution has not proven smooth or straightforward. Perhaps surprisingly, the problems have not, in the main, stemmed from the public: although the NAW began its life with little public enthusiasm behind it, attitudes changed with surprising rapidity in a more supportive direction after the Assembly began its work in 1999. Rather, problems have been rooted in the very design of the Assembly and devolved government in Wales. No stable, workable constitutional settlement for devolved Wales has yet been found. The Conservative–Liberal Democrat Coalition inherited this running sore in Welsh politics, and had to deal with it. In this section of the chapter I will consider the Coalition's influence on constitutional politics in

Wales. The discussion here falls fairly readily into two parts: the period leading up to the Welsh referendum of March 2011, and post-referendum constitutional debates.

Referendum 2011[1]

The Government of Wales Act 2006 (GOWA) had been an attempt by the Labour government, and particularly Secretary of State for Wales Peter Hain, to deal with many of the flaws of the original Welsh devolution design. GOWA made some immediate changes – notably by abolishing the original 'Body Corporate' structure of the Assembly and formally recognising the de facto division between Assembly and Government that had been established on the ground in the preceding years. But GOWA also provided for possible further change in the future. Most particularly, it made provision for a potential future referendum on the issue of whether full, primary legislative powers should be passed to the NAW in the 20 main areas of devolved responsibility in Wales.

But while GOWA had set out a legal basis for a referendum on primary law-making powers, at the time of the passage of the Act that referendum still seemed some years away. There remained internal divisions within the Labour Party: many of its representatives at Westminster, in particular, seemed reluctant to see Welsh political autonomy advance further. At the time of GOWA, enthusiasts for greater devolution within the Labour Party appeared to accept the primacy of party unity. However, Labour's relative lack of success in 2007 NAW elections meant that a coalition deal with Plaid Cymru was needed for Labour to retain power in Wales. Plaid's price was a significant one: a clear Labour commitment to hold the referendum within the 2007–11 Assembly term. That commitment was made by Labour's leadership within the Assembly, and formally endorsed by the wider Labour Party, but evident unease at moving forward, particularly within the Westminster parliamentary party, remained.

GOWA had put in place several hurdles before the referendum could be held. The first was a 'trigger' vote in the NAW, requiring a super-majority, to request the referendum. After some internal difficulties within the Cardiff coalition, this vote was held and passed – unanimously – by the NAW in February 2010. The process that this vote started required the Secretary of State then to move ahead with laying an Order in Council before Parliament, and for Westminster to formally approve the holding of the referendum. However, perhaps mindful of the continuing lack of enthusiasm among some of his Welsh parliamentary colleagues, Peter

Hain did little or nothing to move forward on the referendum before parliament was prorogued for the May 2010 general election.

The issue thus lay dormant until inherited by Hain's successor as Welsh Secretary in the new Coalition government, Cheryl Gillan. Like Hain, Gillan faced the possibility of some internal party divisions over the referendum. The Conservative group in the NAW had become, over time, increasingly supportive of a move to full legislative powers for the Assembly. In part this reflected their experiences, and frustrations, of working within the highly convoluted law-making arrangements put in place by GOWA. But in addition, the clear majority of Conservative AMs had come to support the political strategy that had stealthily taken shape over the previous decade under their Assembly leader, Nick Bourne. Initially an opponent of devolution, Bourne had become convinced that the Conservatives needed to develop a more positive agenda: the Tories could not forever be the party of 'No', nor of 'Thus Far if Absolutely Necessary But Not an Inch Further'. But Bourne's views were not shared by much of the party's grass-roots in Wales. And at least some of the increased contingent of Conservative MPs from Wales returned in May 2010 were also known to be more cautious.

However, Gillan had to be concerned not merely with internal Conservative politics on the issue. There was also a coalition partner to be kept happy. Aware that coalition was already impacting heavily on their popularity, and feeling a strong need to be able to show visible achievements from being in government, the Welsh Liberal Democrats pressed strongly for movement forward on the referendum. Agreement was finally reached in autumn 2010 that the referendum would take place on 3 March 2011.

The UK government, and the Welsh Conservative Party as a whole, remained officially neutral on the referendum: their position was that they had simply facilitated allowing the people of Wales to decide on the issue of whether their Assembly should become a full law-making body. In practice, however, official neutrality did not quite work out as neutral in its effects. The Conservative NAW group were clearly in favour of a Yes vote, and many of them campaigned actively for this outcome. Meanwhile, the MP known to be most deeply sceptical about such advances in devolution, David Davies of Monmouthshire, had been effectively neutralised. Davies had been installed as Chair of the Commons' Welsh Affairs select committee, a position which required him to remain above the fray.

Davies might conceivably have made an effective leader of a populist, anti-elitist No campaign. In absence of his open support, and with no other prominent politicians willing to come forward and campaign against the broad consensus backing full law-making powers for the Assembly, the No campaign in the referendum never developed into an effective force. Based around a small group of people styling themselves True Wales, they struggled even to supply sufficient numbers of competent speakers for the various media events held during the lead up to the vote. Their organisational failure is perhaps best illustrated by their fund-raising efforts: True Wales managed to raise barely £5,000 across the whole of Wales for the referendum campaign. By contrast, the Yes for Wales campaign received support from major figures across much of the political spectrum in Wales, and had serious political operators at its organisational centre. Although the referendum in Wales never managed to generate anywhere near the same level of passion and interest as the 2014 independence referendum in Scotland, Yes for Wales steadily got their message across. As referendum day approached, the polls indicated that the Yes campaign was on course for a decisive victory.

The final result of the referendum (see Table 12.5) was indeed a clear victory for Yes. The Welsh people, who had only very narrowly supported creating a National Assembly in 1997, now voted by an almost two-to-one majority to give that Assembly substantially greater law-making powers. There seemed little question that devolution within the UK, and quite powerful devolution at that, was now the 'settled will' of the Welsh people. However, while the verdict delivered by those who voted was clear, the referendum was also notable for generating a rather pitiful turnout of only 35.6 per cent. The decision had been clear, but the whole experience had hardly been a triumph of participatory democracy.

Table 12.5 March 2011 Welsh referendum

	Yes	No
Number of votes	517,132	297,380
% Share	63.5	36.5
Turnout = 35.6%		

Source: http://www.bbc.co.uk/news/uk-wales-12482561

Taking Silk: constitutional debate after the referendum

As part of the commitment it made when agreeing to the holding of the referendum, the UK government had also promised to conduct a wide-ranging review of Welsh devolution after the vote. This had been a particular priority for the Liberal Democrats. After the result of the referendum, the new law-making powers were rapidly put in place (being implemented immediately the new Assembly gathered after the May 2011 election). There was also rapid progress on the devolution review, which it was agreed would take the form of an expert Commission of Inquiry – one which followed in a fairly lengthy line of such expert commissions on devolution and related matters in Wales.[2]

This new inquiry became known in Wales, informally, as the 'ap Calman' Commission until its final membership had been agreed.[3] The terms of reference were constructed on a strikingly similar basis to that of the Calman Commission on Scottish Devolution that had operated between 2007 and 2009: thus, the body was given a broad mandate to review the Welsh devolution settlement. The first part of its work was to involve looking at issues of financial accountability, and consider the possible devolution to the National Assembly of some taxation powers. This was then to be followed by a second stage: this latter element would examine the remainder of the devolution settlement, and consider such matters as the basic model of Welsh devolution and the scope of powers that were devolved in Wales.

This Welsh Commission, however, was to have one very important difference from its forerunner in Scotland. Like Calman, membership of the Welsh Commission was to include several independent figures of high standing, as well as representatives of the three main Westminster parties. But in Scotland, the governing SNP had not participated in Calman, running its own parallel exercise, the 'National Conversation'. In Wales, Plaid Cymru was fully signed up and involved in the process from the start, which was therefore more inherently inclusive. The commission was to be chaired by Paul Silk: a highly distinguished former senior official in the House of Commons who had also served for several years as Clerk of the NAW. He therefore came to the task with a considerable understanding both of the substantive issues at stake as well as many of the political sensitivities that existed at both ends of the M4.

The Silk Commission began its work in late 2011. It followed the fairly typical pattern for such an expert commission: it held evidence sessions around Wales with invited experts, and also gave ample opportunities for civil society organisations and members of the public to submit written and oral evidence. In addition, Silk commissioned its own evidence-gathering, notably on public attitudes towards potential proposals for reform. The presence of representatives on the commission from all four established parties in Wales also meant that lines of communication were open to the main parties: it is impossible to know to what extent consultation went on, but we must expect that senior figures in the parties were at least consulted on Silk's main recommendations.

Despite the diversity of views within its membership, the Silk Commission appears to have worked fairly harmoniously. There were no public reports of major splits in the commission; no minority or dissenting reports were issued; and there was no evident tension between commission members during their public sessions. The very high calibre of the membership showed in the quality of reports produced. Whatever one might have thought of Silk's recommendations, the reports the commission produced were, almost without exception, clearly-argued and developed logical and evidence-based arguments for their main conclusions.

The first report (Silk I) was produced in November 2012. Entitled *Empowerment and Responsibility: Financial Powers to Strengthen Wales*, it addressed the financial side of devolution. Its main recommendations included the transfer from Westminster to the NAW of some powers over minor taxes (including Stamp Duty and Landfill Tax); the establishment of some, limited, borrowing powers for the Welsh Government; and the possible partial devolution of income tax. However, Silk argued that the latter should be subject to a referendum. The arguments put forward on the latter point were probably the weakest point of Silk I: no very compelling case was articulated as to why this particular change, and not others, should warrant or require plebiscitary endorsement. But there seemed to be widespread political fear, particularly among the Labour and Conservative parties, that devolution of a major tax such as income tax would be seen as illegitimate if it were not given some explicit public endorsement – in the manner that the second question in the 1997 Scottish referendum had endorsed the Scottish Parliament having powers over taxation.

The commission's second report (Silk II) inevitably had a broader remit, and took slightly longer to produce. Published in March 2014, *Empowerment and Responsibility: Legislative Powers to Strengthen Wales* reflected the commission's examination of the whole basis of Welsh devolution. Silk recommended some fundamental reforms. Among these was a change to the basic principle of the Welsh devolution settlement. Hitherto, the NAW has operated under a conferred powers model of devolution in which it was only entitled to act in areas where powers had been explicitly conferred upon it. Silk recommended a move to a reserved powers model, as existed already in Scotland and (in a slightly different form) Northern Ireland: where the devolved legislature and government were assumed to have the power to act in any policy field *except* for those that were explicitly reserved to Westminster. While the two models might logically appear to be simply opposite sides of the same coin, in practice the conferred powers model has long been regarded by most constitutional experts as being both inherently more restrictive and less clear. In the first three years after it acquired primary law-making powers following the 2011 referendum, three Acts passed by the NAW were referred to the UK's Supreme Court to review whether they exceeded the powers of the Assembly; this was more than the total number of such cases arising in the entire lifetime of the Scottish and Northern Irish devolution settlements.

Among the other recommendations of Silk II were significant extensions of the scope of devolution to Wales in a number of areas, including transport, energy generation and policing, as well as the greater involvement of Welsh authorities in regulation of public service broadcasting in Wales. Overall, Silk II pointed the way towards a significant further extension of Welsh devolution.

For better or worse, however, the success of the Silk recommendations depended not only on the intellectual strength of the case that the commission could develop. There were also crude political realities that had to be dealt with. One of these realities was that few politicians in Wales seemed very keen to move ahead with the proposed income tax referendum. The First Minister, Labour's Carwyn Jones, argued that income tax devolution should not move forward before another issue had been dealt with: the relatively unfavourable treatment that Wales received under the Barnett funding formula. More generally, there remained significant figures within the Welsh Labour Party who appeared unenthusiastic about substantial tax devolution in principle. And even among those who liked the idea, there was considerable scepticism about the prospects for success in a referendum. The experience of March 2011 had shown how difficult it could be to get much of the Welsh public engaged in a vote on a relatively abstruse matter; the rising tide of UKIP support also suggested that however compelling the case might be that the Assembly should be responsible for raising at least some of the money that it spent, the idea of tax devolution might fall victim in any referendum to the forces of political populism.

Another political reality was that, whatever the mood in Cardiff, implementation of the Silk recommendations depended ultimately on agreement from the key political players in London. The Liberal Democrats, who viewed Silk as one of their key achievements for Wales, remained keen to move forward on most of the Silk recommendations, and continued to exert pressure in this direction within the Coalition. But Cheryl Gillan had been replaced as Welsh Secretary in September 2012 by David Jones, the Conservative MP for Clwyd West. Jones radiated a lack of enthusiasm for further devolution – though rarely explicit in outright hostility, his speeches and other public pronouncements made it abundantly clear that he had no desire to extend Welsh political autonomy significantly further.

Jones became a road-block to progress in the implementation of the Silk agenda. After Silk I was published in December 2012, an agreed government response was promised by 'the spring'. Spring 2013 arrived, and then departed, with no official response from the government to the report. All through summer 2013 no response was delivered. It was clear that there was a substantial internal battle within government as to what the nature of its response to Silk should be. As summer turned into autumn, with only bland statements emerging from the Wales Office that the response would be delivered 'soon', the situation was becoming farcical.

Finally, the official government response was delivered at the start of November 2013. It was widely rumoured that the leaders of their respective Welsh parties had gone over the head of the Welsh Secretary to appeal to the Prime Minister and his deputy to put an end to the stalemate. When it finally came, the government's response, which formed the basis for the Wales Bill introduced in 2014, agreed with most of the key Silk I recommendations. The Assembly was to get control over some minor taxes, and the Welsh Government would receive limited borrowing powers. However, income tax powers would only be devolved in a manner that made them virtually unusable, and thus made it appear even less likely that leading Welsh politicians would press for a referendum to be granted these powers.[4] In addition, the government proposed to place into the Bill a change not discussed by Silk: this would reverse the ban on 'dual candidacy' in NAW elections that had been first introduced in 2006 by GOWA.[5]

A similar political stalemate seemed plausible after the publication of Silk II in spring 2014. Jones had already gone public on his scepticism about any move to a reserved powers model, and seemed most unlikely to favour the extensions in the scope of devolution proposed in the report. Another bout of lengthy internal government trench warfare seemed in prospect. However, this changed when Jones was sacked in July 2014. His departure was, by now, unlamented by most of the Welsh political establishment, including many in his own party.

The new Secretary of State was another Welsh Conservative MP, Stephen Crabb. Crabb was not known for having tremendous enthusiasm for greater devolution, but from the start he appeared determined to strike a more positive note than his predecessor. (Which was, it must be said, not that difficult). As the Wales Bill to implement Silk I was working its way through parliament, Crabb indicated his willingness to consider significant amendments to the Bill. He also made clear in autumn 2014 that plans were being developed for a further Bill to implement much of Silk II – including putting in place a reserved powers model of devolution for Wales. This was a major change in the government's stance. Media reports suggested that the influence of the Liberal Democrats, and in this instance Baroness Jenny Randerson, junior Welsh Office Minister in the Lords, had again been crucial. But Crabb's more emollient approach had also been highly important: it was difficult if not impossible to imagine such a fundamentally important change having been approved by David Jones. Late in 2014, Crabb announced all-party talks, aiming to reach agreement on implementing the bulk of the Silk II agenda as well as providing a Welsh response to potential constitutional changes in Scotland. The aim was to reach agreement by 1 March 2015, and for all parties to make manifesto commitments to implement what was agreed.

Conclusion

For a party with a long history of caution, or even downright hostility to Welsh devolution, the Conservatives in government have presided over a period of striking advances. When David Cameron entered 10 Downing Street, the NAW still had very limited powers. By the end of the Coalition's five-year term, the Assembly was a primary law-making parliament; was likely soon to be able to pass laws over an enhanced range of policy areas; and was due soon to acquire at least some taxation and borrowing powers. In part, these changes reflected broad shifts in public attitudes in Wales since the NAW had first been created. In part, they also reflected some – though not universal – changed attitudes within the Conservative Party. But Welsh devolution was one area where the influence of the Liberal Democrats in coalition had really mattered. They had pushed for the referendum, for the Silk Commission, and then for the implementation of Silk's proposals. There was little sign of public gratitude in Wales for this: the Liberal Democrats approached the 2015 general election with no higher ambition than to avoid wipeout. But even if their fate at the hands of the electorate should prove savage, the Welsh Liberal Democrats may take at least minor consolation from the fact that their period in coalition has seen substantial moves forward towards the more than century-old Liberal objective of Welsh home rule.

Notes

1. The following section draws heavily on Wyn Jones and Scully (2012).
2. Previous expert commissions had included the Sunderland Commission (2001–02), which examined the conduct of local elections in Wales; the Richard Commission on the Powers and Electoral Arrangements of the National Assembly for Wales (2002–04); the Holtham Commission on Funding and Finance for Wales (2007–10); and the All Wales Convention (2007–10), which was chaired by Sir Emyr Jones-Parry.
3. 'Ap' is part of the traditional Welsh structure of names. It literally means 'son of': the implication was that what became the Silk Commission was the direct offspring of the Calman Commission.
4. The Wales Bill included what became known as a 'lockstep' provision. This meant that if income tax powers were partially devolved, the NAW would only be able to move all income tax bands upwards or downwards together, rather than make more fine-grained adjustments to the individual bands separately. The lockstep was very similar to a recommendation of the Calman Commission that had been enacted in the Scotland Act (2012).
5. 'Dual candidacy' concerned whether candidates for the NAW would be able to stand both in a constituency contest and on the regional list.

References

BBC Summary of 2011 Welsh Referendum Results: http://www.bbc.co.uk/news/uk-wales-12482561

Cracknell, R., McGuiness, F. and Rhodes, C. (2011) 'General Election 2010: Research Paper 10/36', House of Commons Library.

Hawkins, O. and Miller, V. (2014) 'European Parliament Elections 2014: Research Paper 14/32', House of Commons Library.

Scully, R. (2013) 'More Scottish than Welsh? Understanding the 2011 Devolved Elections in Scotland and Wales', *Regional and Federal Studies*, 23: 591–612.

Scully, R. (2014a) '1859 and All That: The Enduring Failure of Welsh Conservatism', in P. Cowley and R. Ford (eds), *Sex, Lies and the Ballot Box: 50 Things You Need To Know about British Elections*. London: Biteback.

Scully, R. (2014b) 'Ernie Wise and Welsh Politics', *Elections in Wales Blog*: http://blogs.cardiff.ac.uk/electionsinwales/2014/02/24/ernie-wise-and-welsh-politics/

Wyn Jones, R. and Scully, R. (2012) *Wales Says Yes: Devolution and the 2011 Welsh Referendum*. Cardiff: University of Wales Press.

13
The Coalition's Impact on Northern Ireland

Cathy Gormley-Heenan and Arthur Aughey

Introduction

The Coalition had set out clearly its strategic objective. By restricting the claims of the public sector on the nation's resources the intention was to restore incentives, encourage efficiency and to create a climate in which commerce and industry would flourish, laying a secure basis for investment, productivity and increased employment (cited in Fry, 2008: 71). This prospectus is not taken from the Coalition's Programme for Government in 2010. It is taken from the Queen's Speech of 15 May 1979, announcing the radical intent of the first Thatcher administration. It reveals an interesting echo of a recurring political problem for British government: an end can be identified and the policy means may be assembled but the outcome is far from assured. In 1979, as the Queen's Speech made clear, 'all parts of the United Kingdom' were to benefit from the new dispensation (ibid.). There was the same expectation after 2010 that by cutting public spending and accelerating 'the reduction of the structural deficit over the course of a Parliament', all parts of the United Kingdom would benefit (HM Government, 2010: 15). One crucial difference between 1979 and 2010 was devolution and the Coalition accepted that the Northern Ireland Executive, the Scottish Executive and the Welsh Assembly Government would 'make their own policy on their devolved issues' (ibid.: 35).

As in 1979, the Coalition sought to create a 'more balanced economy'. That is a simple phrase but it involved different interpretations. On the one hand, the imbalance was defined as dependence 'on a narrow range of economic sectors', mainly in banking and financial services, and rebalancing meant promoting manufacturing industry and other services (HM Government, 2010: 9). This implied 'a more evenly shared' economy between regions, if only because banking and financial services were concentrated predominantly in London (ibid.). On the other hand, there still obtained the notion of a more productive, market-driven, re-distribution of activity between the public and private sectors. Northern Ireland had provided an illustration of that problem during the general election campaign. David Cameron had spoken of the 'unsustainable' share of the public sector in some parts of the country and he pointed specifically to Northern Ireland where 'the size of the state has got too big' (Crichton, 2010). Reducing government expenditure, achieving greater efficiency in public services and changing the economic culture were here intimately connected. In 2006 the problem of an 'over-large' public sector acting as a disincentive to private enterprise had been recognised by Northern Ireland's First Minister, Peter Robinson – though it was an indication of problems of delivery when later he challenged the Coalition's view of what needed to be done to rectify it (Gordon, 2010).

This chapter evaluates how the Northern Ireland Executive has attempted to meet the two related challenges of the politics of austerity: to rebalance the local economy, bringing its performance more into line with the United Kingdom average; and to meet its obligations of public expenditure retrenchment. The chapter incorporates in both cases a third factor, Northern Ireland's distinctive context of institutional instability.

The economic challenge

If there were echoes of 30 years before in the project of the Coalition then there were clear reverberations of previous studies of Northern Ireland's economic problems. A report by PricewaterhouseCoopers noted the consistency of these 15 major economic reviews conducted over half a century, observing that the very fact of so many reviews 'suggests that not much has actually been achieved' (Birnie, 2012: 10). Their similarity indicated real difficulties in carrying out in practice what analysis implied. One further consistent feature of public statements on the economy was remarked upon: rhetorical aspiration. Policy-makers have accepted, as have politicians since the Good Friday/Belfast Agreement of 1998, that the objective should be a competitive and growing economy based on high-tech, creative industries and services, providing well-paid employment for a highly skilled workforce. The consistent re-iteration of that objective equally suggests that the gap between aspiration and reality remains wide, despite the best efforts of officials and ministers. The report concluded with the observation that the Northern Ireland economy chronically underperforms compared to its potential and that this has serious consequences for the general well-being of society (ibid.: 50). This is not a matter peculiar to Northern Ireland and the persistence of some problems it shares with other regions of the UK, such as Wales. These include low productivity, high levels of youth and long-term unemployment as well as outward migration of skilled workers. However, as the Treasury Report *Rebalancing the Northern Ireland economy* (HM Treasury, 2011) detailed, there are several distinctive factors. Political factors include the legacy of 30 years of violence and, uniquely, the land border with the Republic of Ireland (ibid.: 7–9). Economically, Northern Ireland continues to be more reliant than other parts of the UK on public sector employment (30 per cent compared to a UK average of 21 per cent); to have the highest proportion of economically inactive workers (28 per cent); low productivity; and a private sector 'more concentrated on low value-added sectors than other parts of the UK' (ibid.: 9). If the common purpose of HM Government and the Northern Ireland Executive has been to 'rebalance' the economy, then it involves two aspects. The first is to shift employment from the public to the private sector. The second is to move from low value-added to high value-added enterprises. The consequence of both shifts, it is expected, will transform an economic culture heavily dependent on public spending. For example, the Northern Ireland Executive calculated that public spending on activities undertaken by the private sector represented over 60 per cent of total output (Northern Ireland Executive, 2011: 14). Unfortunately, the spectre haunting such prescription is familiar: the failure of implementation. With such a history of policy disappointment it is understandable that most politicians, policy-makers and economists should be attracted to a strategic 'game-changer'. Reducing the rate of corporation tax in Northern Ireland to the same level as the Republic of Ireland (12.5 per cent) has become that game-changer as well as an article of faith.

The practicality of varying the rate of corporation tax had been considered by Sir David Varney under the previous Labour government. Varney had ruled out the proposal not only on grounds of the likely effect on investment and public expenditure in Northern Ireland but also on the grounds of the potential loss of revenue to the UK Exchequer as profits were displaced from Great Britain to Northern Ireland (Varney, 2007). The response to Varney's report by Peter Robinson captured well the local political consensus: 'We will continue to argue the case for a reduction in corporation tax. The issue will not go away' (BBC, 2007). It did not go away and the principle of devolving corporation tax was given a fair wind by the Coalition. The Programme for Government explicitly committed to a 'paper examining potential mechanisms for changing the corporation tax rate in Northern Ireland' (HM Government, 2010: 28). This paper was the 52-page document *Rebalancing the Northern Ireland economy* cited above. The first Coalition Secretary of State for Northern Ireland, Owen Paterson, was sympathetic but he always linked support to the requirement for welfare reform being implemented elsewhere in the UK by the Secretary of State for Work and Pensions, Iain Duncan Smith, a connection also made by the Treasury report. Though the headline case for devolving corporation tax concentrated on the assumed economic advantages, there was a more subtle contextual view that it would deliver two additional benefits. First, it would unlock social potential now stifled by a culture of dependency, sometimes described as transforming Northern Ireland from a 'grantpreneurial' to an entrepreneurial society (HM Treasury, 2011: 7). Second, it would help foster greater responsibility within the Assembly and greater accountability by the Executive (ibid.: 4).

A succinct case in favour of devolving corporation tax can be found in the summary report of the Northern Ireland Economic Reform Group (NIERG, 2011). It estimated that by 2030, with a rate of 12.5 per cent, job creation would be around 90,000, transforming not only the private sector but also higher education and thus solving Northern Ireland's skills exodus (ibid.: 2). These jobs would be in pharmaceuticals, health sciences, communications and financial services, precisely those companies that would deliver high value-added, research-driven, growth. Finally Northern Ireland would be able to compete on a level playing field with the Republic of Ireland. The report underlined the necessity of the initiative because investment grants and incentives, for long the backbone of industrial strategy and central to the performance of Invest NI, were no longer acceptable to the European Commission. However, the key proposition was the expectation of a substantial behavioural effect, intimating a close relationship between business enterprise and wider social and cultural change:

> An inflow of such companies, expecting and demanding a world-class business environment, would set the benchmark which Northern Ireland's continuing efforts to enhance that environment would have to match. As was the case in the Republic, demand and supply factors would be linked in a virtuous circle. (ibid.)

Or as the economist Mike Smyth put it pithily, given the choice of all policy options open to the Local Assembly, corporation tax was the one to go for because, 'It gives us the chance to do all the other things that we need to do' (Gosling, 2013). The correspondence was close between this considered view and the narrative of political reform in London, especially the new emphasis on localism by all parties at Westminster. The full NIERG report not only pointed to the greater ability to finance local public spending but also to something increasingly close to Conservative Party hearts, 'less dependence on a subvention from taxpayers in South East England' (NIERG, 2010: 1). Furthermore, here was a new path to overcome at last the 'failure of existing economic development policy' (ibid.). Though the former Minister for Finance, Sammy Wilson, was sceptical of those claims, two of the key local players, his successor Simon Hamilton and the Minister of Enterprise, Trade and Investment, Arlene Foster, remain firm advocates.

The case has been powerfully made and it has become 'conventional wisdom' which, as J. K. Galbraith observed, is not necessarily the same thing as 'good sense' (Wilson, 2011). Significant doubts remain about the truth of those claims. The Treasury report had cautioned, as did Varney, against the easy assumption that reducing corporation tax to the same level as the Republic of Ireland would have an equal prosperity effect (HM Treasury, 2011: 21). There are so many other factors to be taken into account that the case remains 'unproven', the term used by the Northern Ireland Assembly Research and Information Service paper setting out the challenges facing the new Assembly elected in 2011 (Northern Ireland Assembly Research and Information Service, 2011: 25). Moreover, the operation of the Republic's tax regime and its industrial policy consequences have become subject to recent severe academic interrogation as to whether they produce an innovative economy or whether they encourage an emphasis on tax reduction and avoidance (Stewart, 2014). Of course, it is that concern which also informed Varney's rejection of the proposition, fearing for its detrimental impact on the rest of the UK in terms of profit-shifting and displaced investment. The main attraction of the case for the devolution of corporation tax is its long-term, 30-year vision of both economic regeneration *and* behavioural change. That also happens to be its weakness. The costs would be felt immediately and are certain, the benefits long-term and uncertain. There is perhaps justified scepticism of predictions for significant job gains a generation hence and it is easier to point to the serious short-term consequences for the budget and for public services. Devolution of corporation tax would entail a corresponding reduction in the Treasury's block grant for Northern Ireland. Estimates of this vary but the immediate cost is likely to be at least £300 million but could be as much as £700 million. A critical estimate prepared for the Irish Congress of Trade Unions argued that whatever Northern Ireland's pressing needs, reducing its corporation tax rate to 12.5 per cent is not the answer (Murphy, 2010: 5). It could never properly compete with the Republic of Ireland on tax and far 'from solving its problems such a tax rate could only increase the isolation, uncertainty and cost of trading from Northern Ireland' (ibid.). Indeed, at a time of public austerity and falling living standards, the real effect would be to relieve one burden on business and to shift it onto households. Therefore, the political consensus on the issue is surprising and entails a remarkable leap of faith which may be explained by the following calculations. For the unionist parties, it reflects faith in the attractiveness of Northern Ireland as a place to do business, a rediscovery of its former enterprise culture. For the nationalist parties, it establishes a common tax level throughout the island and potentially another step towards unity.

What struck one expert about the debate were not the certainties of the claims made by either side but the very uncertainties surrounding the details. It was astonishing that things appeared to have got so far without either firm knowledge of the amount of tax generated in Northern Ireland or the likely impact on the block grant:

> To proceed with work on devolving the tax without making that the first priority shows a fatal lack of seriousness, either by those who advocate devolution – who are inviting Northern Ireland to buy a pig in a poke – or those who may be opposed, who are ensuring that the effects of fiscal decentralisation cannot be understood. (Trench, 2012)

This interesting contrast between a fog of practical unknowing and the clarity of favourable consensus suggests that the Coalition's appearance of support for the devolution of corporation tax is not fully matched by the reality of its commitment. One is reminded of the exchange in *Yes, Prime Minister* between Sir Humphrey and Jim Hacker. The latter was restless to make his mark, the former to resist unwise innovation. The compromise which Sir Humphrey suggested was 'firm masterly inactivity'. There is a good case for arguing that 'firm masterly inactivity' is a reasonably accurate description of Coalition policy. Its commitment has never been certain and the opportunity to do something has always been postponed. Early in 2013, the decision was postponed until after the referendum on Scottish independence on 18 September 2014. A new reason for the Coalition to be wary of moving on Northern Ireland arose after the Scottish 'No' vote. The general interest of UK cohesion is now a factor in deliberation about new powers for Holyrood. There is an obvious reluctance to give the Scottish National Party an excuse to demand a similar concession, arousing public expectations which cannot be fulfilled and making it even more difficult to manage the Union (Constitution Unit, 2014: 5).

Moreover, in an address to a fringe event at the Conservative Party Conference in 2014, the Secretary of State for Northern Ireland, Theresa Villiers, said that it was 'hard to see how the Executive could fund a corporation tax cut as well as meeting mounting bills to run a more expensive welfare system' (Walker, 2014). And it was clear that 'masterly inactivity' was firmly expressed in the very active business of official deliberation: devolution of corporation tax involves complex legislation 'and various work streams are yet to be completed' (ibid.). In her platform speech at Party Conference in 2014, Villiers emphasised the UK-wide policy of reducing corporation tax which was at the heart of Chancellor George Osborne's economic strategy. The decision on whether to devolve corporation tax powers so Northern Ireland can set its own rate, she noted, is deferred. She observed that 'Stormont needs to be in the best possible shape if it's to be able to take full advantage of what would be a significant change if it were to go ahead' (UTV, 2014). What Villiers was referring to was the impasse in the Executive on welfare reform and the budget upon which devolution of corporation tax now depended. This is another sort of political inactivity which, as one journalist put it, is 'like a society living on a loan from Wonga' (Clarke, 2014).

The welfare challenge

The Coalition's Welfare Reform Act 2012 was designed to achieve a number of related objectives: to resolve the complexities of the existing benefits system in the UK by introducing a single 'universal credit'; to bring greater efficiencies to the system through measures such as the 'bedroom tax' for those living in housing deemed to be too large for their needs; to remove the Disability Living Allowance; and to introduce a Personal Independence Payment (PIPs) (HM Government, 2012). An essential element of welfare reform was also the introduction of an overall cap on the benefits people could draw.

Unlike the present arrangements in Scotland and Wales, however, welfare reform is a devolved matter for Northern Ireland. Considered as something of a historical anomaly, the devolution of social security exists because neither the Government of Ireland Act (HM Government, 1920) nor the Northern Ireland Constitutional Act (HM Government, 1973) had added social security to the lists of non-devolved matters (Birrell, 2009). The Northern Ireland Act (1998) did not seek to change the status of social security from a devolved matter but instead noted that the Secretary of State and the appropriate Northern Ireland Minister 'shall from time to time consult one another with a view to securing that, to the extent agreed between them, the legislation ... provides single systems of social security, child support and pensions for the United Kingdom' (HM Government, 1998: c:47; section 87). Though not enshrined in any specific legislation, such a principle of parity has – at least in the post-war era – been used to ensure that social security benefits in Northern Ireland were similar to those awarded across the rest of the UK. In short, social security in Northern Ireland, despite some minor administrative breaches of the parity principle from time to time, was always considered to be the 'same but different' (Birrell and Heenan, 2010). And so it was expected that the Welfare Reform Act of 2012 would have an accelerated passage through the legislative process at Stormont to maintain Northern Ireland's parity with the changes made in the rest of the UK.

While there were grave concerns about the introduction of the Welfare Reform Act to Northern Ireland, matching those expressed elsewhere in the UK, it appeared initially that the general acceptance of the parity principle would trump any local political reservations about its social impact. Moreover, it was made clear by the Treasury that any deviation from the parity principle in order to maintain existing levels of welfare payments in Northern Ireland would result in an automatic reduction in the annual block grant (HM Treasury, 2010; Clarke, 2014a). This was calculated using the Barnett formula and estimated to be around £10bn per annum; the block grant amounts to 93 per cent of Northern Ireland's total budget with the remaining 7 per cent generated from revenue raised and borrowed by the Executive (Northern Ireland Executive, 2011). Conscious of its financial dependence, the Northern Ireland Executive tabled the Coalition's proposals for welfare reform in October 2012. While the proposed Bill progressed with relative ease through its first stage (October 2012), second stage (October 2012) and committee stage (February 2013), it was stalled at the consideration stage scheduled for April 2013. The Minister for Social Development, Nelson McCausland

MLA (DUP), withdrew the Bill because of disagreements over its intent between the main political parties. Sinn Fein and the Social Democratic and Labour Party (SDLP) both argued that the Bill was unacceptably partisan, constituting the implementation of a Conservative austerity programme, with little regard for the impact that the changes would have on people in Northern Ireland. On that basis – implicitly one of an absent local mandate for reform – both nationalist parties were set to oppose the Bill. However, Villiers argued that the Bill was not only about austerity but also about designing a welfare system that was fair both to those who need assistance and to those taxpayers who pay for that assistance. The DUP proposed a series of talks with Sinn Fein to try to put in place a package of measures which, in their view, would not only alleviate some of the likely disadvantages but also give reform a sufficient local mandate.

Much speculation ensued about why Sinn Fein, particularly, had gone cold on the Bill. It was suggested that standing on an anti-austerity ticket in the 2014 Local Elections in the Republic of Ireland would have sat uneasily with agreement to introduce further austerity measures in Northern Ireland. In addition, much emphasis was placed on the findings of a report commissioned by the Northern Ireland Council for Voluntary Action (NICVA) *The Impact of Welfare Reform on Northern Ireland*, the research for which was conducted by academics at Sheffield Hallam University. The report suggested that full implementation of welfare reform would equate to a loss of £750m per year from the local economy (Beatty and Fothergill, 2013). This research also claimed to show that Northern Ireland had higher numbers of people living with a disability than elsewhere in the UK, as well as much higher instances of mental health problems presenting as post-traumatic stress disorder (ibid.). Thus the report's figures seemed to demonstrate that Northern Ireland was indeed a special case and that the proposed reforms were likely to hit the most vulnerable hardest. Political and public debate on welfare reform now became a fight about figures and there was much confusion on the relative weight to be given to costs of implementation versus penalties for non-implementation. Sinn Fein referred to the loss to the economy of £750m while the DUP referred to the increasing penalties that would be imposed by the Treasury, beginning at £5m a month and rising to more than £200m a year. It also pointed out the additional cost of building and sustaining a new IT infrastructure needed to manage the different benefits in Northern Ireland once the rest of the UK had moved to the new system. In this battle of perspectives, both claimed that the other did not understand the real economics of the situation.

Of course, such a lack of understanding is not unusual in politics. In 1851, when Prime Minster Lord Derby invited Disraeli to become Chancellor of the Exchequer, Disraeli initially refused, claiming that the Exchequer was a 'branch of which I had not knowledge'; Derby's celebrated retort to this was for Disraeli not to worry, 'They give you the figures', at which point Disraeli accepted (Blake, 1966: 311). With the welfare reform impasse, the government, civil servants, the media, the community and voluntary sector and academic researchers all gave politicians 'the figures': conflicting figures and at cross purposes. Politicians, as ever, drew their own conclusions and made their own public claims. This might count as another example of 'masterly inactivity' but the public tended to read it as confusion and stalemate. Not until the autumn of 2014 did it become clear that almost £500m per year had already been 'lost' from the local economy due to welfare changes agreed and implemented before 2012 if reforms by the former Labour government were included alongside those of the Coalition (Black, 2014). In some instances this was the result of changes at Westminster over which the Northern Ireland Assembly had no control; in other instances the Assembly had voted in favour of the changes (Northern Ireland Assembly Official Report, 2014). Indeed, since 2007 there have been two Welfare Reform Acts passed by the Assembly, the first in 2007 and the second in 2010. The 'cost' of implementing the remaining proposed changes would amount to the loss to the economy of a further £250m per year (NICVA, 2014). The Treasury 'fine', which would be deducted from the annual block grant for continued failure to implement the remaining changes, was calculated to be £87m for 2104, rising to £114m in 2015 and in excess of £200m thereafter (NIA Official Report, 2014).

As a consequence of the shifting interpretations of the financial impact, attention has more recently turned towards a more subtle compromise between principle and pragmatism. Northern Ireland could be seen to maintain parity with the rest of the UK on welfare reform while at the same time exploiting the flexibility afforded in terms of its implementation, particularly through the regulatory framework accompanying the relevant legislation. As the Northern Ireland Welfare Reform Group (NIWRG) observed in 2012 'the flexibility to do things differently in a Northern Ireland context lies very much within the detail of the regulations' (NIWRG, 2012). Here is the 'same but different' principle in another guise. Thus, some deviation from practice in the rest of the UK had already been the subject of negotiation by the Department of Social Development (DSD) with Department for Work and Pensions (DWP) in Westminster. There was agreement, at least in principle, that universal credit in Northern Ireland would be paid fortnightly as opposed to monthly, with split payments to each partner rather than a single payment per household; that there would be a transitional fund put in place until 2019 to protect those 86,000 people who would lose out from the proposed changes; that only new claimants would go onto the British system immediately; that a fund would be established to protect current tenants from the impact of the bedroom tax until such time as a suitable alternative could be found; that the housing element of universal credit would continue to be paid to landlords, rather than to claimants, as elsewhere in the UK; and that the sanctions levied against those who either make false claims or who refuse employment opportunities would be reduced from three years to two years (Northern Ireland Executive, 2012).

Nevertheless, the First Minister has held out the possibility that if an agreement cannot be reached then responsibility for welfare should be handed back to the Coalition to administer on Northern Ireland's behalf (BBC News Online, 2014b). If this were to happen it would constitute a major admission of defeat by the local political class. The suggestion that powers might be handed back to Westminster at a time when both Scotland and Wales are demanding greater devolution and at a time when the Northern Ireland parties are asking for the devolution of corporation tax is – to use a polite expression – paradoxical. Some might express it as the Northern Irish attempt to develop a bespoke brand of 'à la carte devolution' rather than the much sought after, and commonly cited, 'devo max'. But it would look more like incompetence. Possibly in the light of this, Sinn Fein have now called for the Welfare Reform Bill to be debated on the floor of the Assembly while the DUP Minister for Finance has not included the estimated Treasury 'fine' for non-implementation in his draft 2015–16 budget (BBC News Online, 2014). This suggests that the impasse on welfare reform, of two years' standing, may be addressed finally within the financial year (BBC News Online, 2014a). This is far from being a certainty.

The accepted political narrative, until recently, has been simple. It states that the financial difficulties experienced by the Stormont administration were wholly as a consequence of the failure to implement welfare reform. However, this was only partly true. Focusing on the one issue has allowed the Executive to mask a broader problem of financial mismanagement at a time when the Coalition was implementing austerity elsewhere in the UK. Although the Executive adopted the common political language of austerity, in reality it stopped far short of implementing its harsh realities. Northern Ireland continues to see itself as a special case and this thinking has become an ingrained political response to events. It has thus become an austerity-resisting region. Rather than cutting costs and/or raising revenue in a manner similar to the rest of the UK or the rest of Ireland, the Executive did the reverse. It promised not to introduce water rates across the region; it levied the lowest regional rates in the UK; and it introduced universal free prescriptions along with free public transport for the over 60s. Such popular, if expensive, policies could never be sustained while the budget faced year-on-year cuts from Westminster. The Head of the Northern Ireland Civil Service, Malcom McKibbin, warned that the devolved administration would run out of funding by the end of 2014 if changes were not made (BBC News Online, 2014c). In a letter to George Osborne in October 2014, he confirmed that the Executive would soon breach the spending limit determined by the Treasury (ibid.). The Finance Minister quickly secured a £100m emergency loan from the Treasury in order to avoid that eventuality (BBC News Online, 2014d). The irony of borrowing £100m from the Treasury in order to pay back to the Treasury the £87m welfare fine did not go unremarked, with the leader of the Ulster Unionist Party (UUP), Mike Nesbitt, suggesting that the loan would 'make Wonga look like amateurs' (Williamson, 2014). The emergency loan came with strings attached. It was conditional on the Executive agreeing its draft budget for 2015–16, out of which the £100m would be re-paid (BBC News Online, 2014e). Agreement on the draft budget by the two main parties in the Executive, the DUP and Sinn Fein, was sufficient to secure the loan – the other parties in the Executive voted against the draft budget (SDLP) and abstained (UUP and Alliance). The speed with which agreement was found between the two main parties can be explained simply: Northern Ireland was running out of time more quickly than it was running out of money. The emergency loan had bought additional time for the Executive to address the bigger budget deficit (approximately £220m, including the £87m Treasury fine) (ibid.). Therefore, the full figures show that in 2014 two-fifths of the problem is the headline issue of welfare reform but three-fifths can be attributed to poor financial planning.

The budget crisis, however significant, illustrates a deeper political malaise within the Northern Ireland Executive. The Coalition government has shown that, despite ideological and party differences, it is possible to commit to a programme of government and secure collective responsibility. The Northern Ireland Executive has failed demonstrably to do either of those things because of unresolved legacies of the past and opposing views about the future. For example, talks between the Executive parties in the autumn and winter of 2013, chaired by American diplomat Dr Richard Haas and concerned with flags, parades and dealing with Northern Ireland's past, failed to reach agreement. New talks, which began in the autumn of 2014, needed to address not only these same three issues but also welfare reform, the broader financial crisis and the structure and function of political institutions. To use an American term, that seemed a very odd way to run a railroad.

The Stormont House Agreement (Northern Ireland Office, 2014) was reached days before the end of 2014. As part of the Agreement, the parties appeared to have finally accepted the introduction of the various UK benefit changes though they would pay any additional costs for flexibilities and 'top-ups' from within the Northern Ireland block grant. The implementation of this aspect of the Agreement was to proceed with considerable speed and noting 'Legislation will be brought before the Assembly in January 2015 to give effect to welfare changes alongside further work to develop and implement flexibilities and top-ups from the block grant as part of a package of measures to address local need' (ibid.: 1–2). This did not happen and so the Agreement gives the impression of movement while hiding the fact of continued political inertia. In truth, as with much else in Northern Ireland, it has revealed the contradiction between the provisions of a detailed timetable and the political will (or lack thereof) to give it effect. Furthermore, this raises some doubts about corporation tax too. Point 8 of the Stormont House Agreement provides for legislation to enable its devolution by April 2017. The Secretary of State introduced a Bill to Parliament which is expected to be enacted by March. The Labour Party leadership originally expressed doubts about this process. However, on a visit to Belfast in January 2015, Ed Miliband confirmed his party's support but only if certain conditions have been met. What are those conditions? According to the Stormont House Agreement, the Bill should 'proceed in parallel with the implementation of key measures to deliver sustainable Executive finances' (ibid.: 2). Masterly inactivity may continue to inform the political process at Westminster.

What political options might be available if the parties do fail to implement all aspects of the Stormont House Agreement? The Treasury might decide to change the way in which it currently funds Northern Ireland. For example, it could introduce a 'Whitehall Rule' whereby it would oversee the Northern Ireland budget in order to keep the Executive within its limits; or the historical anomaly that added social security to the lists of non-devolved matters in Northern Ireland but not in Scotland or Wales might be reconsidered by the newly established Cabinet Committee for devolved powers. Either of these options would avoid a reluctant Westminster resuming direct rule (however short-term that might be) but their very consideration might alarm the Executive into taking the appropriate action.

Conclusion

During the talks, which resulted in the 1998 Good Friday/Belfast Agreement, much was made of the use of 'constructive ambiguity' on politically sensitive issues in order to facilitate progress towards an eventual settlement. A similar degree of ambiguity can be detected in relation to the goals of rebalancing the economy and meeting the obligations of public expenditure retrenchment. It has, though, been more destructive in shape and form. We would call it 'destructive ambiguity' and it reveals truths that are often inconvenient to express officially: that there appears to be no plan, no road map and no big ideas for increasing revenue, beyond calls for corporation tax to be devolved. Destructive ambiguity disguises the prospect that the introduction of corporation tax will likely compound the problems of welfare reform as its critics have argued consistently. And what message does the current political instability send out to international corporations and businesses which lowering corporation tax is designed to attract? Will they want to do business in a seemingly unstable and financially embarrassed location? They, too, might play the game of masterly inactivity – and locate elsewhere.

References

BBC News Online (2007) Report rules out tax cut demands, 17 December. Date accessed: 23 January 2015. Available online at: http://news.bbc.co.uk/1/hi/northern_ireland/7148574.stm

BBC News Online (2014) Welfare reform: Simon Hamilton hopeful of NI resolution, 2 November. Date accessed: 13 November 2014. Available online at: http://www.bbc.co.uk/news/uk-northern-ireland-29870996

BBC News Online (2014a) 'No provision' for welfare penalty in draft budget, 31 October. Date accessed: 13 November 2014. Available online at: http://www.bbc.co.uk/news/uk-northern-ireland-29849933

BBC News Online (2014b) DUP to 'bring welfare reform issue to a head', 31 October. Date accessed: 13 November 2014. Available online at: http://www.bbc.co.uk/news/uk-northern-ireland-29850135

BBC News Online (2014c) Treasury warned Northern Ireland Executive to go 'into the red', 2 October. Date accessed: 14 November 2014. Available online at: http://www.bbc.co.uk/news/uk-northern-ireland-29453635

BBC News Online (2014d) Stormont: Loan from Treasury proposed to ease budget crisis, 9 October. Date accessed: 25 January 2015. Available online at: http://www.bbc.co.uk/news/uk-northern-ireland-29546650

BBC News Online (2014e) NI Executive: Ministers agree to £100m loan from Treasury, 10 October. Date accessed: 25 January 2015. Available online at: http://www.bbc.co.uk/news/uk-northern-ireland-29562432

Beatty, C. and Fothergill, S. (2013) *The Impact of Welfare Reforms on Northern Ireland*, Centre for Regional Economic and Social Research, Sheffield Hallam University/NICVA.

Birnie, E. (2012) Northern Ireland: A Tale of Two Economies, 10 September. Date accessed: 14 October 2014. Available online at: http://pwc.blogs.com/economics_in_business/2012/09/northern-ireland-a-tale-of-two-economies.html

Birrell, D. (2009) *The Impact of Devolution on Social Policy*, Bristol: Policy Press.

Birrell, W. D. and Heenan, D. (2010) Devolution and Social Security: the anomaly of Northern Ireland, *Journal of Poverty and Social Justice*, 18(3): 281–293.

Black, R. (2014) '£750m bill for welfare reform dismissed as body reveals the true cost is significantly lower', *Belfast Telegraph*, 8 October. Date accessed: 14 November 2014. Available online at: http://www.belfasttelegraph.co.uk/news/local-national/northern-ireland/750m-bill-for-welfare-reform-dismissed-as-body-reveals-the-true-cost-is-significantly-lower-30647188.html

Blake, R. (1966) *Disraeli*, London: Faber and Faber.

Clarke, L. (2014) 'Northern Ireland is now like a society living on a loan from Wonga', *Belfast Telegraph*, 9 July. Date accessed: 13 October 2014. Available online at: http://www.belfasttelegraph.co.uk/opinion/news-analysis/northern-ireland-is-now-like-a-society-living-on-a-loan-from-wonga-30417084.html

Clarke, L. (2014a) 'Finance Minister Simon Hamilton warns of massive cuts if Northern Ireland does not agree to welfare reform ... but Sinn Fein urges him to defy Westminster', *Belfast Telegraph*, 2 April. Date accessed: 25 January 2015. Available online at: http://www.belfasttelegraph.co.uk/news/local-national/northern-ireland/finance-minister-simon-hamilton-warns-of-massive-cuts-if-northern-ireland-does-not-agree-to-welfare-reform-but-sinn-fein-urges-him-to-defy-westminster-30146434.html

Constitution Unit (2014) *Monitor 58*, October. Date accessed: 13 October 2014: Available online at: https://www.ucl.ac.uk/constitution-unit/publications/tabs/monitor-newsletter/monitor-58

Crichton, T. (2010) 'Election 2010: David Cameron left squirming in Jeremy Paxman interview', *The Daily Record*, 24 April.

Fry, G. K. (2008) *The Politics of the Thatcher Revolution: An Interpretation of British Politics, 1979–1990*, Basingstoke: Palgrave Macmillan.

Gordon, D. (2010) 'First Minister had warned of belt-tightening in 2009', *Belfast Telegraph*, 26 April. Date accessed: 7 October 2014. Available online at: http://

www.belfasttelegraph.co.uk/news/politics/election/first-minister-had-warned-of-belttightening-in-2009-28532072.html

Gosling, P. (2013) 'Northern Ireland's missing ingredient – a USP', *Belfast Telegraph*, 7 November. Date accessed: 14 October 2014. Available online at: http://www.paulgosling.net/2013/11/northern-irelands-missing-ingredient-a-usp/

HM Government (1920) *Government of Ireland Act* [10 & 11 Geo. 5. Ch. 67].

HM Government (1973) *Northern Ireland Constitutional Act.*

HM Government (1998) *Northern Ireland Act.*

HM Government (2010) *The Coalition: Our Programme for Government.* Date accessed: 7 October 2014. Available online at: https://www.gov.uk/government/uploads/system/uploads/attachment_data/file/78977/coalition_programme_for_government.pdf

HM Government (2012) *Welfare Reform Act.*

HM Treasury (2010) *Funding the Scottish Parliament, National Assembly for Wales and Northern Ireland Assembly: Statement of Funding Policy*, London: HM Treasury.

HM Treasury (2011) *Rebalancing the Northern Ireland Economy* (March document), London: HM Treasury.

Murphy, R. (2010) *Lowering Northern Ireland's Corporation Tax: Pot of Gold or Fool's Gold?* Belfast: Irish Congress of Trade Unions Northern Ireland Committee.

Northern Ireland Assembly Official Report (2014) Oral Answers to Questions – Finance and Personnel, 14 October 2014.

Northern Ireland Assembly Research and Information Service (2011) *Consider this...* Belfast: Northern Ireland Assembly.

Northern Ireland Council for Voluntary Action (NICVA) (2014) Welfare Reform and avoiding the worst case scenario. Date accessed: 25 January 2015. Available at: http://www.nicva.org/article/welfare-reform-and-avoiding-worst-case-scenario

Northern Ireland Economic Reform Group (2010) The case for a reduced rate of Corporation Tax in Northern Ireland. Date accessed: 10 October 2014. Available online at: http://www.ergni.org/reports/report_corporation_tax_may_2010.pdf

Northern Ireland Economic Reform Group (2011) 12 key points on Corporation Tax reduction. Date accessed: 10 October 2014. Available online at: http://ergni.org/reports/key_points_feb_2011.pdf

Northern Ireland Executive (2011) *Budget 2011–15.* Date accessed: 25 January 2015. Available online at: http://www.northernireland.gov.uk/revised_budget_-_website_version.pdf

Northern Ireland Executive (2012) Tailoring welfare reforms for Northern Ireland: McCausland, 22 October. Date accessed: 26 January 2015. Available online at: http://www.northernireland.gov.uk/news-dsd-221012-tailoring-welfare-reforms

Northern Ireland Office (2014) The Stormont House Agreement. Date accessed: 25 January 2014. Available online at: https://www.gov.uk/government/publications/the-stormont-house-agreement

Northern Ireland Welfare Reform Group (2012) Social Development Committee: Welfare Reform Bill (Northern Ireland). Date accessed: 13 November 2014. Available online at: http://www.lawcentreni.org/Publications/Policy-Briefings/WRG-Social-Development-Committee-OCT-2012.pdf

PricewaterhouseCoopers (2013) Fiscal powers: A review of the fiscal powers of the Northern Ireland Assembly (prepared on behalf of the Northern Ireland

Council for Voluntary Action), June. Date accessed: 14 October 2014. Available online at: http://pwc.blogs.com/files/fiscalpowers-nicva_final_270613.pdf

Stewart, J. (2014) 'Ireland's tax regime nurtures innovation in avoidance', *Financial Times*, 7 October.

Trench, A. (2012) Corporation tax devolution for Northern Ireland: does anyone care how much corporation tax is generated there? Date accessed: 13 October. Available online at: http://devolutionmatters.wordpress.com/2012/02/02/corporation-tax-devolution-for-northern-ireland-does-anyone-care-how-much-corporation-tax-is-generated-there/

UTV (2014) Villiers warns over corporation tax. Date accessed: 15 February 2015. Available online at: http://www.u.tv/News/Villiers-warns-over-corporation-tax/18983fdb-fab2-4d68-b4c1-bb1fd9b364cc

Varney, D. (2007) Review of tax policy in Northern Ireland. Date accessed: 10 October 2014. Available online at: http://webarchive.nationalarchives.gov.uk/+/http://www.hm-treasury.gov.uk/media/1/3/varney171207.pdf

Walker, S. (2014) Theresa Villiers: Stormont needs to be in 'best possible shape' for tax powers. Date accessed: 13 October 2014. Available online at: http://www.bbc.co.uk/news/uk-northern-ireland-29419647

Williamson, C. (2014) DUP negotiated the ultimate sellout by accepting £100m lifeline loan: Mike Nesbitt, *Belfast Telegraph*, 11 October. Date accessed: 14 November 2014. Available online at: http://www.belfasttelegraph.co.uk/news/politics/dup-negotiated-the-ultimate-sellout-by-accepting-100m-lifeline-loan-mike-nesbitt-30655135.html

Wilson, R. (2011) Conventional wisdom fails us over the economy, *Belfast Telegraph*, 7 May.

14
Defence Under the Coalition: Maintaining Influence Under Continuing Austerity

Christopher Martin

Introduction

The Coalition's Strategic Defence and Strategy Review (SDSR 2010) made the most draconian cuts to the UK's military capability since those made under Duncan Sandys in the late 1950s. Nevertheless, there was a clear commitment given to Future Force 2020 (FF2020). FF2020 is the bedrock of the UK government's plans for defence in the twenty-first century. It is not within the scope of this chapter to detail all of FF2020 but, at its pinnacle, the rationale is the maintenance of the UK's ability to conduct expeditionary operations. This maritime-based capability is centred upon the procurement of two new *Queen Elizabeth* aircraft carriers, six Type-45 destroyers, 13 Type-26 frigates and six *Astute* class hunter-killer submarines. The operational ceiling of this capability is to send and support with all necessary maritime and air elements, and with sufficient warning and for limited time, three army brigades (30,000 troops). Few states can boast such a capability and it is one that marks the UK out among states of similar size and economy. For the UK it is a crucial element of its ability to conduct independent operations and make significant contribution to combined operations, thereby ensuring influence over opponents and with friends. The ultimate purpose of these forces is of course war fighting, but their routine business is to exert where necessary, influence, in any instance where UK interests require it. In this respect, the National Security Strategy (NSS) was explicit in this matter as it stated, 'Britain's national interest requires us to reject any notion of the shrinkage of our influence' (HM Government, 2010a: 10).

This author's review of the 2010 SDSR and NSS concluded with four main assertions. First, that the decisions made were financially driven and not strategic. Second, that the SDSR was a 'jam tomorrow' promise but no faith should be placed in that promise. Third, it was a high-risk policy founded on a hope that no major events would occur that required UK participation above a particular ceiling of operation and independence. Fourth, that the UK risked losing influence over events with adversaries and allies alike (Martin, 2011: 200–1). The first assertion was not prediction, but a statement of fact and one since borne out by the investigations of the House of Commons Defence Select Committee (House of Commons Defence Committee, 2014a). As for the other three, the question arises to what degree were these forecasts realised?

This chapter will explain that the UK government's commitment to its global position is not commensurate with its defence spending capacity. The UK will fall out of the top league of states if the current and projected situation flows through to 2020 and beyond. Key capabilities for influence such as expeditionary operations are under threat. Unless the government makes real-term commitments to defence spending, the UK will lose its position in the global political pecking order. Its problem is, at a time when the worst of the cuts are yet to come, how can it convince a public suffering austerity that defence expenditure is a strategic national priority?

The defence budget

Because the Chancellor has missed his deficit reduction targets for the period 2010–15, there are huge pressures upon defence spending after 2015 not least because of past promises made by the Prime Minister. On 19 October 2010, following the publication of the SDSR and NSS papers, the Prime Minister faced a hostile Commons to which he attempted to justify the huge range and depth of cuts to UK forces. While on his feet he expressed both a personal opinion and made a promise regarding future funding and force structure:

> The White Paper we have published today sets out a clear vision for the future structure of our armed forces. The precise budgets beyond 2015 will be agreed in future spending reviews. My own strong view is that this structure [FF2020] will require year-on-year real-terms growth in the defence budget in the years beyond 2015. Between now

and then the Government are committed to the vision of 2020 set out in the review and we will make decisions accordingly. (Cameron, 2010: c.799)

Let us be clear about what the Prime Minister was stating here. First, in his opinion, FF2020 would require real-term increases after 2015 in the defence *equipment* expenditure of the UK, not *overall* expenditure. Implicit in this assertion is that, should such increases not be made, then the structure of FF2020 might not be met. Second, the government was committed to meeting FF2020 *at the time*, if we interpret 'between now and then' as the period 2010–15. But, and here is the problematic aspect: the deeper the cuts to *overall* defence spending 2010–15, the more money would need to be found post-2015. The Comprehensive Spending Review (CSR) undertaken in 2010 claimed that in the period 2010–15 there would be a real-term cut in defence spending of 8 per cent. The projected expenditure on defence over this period, year-on-year expressed as Total Departmental Expenditure Limit (DEL), was as follows: 2010–11: £32.9bn; 2011–12: £33.8bn; 2012–13: £34.4bn; 2013–14: £34.1bn; and 2014–15: £33.5bn (HM Treasury, 2010: 57). On this particular point, the Prime Minister was once again explicit in his statement to the House of Commons:

The whole point about this review is that it has a vision for what our forces should look like in 2020 – 10 years' time rather than just five years' time. Because the Ministry of Defence and the service chiefs can now see their budgets for the whole of the spending review period, they can make proper plans and try to drive some efficiencies through the MOD so that they get even more for the money that they have. (Cameron, 2010: c.809)

The SDSR was also clear, insofar as it stated: 'The defence budget will rise in cash terms. It will meet the NATO 2% target throughout the next four years. We expect to continue with the fourth largest military budget in the world' (HM Government, 2010b: 3).

The service chiefs certainly took the view that they were entitled to make certain assumptions about the direction of defence spending over the round, but any assumption that they would be able to 'see their budgets for the whole of the spending review period' from 2010 were misplaced. The 2012 Autumn Statement cut spending on the defence Resource Budget by 1 per cent for the FY 2013/14 and by another 2 per cent for the FY 2014/15. What this meant was that rather than having an estimated resource DEL of £24.7 billion as projected under CSR2010, the projected resource DEL for 2015/16 was £23.9 billion (HM Treasury, 2013: 43). The Spending Round 2013 cut another £1 billion from overall spending but maintained the promise of a 1 per cent increase in real-term spending on the equipment plan and the notion that, post 2015, defence would have a flat rate (i.e. no cuts) but a 1 per cent real-term increase to the equipment budget continued to determine MoD planning (House of Commons Defence Committee, 2014b: 4). This much had been made clear by Defence Secretary Philip Hammond at the House of Commons Defence Select Committee on 9 October 2013 (House of Commons Defence Committee, 2014a: Ev.43). Nevertheless, Hammond, probably more with the Chancellor in mind than the Defence Committee, added a very strong caveat to his statement, in that his claim was based upon an understanding that, 'we are left alone, in peace, with the budget we have assumed' (House of Commons Defence Committee, 2014a: Ev 44).

The fact is that the claim made in the SDSR, to the effect that actual expenditure on defence 2010–15 would rise in actual cash terms, has proven false. It has actually fallen from a DEL of £32.9 billion in 2010 to £32.6 billion. Consequently, in real terms, the MoD budget has contracted by 9.6 per cent since 2010 and, when the elimination of spending on Afghanistan is taken into account (as it was included in calculations), total defence spending will have contracted by 15 per cent in real terms (Chalmers, 2013: 4). However, the Spending Round 2013 did not hit defence as hard as many had feared. In real terms, the effect was near stasis. Of the £1 billion savings announced, 75 per cent were, by sleight of hand, shifted to renegotiating existing contracts. Because of the pressure on the future equipment budget the MoD also benefited in that reductions to the Resource Budget avoided being allocated to the equipment proportion of that budget. However, the promise of a 1 per cent increase in real terms on equipment is from the overall baseline that will exist in 2015–16. It will no doubt be noted that this baseline (2015–16) is not quite in line with what Cameron stated in the Commons in October 2010 (i.e. a baseline of 2015). Since 2010, considerable concern has been expressed that Cameron has not been willing to keep his promise on defence spending (Kirkup, 2013). When it was confirmed that Cameron would stand by his statement, it is noteworthy that the position had shifted slightly: 2015 had become FY 2015/16. This might not sound significant except for the fact that the increases to equipment spending are 'guaranteed' to FY 2020/21 only, and that the equipment budget is only 40 per cent of overall defence spending. It is rather more sobering therefore to recognise just what Cameron's statement means, assuming he does not resile from it: an increase in defence spending in real terms for five years of about 0.4 per cent of overall spending. Equipment therefore has an effective 'internal ring fence' but it only applies to 40 per cent of the budget; the other 60 per cent is up for grabs in any further spending cuts.

Defence, unlike most other government departments, is not insular. Defence in the UK is intimately tied to NATO. One aspect of NATO membership that has been a matter of contention for many years is the agreed 'minimum' level of defence spending for NATO members of 2 per cent of Gross Domestic Product (GDP) per annum. Historically, the UK has always exceeded this figure and often by a very large amount, but it is almost certain that the UK will fall below this figure after 2015 and that could have considerable effect on the future of UK defence capabilities and the future of NATO.

The SDSR 2010 confirmed a commitment to a minimum of 2 per cent GDP on defence as did the Spending Round 2013. However, we can only take those commitments for as long as the remit of those policies runs, i.e. until 2015. The fact that the UK has traditionally exceeded the 2 per cent target has always been recognised as a point of vital principle. It demonstrates to the senior partner, the United States, the UK's commitment, while to the other NATO members the UK has been able to use this as an example to be followed and it has given the UK a place of authority and influence.

The failure of most European NATO members to meet this target has often been a point of frustration especially with the USA. Not only do European members consistently fail to meet the target, they do not spend on the kind of capability in equipment that enables them to easily deploy at distance from NATO's core European area. Before the 2014 NATO Summit David Cameron made a speech in which he stated, 'I hope today we [NATO] can reaffirm our public commitment to spend 2% of our GDP on defence and 20% of that money on equipment' (Cameron, 2014). The irony is that Cameron's next government, assuming he is in office after 2015, will fail to meet this target. At the end of the summit the NATO leaders released an agreed statement in which it was stated:

> We agree to reverse the trend of declining defence budgets ... Allies currently meeting the NATO guideline to spend a minimum of 2% of their Gross Domestic Product (GDP) on defence will aim to continue to do so. Likewise, Allies spending more than 20% of their

defence budgets on major equipment, including related Research & Development, will continue to do so. (NATO, 2014: para. 14)

It was noted before that the UK spends 40 per cent of its defence budget on equipment. This is much higher proportionately than most other NATO members. The UK has always pursued this policy (high spending on equipment) because technology substitutes for personnel, which the UK lacks. It would be most unlikely that the UK would dip below 20 per cent as this would imply a complete collapse in spending, so this target is well within UK parameters and no real problem. It is in regard to the remarks on the 2 per cent proportion of GDP that we need to look closely. The commitment is only 'to aim to continue to do so'. This is hardly a firm commitment and, indeed, post 2015 when SDSR 10 and Spending Round 2013 expire there is no absolute commitment to maintaining the 2 per cent threshold of GDP on defence. In fact there are very good reasons why the UK *will not* maintain its commitment at 2 per cent or more of GDP on defence. Malcolm Chalmers of RUSI has made some interesting calculations concerning the UK's projected defence spending. They are worth examining if for no other reasons than Chalmers' other papers on UK defence spending over the last parliament have been prescient.

Chalmers considers three possible scenarios for UK defence spending after the post General Election 2015 Spending Review (Chalmers, 2014: 4). First, the UK meets the 2 per cent target through to 2020. Second, the UK sustains a flat rate +1 per cent increase in real-terms expenditure on equipment to 2020 (current planning assumptions). Third, UK defence expenditure suffers two or more years of real cuts.

These scenarios, when projected out to 2025, result in very different situations. By 2025, if the 2 per cent of GDP target is maintained throughout the 2015–25 period (scenario 1), the UK will be spending £10 billion per annum more on defence than if current assumptions are maintained (i.e. scenario 2: flat rate +1 per cent on equipment). This would mean that over the five-year period 2016–21, 'an additional £25 billion would have to be allocated to defence in addition to the level that MoD is now assuming for planning purposes. If the 2 per cent commitment was further extended, through to 2025/26, it would cost an additional £74 billion compared to current MoD assumptions' (Chalmers, 2014: 4). Given that it is clear that the Chancellor will miss all his June/October 2010 targets for deficit reduction, it would be politically unacceptable at home to make the case for a 2 per cent GDP target minimum on defence spending when other departments are undertaking huge cuts to their budgets. But to fail to meet the 2 per cent target could have damaging consequences for the UK and for NATO as a whole, so what is the government's position?

The NATO summit is one indicator but that cannot be taken as the entire position for, while the government overtly gave commitment to a 2 per cent minimum of GDP, it was careful to minimise its exposure to any such commitment. The House of Commons Defence Committee, when investigating some issues pertinent to the next SDSR, made a recommendation to the government to the effect that, 'in opening the NATO summit, the Prime Minister and the Secretary of State should make a commitment to the UK maintaining defence spending at or above 2%' (House of Commons Defence Committee, 2014c: para. 106). In response to the committee's recommendation, the government response is noteworthy for its guarded commitment, stating:

> The Government shares the Committee's view that increasing defence spending must be a priority amongst Allies both to send a strong message of Allies' commitment to collective defence and to enable the required investment in priority capabilities ... the proportion of GDP devoted to defence is an important indicator of how seriously members view collective security ... all Allies agreed to halt any decline in Defence spending, aim to increase it in real terms as GDP grows and to move towards 2% within a decade ... The Government is committed to spending 2% of GDP on Defence. We have consistently met and indeed exceeded the target and will continue to do so until the end of the spending review period. (House of Commons Defence Committee, 2014d: para. 28)

Therefore, within one paragraph, the government had recapitulated its support for the 2 per cent minimum increase in expenditure; made the point that defence spending must be 'a priority' for NATO allies; stated just how important the figure is in representing commitment to NATO; and then made explicit its commitment to the 2 per cent minimum but, only 'until the end of the spending review period' (i.e. 2015).

One can only conclude that the defence budget will continue to be squeezed and the promises made concerning FF2020 look ominously delusional with serious consequences for the standing and ambition of the UK in the world.

A high-risk strategy?

After a decade of war and with the wind-down in Afghanistan a priority, it was important that the period of vulnerability created by the decisions under SDSR 2010 did not coincide with a major international event that threatened the core vital interests of the UK. Unfortunately, the operation in Libya, although short in duration and of low level conflict, occurred and it exposed huge gaps in the capability of the UK (and its NATO-Europe allies). In reference to SDSR 2010, the most obvious issue in regard to deleted capability in such an operation was the loss of carrier strike capability. France and Italy used their carrier capability for limited periods and the United States deployed their Harrier 2 aircraft from amphibious assault ships.

Did the loss of carrier strike adversely affect the UK's contribution? It did not. The deletion of carrier strike was based on the utility of the Harrier vs. Tornado with Afghanistan as the primary consideration, not the value of carrier strike, and the Harrier in use by the UK could not use the latest attack munitions *Brimstone* and *Storm Shadow*. These munitions proved incredibly effective in the Libya operation and quite justified the retention of Tornado – Brimstone was 98.7 per cent on target; the 1.3 per cent that 'missed' was within five feet (House of Commons Defence Committee, 2012: Ev. 46). Nevertheless, as the Defence Select Committee was advised, had carrier strike been available it would have been used despite its limited capacity so as to add to the options commanders had (House of Commons Defence Committee, 2012: Ev. 48). The Royal Navy did deploy HMS *Ocean*, which provided the five Apache ground attack helicopters, verifying the value of air strike from the sea. The lack of any requirement for carrier strike was of course due to the good luck that Libya was on NATO's doorstep and this made it possible for RAF ground attack Tornadoes to fly from Gioia del Colle in Italy.

It was not the loss of carrier strike that is the pertinent issue here, in the context of Libya, for the UK's naval forces. Through the Libya operation the Royal Navy deployed at various times: 1 amphibious assault ship; 2 *Broadsword* class destroyers; 3 *Duke* class frigates; 2 *Sheffield* class destroyers; 1 *Sandown* class mine hunter; 1 *Hunt* class mine countermeasures vessel; 1 landing platform dock; 2 *Trafalgar* class nuclear attack submarines; and 4 Royal Fleet Auxiliary afloat support logistics vessels (RUSI, 2012: xi). The Royal Navy took the greatest hit in the SDSR 2010 but its commitments were not reduced. Clearly, then, when Libya occurred and the Royal Navy was required to deploy, the issue then was, did it have any effect on standing commitments? The service chiefs do not air their grievances in public. Nevertheless, the then First Sea Lord, Admiral Sir Mark Stanhope, found it difficult to hide the fact that the Royal Navy was already stretched:

> Before Libya, we had already recognized stretch in our ability to satisfy our commitment to have a warship in the Caribbean during hurricane season. We were covering that with the Royal Fleet Auxiliary, which is entirely acceptable to do that job, although it did not absolutely satisfy it. (House of Commons Defence Committee, 2012: Ev. 36)

In order for the Royal Navy to meet the demands of Operation ELLAMY and its standing commitments, Stanhope was forced to admit that: 'We managed it for the period of the operation through flexing and stretching some of the deployment baselines' (House of Commons Defence Committee, 2012: Ev. 44). Such a situation could be endured only for a short time. It is just as well Libya was a short operation or the real threadbare state of affairs might have been even more apparent. Little wonder that, in evidence to the Defence Committee, Professor M. J. Williams of Wesleyan University made the point that, 'UK resources had been stretched by the operation ... the UK had been lucky that the operation had ended when it did' (House of Commons Defence Committee, 2012: para. 154). And as for the Defence Committee itself, while it acknowledged the success of the operation, it did note that: 'Operation ELLAMY was conducted prior to the implementation of many of the Strategic Defence and Security Review decisions ... we consider that Operation ELLAMY raises some important questions as to the extent of the United Kingdom's national contingent capability' (House of Commons Defence Committee, 2012: para. 127).

Libya, however, was not just about the UK's forces being stretched. The UK's forces personnel have an uncanny 'can do' ethos that consistently overcomes the hurdles erected by politicians. However, what cannot be overcome is the huge deficit in capability that the UK and other European NATO forces have vis-à-vis the USA. Many of the huge shortfalls were hidden by the fact the operation was at NATO's doorstep. But the gaps are startling. Air Marshal Christopher Harper made the point directly: 'There is no question that this operation throws into stark relief the capability gaps that exist between the non-US members of NATO and the United States' (House of Commons Defence Committee, 2012: Ev. 31). In this operation the US took the view that it would 'lead from the rear'. This decision had two probable purposes: first to avoid being the lead player in another 'anti-Muslim' war; second, to demonstrate to its NATO partners just how things might be if the USA is not available. It must be noted that the US is undertaking cuts to its own forces, and its geo-strategic posture is shifting away from Eurasia to the East Asia-Pacific rim. This shift will have huge consequences for NATO-Europe and the question is: can NATO-Europe stand on its own two feet in defence of its own interests? The answer from Libya is a firm 'no'.

Consider just what the United States contributed when 'leading from the rear'. It equalled the air and maritime assets of the UK and France individually. Of the 40 air-to-air refuelling tankers, it provided 30; it provided all the SEAD (suppression of enemy air defence) capability that made the air campaign possible; it provided almost all the 'drone' capability; it provided 27 per cent of all intelligence gathering assets, and for sheer firepower consider that in respect of TLAM (Tomahawk Land Attack Missile) attacks – a capability owned only in NATO by the US and UK – for every one missile fired by the Royal Navy, the United States Navy fired 32 (RUSI, 2012: 20). Little wonder that the NATO General Secretary stated: '[this] mission could not have been done without capabilities only the United States can offer. Let me put it bluntly: those capabilities are vital for all of us. More allies should be willing to obtain them' (quoted in House of Commons Defence Committee, 2012: para. 88).

But the point from all this is the very pertinent and urgent one: NATO-Europe is toothless without the support of the United States. The Defence Committee regarded this positively: 'We consider that the US decision not to lead the engagement in Libya was positively beneficial, in that it forced European members of NATO to face their own respon-sibilities, and shone a light on the gaps in European capabilities – gaps we consider it essential to be plugged' (House of Commons Defence Committee, 2012: para. 143). A positive view perhaps, but how these gaps will be plugged in an era where NATO-Europe states are struggling to meet their 2 per cent commitment is an open question.

But Libya opened up a further problematic issue, in that one is forced to ask just what NATO is today? Of NATO's 28 member states, only nine contributed to the ground attack campaign. Of those nine, only two were willing to get up-close-and-personal by contributing ground attack helicopters, and this is in a campaign that was right in NATO's strategic area. In any sense of capability, but one still seriously lacking many of the enabling capacities the US provides, NATO-Europe is increasingly looking like being UK-France. These two have traditionally led by example in Europe but at a time when, as stated, the USA is shifting its geo-strategic pivot and the US is increasingly looking at its European partners in despair, just how much burden can France and the UK carry on their shoulders? The Defence Committee was realistic in this assessment in that it stated:

> For the time being, there will still be a heavy reliance on US command and control functions for future operations. It should be a priority for NATO to examine this. However, whilst accepting the current economic climate and its implications for defence capabilities, we are concerned that future operations will not be possible if the US is not willing or able to provide capabilities. (House of Commons Defence Committee, 2012: para. 90)

The US is shifting its priorities; what if it does not turn up to the next crisis? All indicators are that NATO-Europe would be nothing but a spectator to events crucial to its well being, and no amount of bluster by a UK government will change that fact. But, what if the UK takes up the reins and tries to lead NATO-Europe into making real and critical improvements to spending? This is what the US wants and it is certainly a role the UK (and France) would relish. UK-French cooperation in Libya was excellent, and the bi-lateral cooperation much scoffed at in SDSR 2010 has held reasonably well. Cooperation and leadership by example with France would go a long way to dragging NATO-Europe along. The elephant in the room is, of course, the fact that it is certain, as was outlined above, that the UK's spending on defence will drop well under the 2 per cent level and that will hardly impress fellow European NATO members. Indeed there is already in Europe, 'frustration with the UK on the one side making statement about ambition, and on the other side cutting the means to make that ambition real' (House of Commons Defence Committee, 2014a: Ev. 9).

How to exert influence? The UK as a globalised power

Some things never change and at the grand strategic level the fundamental reality is that the UK is, as it has always been, an island, dependent upon the sea as its primary medium to bring its armed forces to the point at which influence and violence can be brought to bear. We should also note that NATO is a maritime-based alliance that uses the sea as its means of access and influence. Additionally, history, wealth and relative standing place burdensome expectations on the UK. Some of these expectations are self-imposed; a sense of responsibility, and some imposed by others – how other states expect the UK to act. The UK is one of the wealthiest countries in the world and a leading member of major international institutions. It would be immoral if the UK turned away from the world and accepted no responsibility for its regulation. British politicians instinctively understand this and so they have always sought influence over events that affect the UK and the globalised system. In the absence of traditional direct military threats to the UK, this is what the UK's military capability is largely for today. As the SDSR 2010 stated:

> Our strategy reflects the country that we want to be: a prosperous, secure, modern and outward-looking nation, confident in its values and ideas. Our national interest comprises our security, prosperity and freedom. We must be a nation that is able to bring together all the instruments of national power to build a secure and resilient UK and to help shape a stable world. Our outlook will be characterised by flexibility and resilience and underpinned by a firm commitment to human rights, justice and the rule of law. (HM Government, 2010a: 10)

This is all very well, but it would be foolish not to acknowledge that the reality is, in a time of austerity, the figures literally just do not add up and, unless the public can be brought on message, funding the requirements for credible armed forces while making savage cuts will not be swallowed, and no amount of government fudging can hide this fact.

We noted that following Libya, the Defence Committee made it clear that the UK had serious deficiencies in capability and it demanded that remedial action be taken, but there has to be some considerable doubt that these deficiencies can be filled, most significantly because the deficiencies are in the types of equipment and capability that the UK, to date, has not planned to acquire and so are outside of an already squeezed budget.

The problem, quite simply, is a lack of money. We have noted above that the baseline for future spending calculations is lower than projected in 2010 when the cuts were applied. In 2013, Philip Hammond, then Secretary of State for Defence, stated clearly that should there be 'significant' reductions in budget then: 'We would have to ask some serious structural questions about the type of forces we were able to maintain' (House of Commons Defence Committee, 2014a: Ev. 44). This should not happen if the flat rate +1 per cent on equipment is maintained, but the budgetary situation will remain very tight. However, as we have noted, there is no commitment to the minimum 2 per cent of GDP expenditure on defence beyond 2015, and any attempt to keep close to this level would require almost exponential increases in the defence budget. As an indication of 'inside thinking', the Prime Minister's National Security advisor, Sir Kim Darroch, indicated that the expeditionary capability was 'discretionary' when he appeared at the Defence Select Committee in September 2013 (House of Commons Defence Committee, 2014a: Ev. 32). However, the Defence Secretary, just one month later, stated to the same committee that this capability 'gives us enormously more reach and enormously more influence' (House of Commons Defence Committee, 2014a: Ev. 40).

Army 2020, with its 30,000 personnel reserve force, is a disaster, having failed to meet every recruitment target, but it is crucial this succeeds if the government is to reduce cost while maintaining the army's scale and capability. In the case of the type 26 Global Combat Ship, the next generation basic but essential naval platform, when the Parliamentary Under-Secretary of State for Defence Philip Dunne was asked if the government was committed to all 13 ships, as under the SDSR, he gave no firm commitment (*Hansard*, 20 October 2014: c.671). If the Royal Navy is to maintain its global presence and undertake its basic commitments, it is vital that the 13 Type 26 committed to in SDSR 2010 are commissioned. From these few examples we can see that FF2020 is under extreme pressure already. Just how can a UK government hope to maintain its commitment to FF2020 as a minimum when the sums indicate huge increases to defence spending are required at the same time that benefits, social services and other 'crucial' sectors face savage cuts after 2015?

It is here we offer a point of departure. Far too often, critics of defence spending argue that this spending is the effort of a post-imperial power to desperately cling to its place in the world. However, we misunderstand UK defence and security policy today if we contextualise it within post-imperial decline, because the system is subtly different now to when western states pursued imperial narrow self-interest. We need to see the UK, not as a global power or a regional power, but as a *globalised* power. A globalised power is a state dependent upon, and enmeshed within, the globalised maritime-based economy, and the greater the degree of a state's globalisation, the greater is its vulnerability to disruptions to the system. A globalised power does not seek to monopolise a stake in the system but recognises it shares the system with others and regards its primary defence and security aims as the successful maintenance of the system. In so doing it recognises that it cannot do things alone and nor, in except the rarest cases, should it: it is a shared system with mutual benefits and mutual responsibilities. For such a state – a post-modern state – the gains to be made from the system are not absolute but relative: the future is cooperation. The fact is that the UK's defence and security policy should be a reflection of how things are today not yesterday.

UKPLC is a globalised player. The global political and economic system is one of extreme complexity and one that requires intimate scales of integration. Manufacturing, raw materials, foodstuffs, energy, finance and services are internationalised in a way not seen before. This globalised system is maritime-based with the overwhelming bulk of goods moving by sea. Additionally, however, it is on land, especially where it meets the sea (the littoral) that the most vital areas of human activity take place. UKPLC would face devastating consequences should this system collapse or face serious disruption. Quite literally the lights would go out; we could not heat our homes; we would not be able to put fuel in our vehicles. In this sense, the UK does not want a capable navy, army or air force because it wants to maintain a facsimile of imperial greatness; it needs these capabilities because it needs to maintain a leading role in ensuring the system, upon which our very wealth depends, works. Because it is that wealth that supports the health system, benefits and social services: expeditionary capabilities are not optional.

Conclusion

Returning to the four 'predictions' reiterated at the start of this chapter, we can state the following. First, *SDSR 2020 was financially driven and not military-strategic*: Given the state of the UK government's finances, it is most likely that the next defence review will also be driven by money not need. Second, *there should be no faith in 'jam tomorrow' promises*: there is no doubt that elements of FF2020 are under threat for various reasons, mostly financial, and promises of 'real-terms' increases to defence spending are nebulous. Various aspects of FF2020 are in disarray, especially Army 2020, and there is a very real possibility that the basic structure of FF2020 as conceived will not be attained. Third, *the UK followed a high-risk policy*: luckily, Libya was at NATO's doorstep, but the operation exposed huge gaps in the capability of the UK in its ability to conduct operations independent of the USA and these gaps leave the UK's credibility open to question. Filling these gaps over and above current spending will be nigh on impossible, leaving the UK dependent on the USA. Fourth, *losing influence with friends and opponents*: at a time when the international situation is becoming ever more volatile and when the USA is shifting its geo-strategic focus to Asia-Pacific, this is a potentially dangerous period for the UK. If, as it seems, the UK will slip below the 2 per cent of GDP level, then in Europe and the USA serious doubt will be expressed as to the UK's commitment. Maintaining a high degree of commitment will be vital to keeping the USA 'in' NATO and the Europeans on track. Cutting back will send the wrong message but making up the shortfall seems financially impossible.

At a time when the government admits that government spending after 2015 will be eviscerated, how can it convince the public that defence spending must remain relatively higher? If it cuts defence further it will alienate friends and reduce its influence; if it does not cut defence in line with other departments it will alienate the public. The sums do not add up and the government has trapped itself with 'jam tomorrow' promises and poorly thought-out cuts, made in 2010.

References

Cameron, D. (2010) Statement: Strategic Defence and Security Review, *Hansard*, 19 October: cc. 797–801.

Cameron, D. (2014) 'NATO Summit 2014: PM speaks at North Atlantic Council meeting', 5 September 2014. www.gov.uk/government/speeches/nato-summit-2014-pm-speaks-at-north-atlantic-council-meeting (accessed 23 September 2014).

Chalmers, M. (2013) *Mid-Term Blues? Defence and the 2013 Spending Review*, RUSI Briefing Paper, February 2013 (London: Royal United Services Institute).

Chalmers, M. (2014) *The Financial Context for the 2015 SDSR: The End of UK Exceptionalism?* RUSI Briefing Paper, SDSR 2015: Hard Choices Ahead, September (London: Royal United Services Institute).

House of Commons Defence Committee (2012) *Operations in Libya*. Ninth report of session 2010–12, HC.950 (London: The Stationery Office).

House of Commons Defence Committee (2014a) *Towards the Next Defence and Security Review: Part One*. Seventh report of session 2013–14, volume 1, HC.197 (London: The Stationery Office).

House of Commons Defence Committee (2014b) *The Ministry of Defence Main Estimates 2014–15*. First report of session 2014–15, HC.469 (London: The Stationery Office).

House of Commons Defence Committee (2014c) *Towards the Next Defence and Security Review: Part Two – NATO*. Third report of session 2014–15, HC.358 (London: The Stationery Office).

House of Commons Defence Committee (2014d) *Towards the Next Defence and Security Review: Part Two – NATO: Government Response to the Committee's Third Report of Session 2014–15*, HC.755 (London: The Stationery Office).

HM Government (2010) *A Strong Britain in an Age of Uncertainty: The National Security Strategy*, Cm.7953 (London: The Stationery Office).

HM Government (2010) *Securing Britain in an Age of Uncertainty: Strategic Defence and Security Review*, Cm.7948 (London: The Stationery Office).

HM Treasury (2010) *Spending Review 2010*, Cm.7942 (London: The Stationery Office).

HM Treasury (2013) *Spending Round 2013*, Cm.8639 (London: The Stationery Office).

Kirkup, J. (2013) 'David Cameron promised to increase defence spending after 2015. Now Downing Street can't say if he'll keep that promise', *Daily Telegraph*, 30 January 2013, http://blogs.telegraph.co.uk/news/jameskirkup/100200808/david-cameron-promised-to-increase-defence-spending-after-2015-now-downing-street-cant-say-if-hell-keep-that-promise/

Martin, C. (2011) The Con-Lib Agenda for National Security and Strategy. In Lee, S. and Beech, M. (eds), *The Cameron–Clegg Government: Coalition Politics in an Age of Austerity* (London: Palgrave Macmillan).

NATO (2014) *Wales Summit Declaration*, 5 September. www.gov.uk/government/publications/nato-summit-2014-wales-summit-declaration (accessed 10 December 2014).

RUSI (2012) Whitehall Report 1-12, *Short War, Long Shadow: The Political and Military Legacies of the 2011 Libya Campaign* (London: Royal United Services Institute).

15
Foreign Policy and International Development

Rhiannon Vickers

This chapter assesses the Coalition's approach to foreign policy, looking specifically at its response to the Libyan revolution of 2011; its attitude and policy towards the Syrian civil war and the rise of ISIS in Syria and Iraq; and its approach towards Russian revanchism in Ukraine. It then examines government's policy on international development, where the Coalition has met the commitment set in place by Labour of spending 0.7 per cent of Gross National Income (GNI) on development aid by 2013, while refocusing aid on conflict prevention rather than post-conflict reconstruction in an attempt to tackle potential security issues at source. Cameron came into power keen to avoid a repeat of the interventionism of the Blair years, and it was hoped that this new cross-government strategy would help limit the need for Britain to intervene militarily in conflict prone situations by building resilience on the ground. The chapter begins by outlining the government's foreign policy perspective, arguing that it is possible to discern an overall foreign policy approach of liberal Conservatism that was liberal enough to satisfy the Conservatives' Coalition partners, while rejecting the more idealistic tenets of New Labour's foreign policy. However, it concludes by suggesting that Cameron, rather than charting a new, post-interventionist foreign policy, has, as a result of the Arab uprisings, ended up embracing some of the same interventionist impulses as Blair, but has been limited in his ability to turn these into policy given the ongoing unpopularity of intervention in a post-Iraq era.

The Coalition's liberal Conservatism in foreign policy

At his first conference as party leader Cameron said that, in terms of foreign policy:

> I'm a liberal Conservative. Liberal – because I believe in spreading freedom and democracy, and supporting humanitarian intervention. That is why we cannot stand by and watch further genocide in Darfur. But Conservative – because I also recognise the complexities of human nature, and will always be sceptical of grand schemes to remake the world. We need more patience, more humility in the way we engage with the world. (Cameron, 2006)

This theme of liberal Conservatism continued throughout Cameron's time as Leader of the Opposition and in the run up to the 2010 general election. Cameron appeared to be signalling a break with earlier Conservative foreign policy, in that he was willing to support intervention on humanitarian grounds, and moving away from a traditional realpolitik approach to foreign policy which tended to see the national interest and international interest as mutually exclusive. As Beech has compellingly argued, Cameron was drawing on ideas associated with Liberal traditions as well as Conservative ones (Beech, 2011). This chapter argues that this is not necessarily due to any rejection of traditional Conservative shibboleths, such as the importance of the Anglo-American relationship. Rather, it is due to the fact that Cameron became leader of the Conservative Party and then Prime Minister in a world that he accepts as being significantly different from that of his predecessors. During previous Conservative premierships, including most recently John Major and Margaret Thatcher, threats came from states; security was viewed as security of the state, rather than individuals or groups; and liberal internationalism was the preserve of the Labour Party (Vickers, 2003). Cameron came to power in a very different world, where threats come from non-state actors as well as states, where security includes human as well as state security, and where there has been a normative shift so that there is greater concern for the lives of people in other countries. Thus, it is hardly surprising that a man of his generation would have a more liberal internationalist perspective on the world than his predecessors.

Attempting to define liberal Conservatism is complex, but at its heart is the idea that while promoting the national interest is of course central to any foreign policy agenda, this must be tempered by consideration of the rights and interests of people in other states, with a sense of global responsibility. Cameron's Conservative Party had moved on from the realpolitik of the Cold War. As the 2010 election manifesto explained:

> A Conservative government's approach to foreign affairs will be based on liberal Conservative principles. Liberal, because Britain must be open and engaged with the world, supporting human rights and championing the cause of democracy and the rule of law at every opportunity. But Conservative, because our policy must be hard-headed and practical, dealing with the world as it is and not as we wish it were. (Conservative Party, 2010: 109)

There was little here that any party could really disagree with, which explains why the Liberal Democrats have accepted the foreign policy approach under what is largely a Conservative dominated Foreign and Commonwealth Office (FCO) and Department for International Development (DFID). Cameron would not follow the idealism that he equated with the Blair years – as Hague said on several occasions, 'idealism in foreign policy always needs to be tempered with realism' (Hague, 2010b) – but neither would he return to the traditional Conservative foreign policy that had been practised under John Major, where events such as Bosnia were largely seen as none of Britain's concern.

However, like any incoming Prime Minister, Cameron took office promising a foreign policy that was distinct from that of his predecessors. Cameron signalled a number of changes. Among these were reforms to the way that foreign policy is made in the UK; a focus on building stronger relationships with what Britain has termed 'emerging economies', in particular China, India and Brazil; forging an enhanced global role for the UK, complaining that under Labour, Britain had declined in importance and had lost some of its global presence; and lastly, an end to the liberal interventionism carried out by Blair, with a greater focus on conflict prevention instead (Conservative Party, 2010: 109–10). He said that under Blair and Brown, British foreign policy had at times 'lacked humility', and that the lesson of Iraq was that military intervention was costly (see Vickers, 2011).

The first two of these changes, with a more public focus on developing stronger links with what the Coalition government calls 'emerging powers', in particular China, India and Brazil, has been relatively easy to achieve. There have been an unusually large number of trips to these states, which have had a strongly economic basis and have focused on trade diplomacy. In terms of foreign policy-making reforms, Cameron set up an American style National Security Council (NSC) to bring together the key figures in foreign and security policy, and appointed Sir Peter Ricketts (Permanent Undersecretary at the FCO) to the newly created post of National Security Advisor. A new version of the National Security Strategy was drawn up, and an inquiry was announced into 'The Role of the FCO in UK Government'. Cameron and Hague had been highly critical of Blair's 'sofa style decision making' when it came to foreign and security policy, especially over the decisions around the invasion of Iraq, and were determined to have a more formalised system in which, it was thought, mistakes were less likely to occur, and misperceptions were less likely to influence British foreign policy. Again, this was uncontroversial in a post-Blair era, where a more robust approach to policy-making was seen as highly desirable by most politicians.

It is the other changes that proved more problematic. Cameron promised an enhanced global role for Britain under the new government. Both Cameron and Foreign Secretary William Hague argued that it was in Britain's national interest to expand its global role. Hague outlined at the start of the FCO 2010 Business Plan that: 'My vision is of a distinctive British foreign policy promoting our enlightened national interest while standing up for freedom, fairness and responsibility. It should extend our global reach and influence and be agile and energetic in a networked world' (Hague, 2010c: x).

Indeed, Hague had argued while still in Opposition that despite Britain's economic problems – or 'economic shrinkage' as he referred to it – relative to the rest of the world, a Conservative government would reject the notion that there needed to be any subsequent 'strategic shrinkage' (Hague, 2010a). Delivering this, of course, has been deeply problematic, given that the government's foreign policy has been made within the context of a budget deficit and a Comprehensive Spending Review designed to significantly cut expenditure during a new age of austerity necessitated by the recession. The Strategic Defence and Security Review reported its findings in October 2010 (HM Government, 2010b), and since then commentators have questioned whether Britain will be able to fulfil its military and foreign policy commitments in the light of the cuts made as a result of the Review's recommendations, not least as these seem to have again expanded. While the Coalition government signalled that there needed to be more consideration given to whether foreign policy was achievable, Britain continues to suffer today – as it has for most of the post-Second World War period – from a problem of military over-stretch.

It is the last change highlighted by Cameron, namely an end to the military interventionism that occurred under Blair, which has proved to be the most unexpected challenge. The 2010 National Security Strategy focused on preventing conflict, rather than on intervening in it, and appeared to herald the end of liberal interventionism; the suggestion was made that if a Kosovo-type situation arose again, the new government might take a different approach than Blair had done (HM Government, 2010a). Of course, this was written and published shortly before the start of the Arab uprisings, and Cameron quickly found himself having to respond to situations where, yet again, there were conflicting views on intervention, and where the desire for Britain to be seen as using force for good, as playing a leadership role in the response to a crisis, was simply too strong for a British Prime Minister to resist, and that indeed, it is difficult for Britain to act 'with humility'. It is Britain's response to events in the Middle East that this chapter turns to next, and which takes up a large portion of this discussion, as under Cameron, there has, unexpectedly, been a resurgence in Britain's 'east of Suez' role.

The uprising in Libya

The so-called 'Arab Spring' began with protests in Tunisia in December 2010, which then spread to Algeria, Egypt, Oman, Syria and Yemen. The demands of the protesters varied, but they included improved living and employment conditions, an end to corruption, political reform, constitutional change and, in some cases, the overthrow of the existing government. Demonstrations began in Libya on 15 February 2011, and momentum rapidly developed into a widespread movement to oust Gaddafi. The Gaddafi regime was quick to respond with force, with security forces firing on protesters, and hundreds of civilians were killed within days. On 28 February Cameron announced to the House of Commons that, 'We should be clear that for the future of Libya and its people, Colonel Gaddafi's regime must end and he must leave' (Cameron, 2011). While in Opposition, Cameron had been critical of Blair's rehabilitation of Gaddafi from enemy to potential ally, and had strongly condemned the decision to release the Lockerbie bomber, al-Megrahi, in 2009. Cameron was determined to be seen as at the forefront of coordinating the international response to the deepening crisis in Libya in February 2011, by applying pressure by isolating the Gaddafi regime financially and diplomatically, and to call for the establishment of a no-fly zone, which would require limited military intervention. In a remarkably short period of time, Cameron turned from being 'a reluctant to a passionate interventionist' (Wintour and Watt, 2011).

In the case of Libya, Cameron was pushing at an open door. Gaddafi lacked support regionally and internationally. Libya's neighbours, Tunisia and Egypt, were too caught up in their own internal unrest to want, or be able to, get involved. The Arab League quickly suspended Libya as a result of Gaddafi's crackdown, and in an unprecedented move, called on the United Nations Security Council (UNSC) to impose a no-fly zone over Libya. The Gulf Cooperation Council states were strongly anti-Gaddafi: Saudi Arabia had never forgiven him for funding a bungled assassination attempt on King Abdullah, while Qatar and the United Arab Emirates provided military, logistical and financial support to the opposition National Transition Council in Libya (Noueihed and Warren, 2012: 182). Even the Western businesses that had flooded Libya with investment for oil and gas exploration and extraction had lost faith with Libya by this point. Thus, limited military intervention in the case of Libya quickly came to be seen by Cameron as a viable option, especially in the face of air attacks on the Libyan population. Britain, France and Lebanon jointly proposed resolution 1973 to the UNSC, which was passed on 17 March 2011. Acting under Chapter VII of the UN Charter, the resolution identified events in Libya as a 'threat to international peace and security' (UN, 2011). This called for an immediate ceasefire in Libya, imposed a no-fly-zone over Libya, and extended the arms embargo, assets freeze and travel bans already in place. In particular, it authorised the use of all necessary means to protect civilians and civilian areas, except for a foreign intervention force (i.e. a ground invasion). The resolution accused the Gaddafi government of gross and systematic human rights abuses, and said that the attacks against the civilian population may amount to 'crimes against humanity' (ibid.). Military intervention began on 19 March, with attacks on Libya's air defence systems by a coalition of ten states including Britain, France, and the US. Thus, within less than a year of taking office, Cameron had committed Britain to humanitarian intervention which basically had regime change as its end goal.

Libya appeared to galvanise Cameron in the same way that Kosovo had Blair. The Opposition leadership, the National Transitional Council (NTC), was officially recognised by the UK as the sole governmental authority in Libya on 27 July 2011, when the Libyan chargé d'affaires was summoned to the FCO to be informed 'that he and other regime diplomats from the Qadhafi regime must leave the UK' (Hague, 2011).

The NTC was invited to appoint a new Libyan envoy, and Hague said that 'This decision marks another step towards a better, democratic future for Libya' (ibid.). However, the outcome of the overthrow of Colonel Gaddafi is still uncertain. After initial optimism about success of the ousting of the old regime, with Cameron receiving a hero's welcome and praising 'free Libya' during a trip to Benghazi in September 2011, Libya has become a fragile country, dominated by rival militias. In September 2012, the US Ambassador and three other embassy staff were killed in an attack on the Benghazi consulate by extremists, thought to belong to Islamist group Ansar al-Sharia. Women's rights have been suppressed, politicians and activists have been kidnapped and assassinated. The governing body, the General National Congress, has collapsed. Since May 2014, rival Islamist militias, non-Islamist militias, and militias loyal to various political groups and politicians, have been involved in a low-level civil war. As the Coalition government approaches the 2015 general election, Libya resembles post-invasion Iraq at its worst, but without Western troops on the ground. Unsurprisingly, the Coalition government has said little about the appalling situation that Libyans now find themselves in.

Syria and Iraq and the rise of ISIS

Libya is not the only country where Cameron has ended up considering military intervention, as protests in Syria turned into armed rebellion following the military response from the al-Assad government, with disparate state and non-state groups involved. The conflict became increasingly sectarian on the one hand, and globalised on the other, with an influx of foreign fighters. The opposition in Syria – the disparate groups doing the fighting on the ground – became increasingly radicalised with the arrival of fighters from Iraq and elsewhere, and the growing support for Jabhat al-Nusra, and for Islamic State of Iraq and the Levant (ISIS or ISIL, later renaming itself the Islamic State). Both these groups had as their goals the establishment of Sharia law and the creation of a pan-Islamic territory under its control.

Syria appeared to demonstrate the limits of Western power and influence. With increasing concern over the use of chemical weapons by the Assad government, the government proposed a motion that proposed a military response in Syria following a suspected chemical weapons attack on the outskirts of Damascus on 21 August 2013, in which hundreds of people were reported to have been killed. The motion that Cameron proposed, which was vaguely worded and rather difficult to understand, was that once the UN team investigating the use of chemical weapons had reported to the UN, and once every effort had been made to secure a UNSC resolution supporting the use of military force, and once a further vote on the use of military force had been made in the House of Commons, then the situation 'may, if necessary, require military action [involving Britain] that is legal, proportionate and focused on saving lives by preventing and deterring further use of Syria's chemical weapons' (Cameron, 2013). The motion was defeated by 285 votes to 272, with 30 Conservative and nine Liberal Democrat MPs voting against it.

In the discussion of the 'defeat' in Parliament on 29 August of the government's motion to support limited air strikes, much of the focus was on Cameron's political tactics and party management. However, while it was a humiliation for Cameron, and Hague has described it as the 'worst moment' during his tenure as Foreign Secretary (Hague, 2014), it was of deeper significance than that. It demonstrated the lack of confidence that MPs and the public had that any limited action, however small, would remain limited, and could achieve its goals. Afghanistan and Iraq have shown that despite the best of intentions, goals and strategy change during a conflict to reflect circumstances on the ground. In 2013, there was no appetite for military operations among the public in the West.

However, this did not signal the end of British policy on Syria or involvement in the wider consequences of the Arab uprisings. On 26 September, Nick Clegg, Deputy PM, announced to a meeting at the UN that Britain would be pledging another £100 million in humanitarian aid to the relief effort aimed at helping those displaced by the war, while Cameron increased Britain's military commitment to the Gulf region. There was an increase in the use of the naval base at Bahrain, and it was announced in January that a squadron of RAF Tornado jets were to be based at the al Minhad airbase south of Dubai (MOD, 2013). The UK increased the amount of training it was providing in Oman. Both the US and UK continued to provide security-related assistance and expertise to the Kurdish regional government, which was seen as a responsible ally in the region. This was at a time when the conflict in Syria was increasingly having an impact on its neighbours, in particular Iraq, where sectarian differences were intensified by the civil war in Syria. Sunnis tended to support the opposition groups, while Shias tended to support the Assad regime. Individuals and groups in Iraq have gone to Syria to take part in the fighting, on both sides. The government in Baghdad claimed to be neutral, but was concerned that if the Assad regime was replaced, either by the 'moderate' opposition or by more radical groups, then this would incite Sunnis in Iraq to try to overturn their government. This was what then happened, as political instability and sectarianism in Iraq intensified, and Sunni groups, demanding the overthrow of unpopular Prime Minister, Al Malaki, joined with the increasingly powerful jihadist group ISIS.

Within a few months, ISIS had managed to take nearly a third of Iraq with little resistance, with Iraqi forces and civilians fleeing from their onslaught. No longer was it the Assad regime that was seen as the problem, rather it was the unprecedented rise of ISIS. That ISIS had turned much of its attention to Iraq was not that surprising, as ISIS had its roots in Al Qaeda in Iraq (AQI), which had been formed by the Jordanian extremist, al-Zarqawi, and from May 2010 was led by Abu-Baker al-Baghdadi, who was of Iraqi origin, and who established ISIS headquarters in Iraq. However, the speed with which ISIS, a non-state actor, took control of northern and western Iraq, moving to within 50 miles of Baghdad, was shocking. While it was well funded, it is only estimated to have several thousand fighters, but was able to defeat the Iraqi national army. It was able to exploit sectarian differences, especially from Sunnis unhappy with the Baghdad government, and in particular with Iraqi Prime Minister, Nouri-al Malaki, who they argued had marginalised and victimised Sunni groups. The brutal behaviour of ISIS, including the mass executions of members of rival militant groups and civilians in addition to soldiers in Syria and Iraq, along with its actions in setting up an Islamic caliphate under its leadership, with state-like institutions in the areas it controls, even led Al Qaeda to disown ISIS in 2013. Preventing ISIS from taking control of a vast swath of the Middle East became a priority. Cameron declared in June 2014 that ISIS was also a threat to Britain, not only in terms of young British men becoming jihadists and then returning from fighting with ISIS in Syria and Iraq, but also in terms of ISIS planning direct attacks on the UK (Cameron, 2014a). The Iraqi government requested assistance, and following the resignation of Malaki, the US along with a coalition including Jordan and Saudi Arabia, began air strikes against ISIS in August. Later that month, ISIS released a propaganda video showing American hostage James Foley being beheaded by a militant with a British accent. The beheading of Western hostages, and the ethnic cleansing of non-Sunni civilians in the territories under ISIS control, resulted in a shift in British opinion. In September Cameron moved another motion on the limited use of force, this time in Iraq. Cameron condemned:

the barbaric acts of ISIL against the peoples of Iraq including the Sunni, Shia, Kurds, Christians and Yazidi and the humanitarian crisis this is causing; recognises the clear threat ISIL poses to the territorial integrity of Iraq and the request from the Government of Iraq for military support from the international community and the specific request to the UK Government for such support; further recognises the threat ISIL poses to wider international security and the UK directly through its sponsorship of terrorist attacks and its murder of a British hostage. (Cameron, 2014c)

He proposed, 'the use of UK air strikes to support Iraqi, including Kurdish, security forces' efforts against ISIL in Iraq' (ibid.). This time, the motion was comfortably passed, with 524 MPs supporting it, 43 voting against, and 59 abstaining. While avoiding the use of the term 'war on terror', this is what appeared to be happening.

However, at the same time as Britain's commitments in Iraq were unexpectedly increasing, Britain was withdrawing from Afghanistan. With the NATO mandate due to expire at the end of 2014, the last of the British troops were withdrawn from Helmand Province in October 2014, in line with the timetable announced by Cameron in 2012. The official end of Britain's 13-year campaign in Afghanistan received little publicity. After more than a decade of conflict, which had cost the lives of 453 British military personnel, the Taliban still controlled large swaths of Afghanistan, opium poppy cultivation was reported to be at an all time high (SIGAR, 2014), and any gains made in terms of human rights and education were fragile in the extreme. The first two Anglo-Afghan wars of 1839–42 and 1878–80, had been relatively short compared with this one. The longest, and one of the most intense conflicts that Britain had been involved in since the Second World War, Afghanistan had become so intractable, that the British public came to see intervention in Afghanistan as a failure. There was little in the way of optimism that Afghan security forces would be able to maintain stability and security, and the warning from history was that once foreign troops were withdrawn, the government left in place would have little legitimacy, being associated with a foreign power, and would be lucky to maintain control over Kabul and the main cities following a resurgence in conflict. The lesson that the Conservative Party took from the British experience in Helmand Province was that military intervention could not be successful without development intervention, and that Britain under Blair and Brown had not managed to combine the two.

Ukraine and Russian revanchism

One of the most unexpected challenges that the Coalition government had to face was Russian revanchism, and a rapid freeze in the West's relationship with Russia. Whereas Cameron had appeared relatively sanguine about relations with Russia in the early years of his premiership, he was quick to condemn Russia's actions towards Ukraine, and to work with the interim government following the ousting of President Victor Yanukovich. Yanukovich had been due to sign an 'association agreement' with the EU, but baulked at the last moment, presumably as a result of pressure from the Kremlin. Putin wanted Ukraine to join his new 'Eurasian Economic Union' of post-Soviet states instead. The resulting wave of protest led to the collapse of the government, and Yanukovich fleeing the country. Putin accused the West of aiding and abetting a coup in Ukraine. The events that followed, with the annexing of the Crimean peninsula and the unofficial role of Russian troops in supporting the pro-Russian paramilitary groups in Western Ukraine, seemed to herald a return to the tensions and distrust of the Cold War.

Britain's response to events was as expected given the circumstances – the government condemned Russia, implemented economic sanctions, suspended military cooperation and exports, while resisting any suggestions that there should be a military response to events in Ukraine. The propaganda war, however, was intense, with each side embracing a highly selective narrative. As far as the majority of the Russian population was concerned, Ukraine was part of their homeland, and not a separate country, and so as Putin argued, Russia had a responsibility to defend the rights of ethnic Russians living in Crimea. For the West, Ukraine was considered to be a sovereign, independent country, seeking to determine its own future. As Ukraine is the most important transit route for Russian oil and gas, this heightened the importance of events to both sides. Russia's military power and its ability to manipulate gas and oil supplies in Europe, meant that many countries were unwilling to get too involved. Diplomatic relations, already somewhat strained between Britain and Russia, deteriorated rapidly. At the NATO summit in Wales in September 2014, Cameron said that 'Russia is ripping up the rule book with its annexation of Crimea and its troops on sovereign soil in Ukraine' (Cameron, 2014b). NATO announced that it would be heightening its responsiveness by reforming the NATO Response Force, and establishing a Very High Readiness Joint Task Force, which could be deployed within two to five days to respond to challenges as they arise, particularly at the periphery of NATO's territory (NATO, 2014). At the end of the government's period in office, Ukraine looked set to become another 'frozen conflict' on the borders of Russia, with Ukraine's geo-strategic importance resulting in it becoming the potential fault line of a new Cold War.

International development

Finally, there have been some unexpected continuities in British external policy. Unusually for a Conservative Prime Minister, Cameron vowed to keep the DFID that had been established by Blair, and to protect the development budget. This was significant, for traditionally the Conservative Party has cut spending on international development when it has come into power, and the decision was taken to protect the development budget and to meet the commitment put in place by Blair of reaching the UN-endorsed target of spending 0.7 per cent of GNI on official development assistance by 2013. This decision was taken against a backdrop of cuts to all government departments apart from health, as Britain faced an austerity drive due to the economic downturn. In part it demonstrates the influence of New Labour on Cameron's Conservatives that there has been a degree of policy continuity in the area of international development. One of the key successes of the New Labour years was that the British focus on international development increased to the extent that it then became untenable for a younger generation of Conservatives to consider undoing the work that their predecessors had done. In 1996 funding for aid and international development was 0.26 per cent of GNI, roughly half the level at which it had stood when Labour had lost power in 1979, and by the time that Labour left office in 2010 expenditure on overseas development assistance stood at £8.45 billion, roughly 0.57 per cent of GNI (Institute for Fiscal Studies, 2012: 144). The 0.7 per cent goal was reached by the Coalition government in 2013, meaning that Britain became the first G7 country to meet this goal (HM Government, 2014: 6). The Coalition government has also continued the practice put in place by New Labour of working closely with international organisations and bringing in outside expertise to advise and sometimes deliver aid programmes.

There has been one perceptible shift in approach, however. While some non-governmental organisations (NGOs) have raised concern that aid distribution under the Coalition government has become 'securitised', in that aid distribution has been based on security value rather than recipient need, others have pointed out that the relationship is the other way round – security has become 'developmentalised' (Pugh *et al.*, 2013: 196). While retaining a commitment to the UN Millennium Development goals, the emphasis has shifted towards viewing development as a potential way of preventing conflict and security threats to the UK from arising. It was thought by those in government that this would allow the debate inherited from the Blair years on whether Britain has a moral responsibility to intervene militarily in order to solve conflict situations, to be bypassed. If, as many analysts and academics had concluded, security and development issues were linked, then the goal would be to focus on building resilience on the ground within the population. The 2010 Strategic Defence and Security Review stated that aid was one of the mechanisms through which threats could be tackled 'at source', by focusing on 'fragile and conflict-affected countries where the risks are high, our interests are most at stake and where we know we can have an impact' (HM Government, 2010b: 44). The National Security Strategy had promised that, 'We will promote development and combat poverty to reduce the causes of potential hostility', because '[f]ragile, failing and failed states around the world provide the environment for terrorists to operate as they look to exploit ungoverned or ill-governed space' (HM Government, 2010a: 25–26).

This new approach was epitomised by the *Building Stability Overseas Strategy* paper jointly produced by the DFID, the FCO and the MOD, in 2011 (HM Government, 2011). This outlined a new, cross-government strategy for dealing with fragile and conflict-affected states which aimed at preventing serious conflict from taking hold in the first place, through development aid and the promotion of democratic and legitimate political institutions. Thus, it represented a shift in strategy from state building and post-conflict reconstruction, to 'upstream' conflict prevention (ibid.). This was praised by NGOs such as Saferworld (Saferworld, 2011). For the first time, a government outlined how conflict prevention could be operationalised. This would be done by providing funding for the existing Conflict Pool so that it could take immediate action in response to warning signs that a conflict might be triggered, and it would be able to draw on Stabilisation Response Teams from across the FCO, DFID and the MOD that could be deployed to deal with conflict situations (HM Government, 2011). It was argued that this sort of approach would not only tackle drivers of instability, but would be vital in attempting to promote human security and to limit the enormous suffering caused by intra-state conflict. It is also likely that this was seen as a step towards developing the capacity to implement state building and development activities alongside future military interventions, and so prevent a repeat of the failures of the interventions in Afghanistan and Iraq.

However, whatever the hopes behind the *Building Stability Overseas Strategy*, the events of the Arab uprisings demonstrated that Britain still lacks the capacity to prevent conflict. Possibly the very idea that Britain has a moral imperative to prevent conflict around the world is something of a hangover from its imperial past. Cameron has been just as quick as Blair to assert Britain's 'moral' leadership, and it appears that he has not yet managed to develop a post-interventionist approach. Nevertheless, Cameron's interventionism 'has been characterised by a concerted effort to divorce himself from the messianic moral fervour of the post-9/11 Blair' (Daddow and Schnapper, 2013: 334). What the Coalition government has succeeded in demonstrating is that, to a large extent, bipartisanship over foreign policy does exist, as the battles between the Coalition partners have rarely been over foreign policy and international development, and that Cameron has managed to chart a more 'liberal' Conservative approach, distinct from the more traditional realpolitik associated with his predecessors, and distinct from the more ideological influences of neo-conservative groups on the fringes of the Conservative Party, such as the Henry Jackson Society. Cameron and Hague worked extremely effectively as partners but, like their Labour predecessors, found that the biggest challenge to charting British foreign policy was the need to respond to unforeseen events and threats in a rapidly changing world.

References

Beech, M. (2011) 'British Conservatism and Foreign Policy: Traditions and Ideas Shaping Cameron's Global View', *British Journal of Politics and International Relations*, 13(3): 348–63.

Cameron, D. (2006) Speech to the Conservative Party Conference, 4 October, http://news.bbc.co.uk/1/hi/uk_politics/5407714.stm (accessed 10 October 2014).

Cameron, D. (2011) Statement on Libya to the House of Commons, 28 February, col. 24, http://www.publications.parliament.uk/pa/cm201011/cmhansrd/cm110228/debtext/110228-0001.htm#11022819000029 (accessed 10 October 2014).

Cameron, D. (2013) Motion on Syria, House of Commons debates, 29 August, cols. 1425–6, http://www.publications.parliament.uk/pa/cm201314/cmhansrd/cm130829/debtext/130829-0001.htm#1308298000001 (accessed 7 October 2014).

Cameron, D. (2014a) Prime Minister's Questions, House of Commons debates, 18 June, col. 1108, http://www.publications.parliament.uk/pa/cm201415/

cmhansrd/cm140618/debtext/140618-0001.htm#14061868000015 (accessed 10 November 2014).

Cameron, D. (2014b) 'PM Speaks at North Atlantic Council Meeting', 5 September, Newport, Wales, https://www.gov.uk/government/speeches/nato-summit-2014-pm-speaks-at-north-atlantic-council-meeting (accessed 6 October 2014).

Cameron, D. (2014c) Motion on Iraq, House of Commons debates, 26 September, cols. 1255–6, http://www.publications.parliament.uk/pa/cm201415/cmhansrd/cm140926/debtext/140926-0001.htm#1409266000001 (accessed 7 October 2014).

Conservative Party (2010) *Invitation to Join the Government of Britain: Conservative Election Manifesto 2010* (London: Conservative Party).

Daddow, O. and Schnapper, P. (2013) 'Liberal Intervention in the Foreign Policy Thinking of Tony Blair and David Cameron', *Cambridge Review of International Affairs*, 26(2): 330–49.

Hague, W. (2010a) 'The biggest risk for Britain is five more years of Brown', Speech, 10 March, http://www.conservatives.com/News/Speeches/2010/03/William_Hague_The_biggest_risk_for_Britain_is_five_more_years_of_Brown.aspx (accessed 15 November 2010).

Hague, W. (2010b) 'Britain's values in a networked world', 15 September, Lincoln's Inn, London, https://www.gov.uk/government/speeches/foreign-secretary-britains-values-in-a-networked-world (accessed 13 October 2014).

Hague, W. (2010c) *Foreign and Commonwealth Office Business Plan 2010–2015* (London: FCO).

Hague, W. (2011) 'Libyan chargé d'affaires to be expelled from UK', 27 July. Available at: https://www.gov.uk/government/news/libyan-charge-d-affaires-to-be-expelled-from-uk (accessed 17 April 2012).

Hague, W. (2014) Interview given to the BBC, broadcast on BBC Parliament, 18 July, http://www.bbc.co.uk/news/uk-politics-28377955 (accessed 10 November 2014).

HM Government (2010a) *A Strong Britain in an Age of Uncertainty: The National Security Strategy*, Cm.7953 (London: The Stationery Office).

HM Government (2010b) *Securing Britain in an Age of Uncertainty: The Strategic Defence and Security Review*, Cm.7948 (London: The Stationery Office).

HM Government (2011) *Building Stability Overseas Strategy* (London: The Stationery Office), https://www.gov.uk/government/uploads/system/uploads/attachment_data/file/32960/bsos-july-11.pdf (accessed 26 November 2013).

HM Government (2014) *Annual Report and Accounts, 2013–14* (London: The Stationery Office), https://www.gov.uk/government/uploads/system/uploads/attachment_data/file/331591/annual-report-accounts-2013-14a.pdf (accessed 4 November 2014). See also https://www.gov.uk/government/statistics/statistics-on-international-development-2014.

Institute for Fiscal Studies, *UK Development Aid*, 2012, http://www.ifs.org.uk/budgets/gb2012/12chap7.pdf.

MOD (2013) 'New RAF unit strengthens relationship with UAE', 23 January, https://www.gov.uk/government/news/906-expeditionary-air-wing-stands-up-in-the-united-arab-emirates (accessed 10 October 2014).

NATO (2014) Wales Summit Declaration, 5 September, Newport, Wales, http://www.nato.int/cps/en/natohq/official_texts_112964.htm (accessed 6 October 2014).

Noueihed, L. and Warren, A. (2012) *The Battle for the Arab Spring: Revolution, Counter-Revolution and the Making of a New Era* (New Haven, CT: Yale University Press).

Pugh, J. *et al.* (2013) 'Beyond the Securitisation of Development: The limits of Intervention, Developmentisation of Security and Repositioning of Purpose in the UK Coalition Government's Policy Agenda', *Geoforum*, 44: 193–201.

Saferworld (2011) 'Saferworld Response to Building Stability Overseas Strategy', 19 July, http://www.saferworld.org.uk/resources/view-resource/563-saferworld-response-to-building-stability-overseas-strategy (accessed 5 November 2014).

SIGAR (Special Inspector General for Afghanistan Reconstruction) (2014) *Special Report, Poppy Cultivation in Afghanistan 2012–13*, SIGAR-15-10-SP, http://www.sigar.mil/pdf/special%20projects/SIGAR-15-10-SP.pdf (accessed 3 November 2014).

UN (2011) United Nations Security Council Resolution 1973, 17 March, http://www.un.org/en/ga/search/view_doc.asp?symbol=S/RES/1973(2011) (accessed 13 October 2014).

Vickers, R. (2003) *The Labour Party and the World. Volume 1. The Evolution of Labour's Foreign Policy 1900–51* (Manchester: Manchester University Press).

Vickers, R. (2011) 'The Con-Lib Agenda for Foreign Policy and International Development', in S. Lee and M. Beech (eds), *The Cameron–Clegg Government: Coalition Politics in an Age of Austerity* (Basingstoke: Palgrave Macmillan), pp. 203–17.

Wintour, P. and Watt, N. (2011) 'David Cameron's Libyan War', *The Guardian*, http://www.theguardian.com/politics/2011/oct/02/david-cameron-libyan-war-analysis (accessed 7 October 2014).

16
The Coalition and the European Union

Philip Lynch

Introduction

The Coalition Agreement stated that there would be no further transfer of powers to the European Union (EU) but promised that the government would be a positive participant. With Conservative proposals for renegotiation of parts of the Lisbon Treaty dropped and no prospect of the UK joining the euro, it appeared that there would be little change to the UK's relationship with the EU. Given the potential for the issue of European integration to both create tensions between the soft Eurosceptic Conservatives and pro-European Liberal Democrats and re-open divisions in the Conservative Party, David Cameron and Nick Clegg would have hoped for an uneventful period in the UK's troubled membership of the EU. However, the Coalition's period in office turned out to be potentially one of the most significant.

Even before the Coalition negotiations had concluded, it was becoming apparent that the EU was entering a critical period in its development and that European integration would become a difficult and divisive issue for the incoming government. Fears that Greece would default on its national debt had emerged during the UK general election campaign. On 2 May 2010, EU finance ministers responded by agreeing a bailout loan. Representing the UK, outgoing Labour Chancellor Alistair Darling committed the incoming government to contribute funds to a temporary bailout mechanism, the European Financial Stability Mechanism (EFSM). New Prime Minister David Cameron and his Chancellor George Osborne faced no-win scenarios: either the euro unravelled with damaging consequences for the

UK economy, or Eurozone Member States forged ahead with further economic integration in an attempt to rescue the euro but in so doing diminished UK influence. They preferred the latter. But Conservative Eurosceptics, who had been relatively quiescent in Opposition, saw the Eurozone sovereign debt crisis as an opportunity to press for radical change to the UK's membership of the EU.

Coalition formation

Differences between the soft Eurosceptic Conservative Party and pro-European Liberal Democrats were more apparent on the EU than on many other policy areas. The 2010 Conservative manifesto promised significant changes to the UK's relationship with the EU (Conservative Party, 2010). A Conservative government would introduce a 'referendum lock' requiring a popular vote to be held when competences were transferred to the EU, provide safeguards on the use of the EU's simplified revision procedure, and introduce a Sovereignty Bill to restate parliamentary authority. In the EU, it would seek to repatriate powers to the UK in three specific areas: the Charter of Fundamental Rights, criminal justice, and social and employment legislation. The UK would not join the euro under the Conservatives. The 2010 Liberal Democrat manifesto had a pro-European flavour but was cautious on Economic and Monetary Union (EMU), noting that the economic conditions for joining the euro were not right, and sought reform of the EU budget and the Common Agricultural Policy. It pledged to remain part of justice and home affairs measures such as the European Arrest Warrant and advocated EU regulation of financial services and banking. The Liberal Democrats also advocated an 'in-out' referendum the next time that a UK government signed up to 'fundamental change in the relationship between the UK and the EU' (Liberal Democrats, 2010).

European integration was a Conservative 'red line' in Coalition negotiations. They were unwilling to concede ground on the referendum lock and opposition to further European integration. But demands for the repatriation of powers were dropped as Nick Clegg insisted that there should be no renegotiation of EU membership under the Coalition (Adonis, 2013: 129). The Liberal Democrats wanted to ensure that the government would play a constructive role in the EU but accepted that there would be no further transfers of power or preparations for joining the euro.

The Coalition Agreement claimed to strike 'the right balance between constructive engagement with the EU to deal with the issues that affect us all and protecting our national sovereignty' (HM Government, 2010: 19). In language that balanced the pro-EU sympathies of the Liberal Democrats with Conservative Euroscepticism (Laws, 2010: 185), it promised that the UK would be a 'positive participant in the European Union, playing a strong and positive role with our partners' but that there would be 'no further transfer of sovereignty or powers over the course of the next Parliament'. The main domestic commitment was the Conservatives' 'referendum lock' but the Coalition would merely 'examine the case' for a Sovereignty Bill. There was common ground on EU reform, notably global competitiveness, completion of the single market, budget reform and ending European Parliament sessions in Strasbourg. Compromise was found on policing and criminal justice where the Agreement ruled out participation in a European Public Prosecutor system, but stated that other measures would be viewed 'on a case-by-case basis, with a view to maximizing our country's security, protecting Britain's civil liberties and preserving the integrity of our criminal justice system' (HM Government, 2010: 19). Conservatives took the key ministerial positions, with William Hague becoming Foreign Secretary and David Lidington Minister for Europe. Philip Hammond replaced Hague in 2014 and took a tougher line, arguing that the UK must be prepared to 'walk away' if attempts to reform the EU were unsuccessful. Unusually for a Minister for Europe, the more consensual Lidington remained in post for the duration of the parliament.

Coalition policy and the EU

The major domestic legislation was the European Union Act 2011. It introduced a 'referendum lock' requiring future treaties transferring powers from the UK to the EU to be put to a binding referendum after receiving parliamentary approval. A referendum will also be held if, for example, the UK joins the euro or abolishes border controls, and in selected cases where the EU uses the simplified revision procedure or enabling clauses. The Act also strengthened requirements for parliamentary approval of EU action. The government decided against a separate Sovereignty Bill. Instead, Section 18 of the European Act 2011 states that EU law only takes effect in the UK through the will of parliament. This is declaratory, has little practical effect and does not change the relationship between UK and EU law (Craig, 2011).

The European Union Act 2011 had little policy impact for the remainder of the Coalition's term in office. Referendums were not required on Croatian accession, Eurozone bailouts, the fiscal compact, or opting back in to the European Arrest Warrant. Although the Act signalled an extension in the use of referendums, requiring them not only on major changes but also on technical matters, it was not part of a wider constitutional reform programme. Nor was it sufficient to satisfy Eurosceptic Conservative MPs hungering for a referendum, as evidenced by Cameron's 2013 pledge to hold an 'in-out' referendum should the Conservatives win the 2015 general election. The referendum lock did, however, make it less likely that the next government would take part in further EU integration. A future parliament might amend the Act but Ed Miliband had promised to strengthen the lock to require an 'in-out' referendum should the UK sign a treaty transferring competences to the EU.

The Coalition Agreement also included a commitment to examine the balance of the EU's existing competences. The Review of the Balance of Competences was duly launched in 2012 and produced 32 reports on individual policy areas by December 2014. This was a technocratic audit led by civil servants which drew upon evidence submitted by a range of organisations. The reports were not intended to produce specific policy recommendations. They did identify divergent views on the EU's current competences but, in the majority of cases, those expressed did not significantly challenge either the status quo or current UK policy. The report on the free movement of persons was delayed after disagreements within the government. It found that the impact on the labour market had been 'largely positive' (HM Government, 2014a: 6) and did not find reliable evidence on the number of EU migrants claiming welfare benefits, but it noted concerns about low skilled migration and criminality. The report on EMU highlighted a number of areas of concern, including the growth of the Eurogroup, the prospect of it caucusing and the complexity of economic governance (HM Government, 2014b). Overall, the reports frustrated Eurosceptics who hoped that they would strengthen the case for a repatriation of powers.

The Eurozone crisis

The Eurozone sovereign debt crisis emerged as the dominant issue in the EU as the Coalition was taking office. It proved to be a critical moment in the evolution of the EU, with Eurozone states agreeing a 'roadmap' for the completion of EMU that hastened the development of a multi-speed Europe. The Coalition accepted that Eurozone states should strengthen EMU in order to resolve the crisis, arguing that this was in the interests of the UK as well as the EU (HM Government,

2014b: 84). But it was unwilling to pay for, and would not take part in, these measures. The UK did not contribute to the European Stability Mechanism, a permanent bailout facility replacing the temporary mechanism agreed by Darling, but did contribute via the International Monetary Fund and a bilateral loan to the Republic of Ireland. Nor did the UK sign the 2011 Euro Plus Pact which introduced greater financial coordination and tougher fiscal rules.

The 'fiscal compact' produced the first major EU policy disagreement between the UK and other Member States, and between Cameron and the Liberal Democrats. Cameron vetoed an EU fiscal compact treaty at a European Council meeting in December 2011 when his demands for additional safeguards on the single market and financial services were rejected. But within months, he accepted that 25 Member States (not the UK or Czech Republic) sign an intergovernmental Treaty on Stability, Coordination and Governance. Its signatories were required to write balanced budget provisions into their national law, with states in breach of deficit or debt criteria liable to face sanctions. Cameron relented on one of his earlier objections by accepting European Court of Justice (ECJ) involvement in non-compliance decisions. Cameron's veto had pleased his party and boosted his opinion poll ratings but angered other EU leaders and the Liberal Democrats.

With Eurozone states pursuing further integration, the Coalition sought additional guarantees that this would neither undermine the single market nor discriminate against non-Eurozone states. A fear was that, under qualified majority voting, Eurozone states could arrange to vote as a bloc on single market measures in order to protect their interests. The UK thus sought tougher voting thresholds. In the agreement on the Single Supervisory Mechanism, the UK secured a system of double majority voting in the European Banking Authority under which proposals require support from a majority of both Eurozone and non-Eurozone states (Dashwood, 2013). The government was also concerned that EU action on financial services would damage the City of London. It launched a series of legal challenges in the ECJ, notably on the Financial Transaction Tax (set to be introduced in ten Member States under the enhanced cooperation procedure), requirements for clearing houses with high-volume euro transactions to locate within the Eurozone, and a cap on bankers' bonuses. But the government withdrew the latter when the ECJ's Advocate General rejected its arguments.

The police and criminal justice opt-out

During the Coalition's tenure, differentiation in the EU also became more pronounced in justice and home affairs. Protocol 36 of the Lisbon Treaty gave the UK the right to opt-in or opt-out of some 130 police and criminal justice measures before they became subject to enforcement by the European Commission and ECJ on 1 December 2014. The Coalition announced in July 2013 that it would exercise this block opt-out but intended to opt back in to 35 measures, including Europol, Eurojust and the European Criminal Records Information System (HM Government, 2013a). MPs endorsed the formal application to rejoin the measures in 2014, but only after criticism of the government's handling of the process.

The most controversial measure was the European Arrest Warrant (EAW). Ministers regarded it as an 'essential weapon in the fight against crime', speeding up the process of extradition and making extradition possible from Member States with whom the UK had not previously had extradition arrangements (Home Affairs Committee, 2014: 2). But ministers had concerns about the disproportionate use of the EAW for minor offences, lengthy pre-trial detention of suspects and extradition for conduct that is not criminal in the UK. The Anti-social Behaviour, Crime and Policing Act 2014 sought to address these, notably by introducing a proportionality test to be applied by judges. But critics argued that tensions between the principle of mutual recognition and variable criminal standards remained.

Institutional issues

These debates reflected wider Conservative concerns about judicial activism. The party's 2010 manifesto had included demands for additional guarantees that the EU Charter of Fundamental Rights did not apply in the UK, but this did survive the Coalition negotiations. The issue resurfaced in 2013 when Justice Mostyn claimed in a High Court ruling that, despite Protocol 30 of the Lisbon Treaty on limits to its applicability in the UK, the Charter was now part of domestic law. The government rejected this interpretation (European Scrutiny Committee, 2014: 39). The government also failed in its attempt to block the nomination of former Luxembourg Prime Minister Jean Claude Juncker as President of the European Commission. Whereas John Major had vetoed Jean-Luc Dehaene's nomination in 1994, the decision was now subject to qualified majority voting rather than unanimity. The Lisbon

Treaty also required the European Council to 'take account' of the result of the elections to the European Parliament (EP) and consult the EP on candidates. The Euro-parties then devised the *Spitzenkandidaten* ('lead candidate') process in which the main political groups in the EP each named a candidate for Commission President. The candidates took part in debates during the elections, but not in the UK where Labour and the Liberal Democrats did not endorse their groups' candidates and the European Conservative and Reformist group did not field a candidate.

Cameron mounted a high-profile campaign to block Juncker's nomination. He argued, first, that Juncker did not have the right qualities to lead the Commission at a time when many voters were demanding reform. Second, he wanted the European Council to remain free to choose its own candidate rather than be required to accept the 'lead candidate'. There was some sympathy from other Member States for this view but once Merkel supported Juncker, Cameron faced a losing battle. The parliament had successfully extended its powers by linking the post of Commission President to the outcome of the elections and then threatening national governments with an inter-institutional crisis unless they approved Juncker. Cameron forced a vote in the European Council but only Hungary joined the UK in voting against Juncker. There was agreement to review the process but Member States will find it difficult to restore their primacy.

Alliance building

The Coalition's Mid-Term Review cited a number of examples of influence in the EU, including reform of the Common Fisheries Policy, agreement on a single European patent and the exemption of micro-businesses from new EU proposals (HM Government, 2013b). The government also helped bring about the first real-terms cut in the EU budget. Net contributors, notably Germany and the UK, demanded a reduction in the EU's 2014–20 Multiannual Financial Framework. Cameron threatened to veto a 5 per cent increase proposed by the Commission, but it was cooperation with Germany that proved decisive when the European Council agreed a 3 per cent reduction. The UK rebate was also maintained. Cameron had more difficulty with the annual EU budget on which he regularly opposed, but eventually accepted, increased expenditure. His exasperation was most apparent in October 2014 when the UK was presented with a £1.7 billion surcharge because of its relatively strong economic performance. Cameron threatened not to pay on time but Osborne struck a deal which he claimed halved the amount due and delayed payment, although the reduction resulted from the automatic application of the UK rebate. Overall, the UK's net annual contribution to the EU rose from £7.4 billion in 2010 to £10.5 billion in 2013, but was expected to decrease thereafter (HM Treasury, 2014).

Twelve Member States supported the government's 2011 'Let's Choose Growth' paper and the Commission launched new initiatives to complete the digital single market and markets in services and energy, and reduce regulation. A report from the Prime Minister's Business Task Force identifying 30 barriers to competitiveness was presented to the European Council and, within a year, 10 of the proposed measures had been delivered and there was progress on another 10 (HM Government, 2014c). The UK was also a strong supporter of the proposed Transatlantic Trade and Investment Partnership with the United States, estimating that liberalisation of non-tariff barriers could be worth up to £10 billion per annum to the UK economy (Centre for Economic Policy Research, 2013).

Although Cameron claimed that his veto of an EU fiscal compact treaty and forcing of a vote on Juncker's nomination showed his determination to fight for the UK's interest, his actions raised questions about his judgement and tactics as they frustrated other Member States without delivering great reward. Ministers from Member States otherwise sympathetic to the UK – including Germany, Poland and Sweden – were also critical of their British counterparts' language on migration and renegotiation.

Unsurprisingly, balancing the objectives of constructive engagement and protection of national sovereignty proved difficult. Although the government had some success in promoting and defending British interests, the UK was less influential in the EU at the end of the Coalition's term in office than it had been at the outset. Whereas previous governments feared the development of a two-speed Europe in which the UK is outside the core, the Coalition supported other Member States in pursuing further economic integration in order to rescue the euro. The price for this support would be safeguards for the UK and on the single market but it was not certain that these demands would be met in full (hence Cameron's fiscal compact veto) and, even if they were, UK influence would still be diminished. Furthermore, the Conservative vision of a flexible EU is not only one in which some Member States forge ahead with further integration, but also one in which some powers flow back to national governments. While further integration occurred there was no reciprocal repatriation of powers.

Cameron's Bloomberg speech

Cameron's January 2013 speech on the EU (the 'Bloomberg speech') was one of the most significant of his premiership. But it was a statement of intent for a future Conservative government not of Coalition policy, and continued the decoupling of Conservative and Liberal Democrat positions on the EU. The key announcement was that, should the Conservatives win the 2015 general election, Cameron would negotiate 'a new settlement' in the EU and then hold an 'in-out' referendum on whether the UK should remain in the EU (Cameron, 2013).

Cameron subsequently identified seven objectives for EU reform (Cameron, 2014). Some were limited and relatively uncontentious. These included national parliaments being able to work together to block EU legislation (replacing the existing 'yellow card' system with a 'red card'), 'businesses liberated from red tape', 'greater free trade with North America and Asia' and new mechanisms to prevent 'vast migrations' when new Member States join the EU. Another objective, UK policing and justice systems 'unencumbered by unnecessary interference from the European institutions' covered the European Court of Human Rights as well as the EU.

But some objectives were more far reaching and would likely require treaty change or a specific UK protocol. The goal of 'powers flowing away from Brussels, not always to it' might be limited to repeal of particular rules (e.g. the Working Time Directive) or encompass significant policy repatriation. Removing the phrase 'ever-closer union' would require treaty change. The June 2014 European Council agreed that 'the concept of ever-closer union allows for different paths of integration for different countries, allowing those that want to deepen integration to move ahead, while respecting the wish of those who do not want to deepen any further' (European Council, 2014: 11). But this did not mention repatriating powers.

Cameron's objective of restricting the right of EU migrants to claim welfare benefits was the most significant and difficult to achieve. This issue came to the fore when temporary restrictions on migrants from Bulgaria and Romania working in the UK expired in 2014. The Coalition introduced a number of restrictions on the benefits that EU migrants could claim. In a speech in November 2014, Cameron sought changes to the rules on free movement of EU citizens: denying access to tax credits and housing benefits for four years, preventing EU jobseekers from claiming Universal Credit, ending payment of child benefit to children living abroad, requiring EU citizens to have a job offer before entry, removing job seekers who do not find work within six months, new restrictions on the entry of non-EU family members, tougher measures to deport EU criminals and stricter bans on re-entry for beggars and others (Cameron, 2014). Some of these might require treaty change (Booth and Chalmers, 2014). Suggestions for an 'emergency brake' or a cap on the number of National Insurance numbers issued to EU migrants did not feature in the speech after they were criticised by other Member States. Some states shared British concerns about EU migrants' access to welfare benefits, but would not countenance the undermining of the principle of free movement.

Cameron's pledge of an 'in-out' referendum marked a change in position. But referendum pledges have often been used to defuse intra-party divisions and gain electoral advantage (Oppermann, 2013). Cameron's position on renegotiation was in tune with public opinion. YouGov consistently reported that, when asked if they would vote to leave or remain in the EU should Cameron renegotiate the UK's relationship with it, a majority of respondents said that they would vote to remain (YouGov, 2014). Parallels are evident with the 1975 referendum on the European Economic Community when Labour Prime Minister Harold Wilson persuaded voters that he had negotiated a better deal for the UK even though the changes he secured were limited. But convincing his party might prove more difficult for Cameron, and he risks leading the campaign to remain in the EU while many Conservatives campaign to leave.

Domestic challenges: tensions, divisions and the rise of UKIP

The domestic obstacles facing Cameron as he forged his EU policy were more challenging than those that had undermined the governments of Margaret Thatcher and John Major. Not only did he have to deal with divisions within the Conservative Party, as Thatcher and Major had done, he also had to manage relations with the Liberal Democrats and respond to the emergence of the UK Independence Party (UKIP) as a significant actor in British politics. The Liberal Democrats sought to prevent Cameron from straying beyond the terms of the Coalition Agreement (Goes, 2014). Tensions between the Coalition partners came to the fore when Cameron vetoed an EU fiscal compact treaty. Clegg had not expected the Prime Minister to resort to a veto and was publically critical of his actions, but he was then able to persuade Cameron to give ground. Following the Bloomberg speech, Clegg criticised Cameron for bowing to Eurosceptic pressure, antagonising other Member States, and setting an arbitrary timetable for a vote. Renegotiation and an 'i referendum were not part of the Coalition Agreement and the Liberaɪ Democrats would not allow Cameron to begin negotiations or introduce a government Bill on an 'in-out' referendum. Liberal Democrat MPs refused to support Private Member's Bills on the latter. Ministers did reach a compromise on police and criminal justice with the Liberal Democrats accepting the exercise of the block opt-out but insisting that the government opt back in to the EAW.

A perfect storm of factors re-opened Conservative divisions on European integration: the Eurozone crisis, the dilution of Conservative EU policy in coalition, the growth of hard Euroscepticism on the Conservative benches, ineffectual party management and the rise of UKIP. In the first three parliamentary sessions (May 2010–May 2014), 101 different Conservative MPs rebelled on EU issues and 44 votes on EU issues saw a rebellion. October 2011 brought the largest ever Conservative rebellion on European integration when 81 Conservative MPs defied a three-line whip to support a backbench motion on policy repatriation and a referendum (Cowley and Stuart, 2012). A year later, the government was defeated when 53 Conservative MPs voted with Labour to demand a real-terms cut to the EU budget. Cameron averted another major rebellion by taking the unprecedented step of granting Conservative backbenchers a free vote on an amendment to the motion on the 2013 Queen's Speech regretting the absence of a Bill on an EU referendum. He then backed Private Member's Bills introduced by James Wharton and Bob Neill requiring an 'in-out' referendum to be held by 2017, but neither was successful. Cameron had initially held his ground against Eurosceptic backbenchers, imposing a three-line whip on the 2011 EU referendum motion. Thereafter, he made concessions but, rather than satisfying Eurosceptic demands, dissent continued. While the renegotiation-referendum formula was one that much of the Conservative Party could agree upon, Eurosceptic MPs distrusted Cameron and scented further concessions.

The fault line in the Conservative Party was now between Eurosceptics seeking limited reform and those demanding fundamental renegotiation or withdrawal (Lynch and Whitaker, 2013a: 319). The Coalition's minimalist brand of Euroscepticism opposed further integration and looked to exploit existing opportunities for EU reform. The Bloomberg speech offered a 'minimal revisionist' strain of Euroscepticism in which some existing EU competences would be returned to the UK. But the centre of gravity in the Conservative Party had already shifted towards a 'maximal revisionist' outlook which demanded a fundamental renegotiation of the UK's relationship with the EU.

Although 'outright rejectionists' seeking immediate withdrawal were in a minority, the balance of Conservative opinion favoured far more radical changes than Cameron advocated. Cameron's reluctance to focus on the EU issue in Opposition, and then to set out objectives for EU reform had allowed harder Eurosceptics to seize the initiative (Copsey and Haughton, 2014). The Fresh Start Project, supported by more than 100 Conservative MPs, thus variously proposed an opt-out from the Charter of Fundamental Rights, an emergency brake mechanism, an unpicking of ECJ judgments and the repatriation of regional policy (Fresh Start Project, 2013). Ninety-five Conservative MPs urged Cameron to accept the European Scrutiny Committee's proposals for a parliamentary veto over current and future EU law (European Scrutiny Committee, 2013: 97). The Liberal Democrats were much more united on the EU issue. In Opposition, three shadow cabinet members – David Heath, Alistair Carmichael and Tim Farron – had resigned and 15 MPs rebelled on a referendum on the Lisbon Treaty (Cowley and Stuart, 2010: 143–4). But the only Liberal Democrat rebellion on EU issues during the Coalition came when Adrian Sanders supported the October 2011 referendum motion.

Historically, challenges to the Conservative Party from the Right have been short lived. In the inter-war years, Rothermere's Anti-Waste League and Beaverbrook's Empire Free Trade Crusade were vanquished or absorbed before they inflicted major damage. The threat posed by UKIP is more significant. The defections of Douglas Carswell and Mark Reckless, and their subsequent by-election victories, signalled that UKIP provided an attractive alternative for some MPs as well as voters from the Conservative Right. UKIP consistently scored over 10 per cent in opinion polls after 2012 and topped the popular vote in the 2014 European elections. The Conservatives lost significantly more of their 2010 general election support (some 20 per cent) to UKIP than did either Labour or the Liberal Democrats. Data from the British Election Study's Continuous Monitoring Survey for June 2010 to April 2013 showed that 42 per cent of UKIP supporters recalled voting for the Conservatives in 2010. UKIP continued to take more voters from the Conservatives than from Labour into late 2014, gaining a higher proportion of voters from the Conservatives in this period than it had taken from Labour under Blair or Brown. Among 2010 Conservative voters, those who disapproved of EU membership, were working class and older were most likely to defect.

The economic interests and social characteristics of working-class UKIP supporters are similar to 'Old Labour' voters (Ford and Goodwin, 2014), but their political attitudes place them on the Right. Some are ex-Conservatives, others the archetypal blue collar voters that the Conservatives used to attract but who now seem beyond their reach. Thatcherism's combination of social conservatism and an appeal to aspirational working-class voters won over the 'Tebbit Tories'. UKIP was now attracting significant support from this demographic, weakening Conservative attempts to establish a broad cross-class, national appeal.

UKIP framed the debates on the EU and immigration, linking the issues together and making it more difficult for the Conservatives to both lower their salience and claim policy success. Conservative efforts to counter UKIP's appeal were ineffective (Lynch and Whitaker, 2013b). Cameron's referendum pledge was a necessary part of the response, but was not sufficient because many defectors had wider concerns and did not trust him (Ford and Goodwin, 2014). His proposals for reform of EU migration rules would be difficult to deliver, thus risking further damage to the party's credibility, and raised the salience of an issue on which UKIP now outpolled the Conservatives. The Liberal Democrats lost more than two-thirds of their 2010 support when in Coalition, but only some 10 per cent of this went to UKIP. However, Clegg took on Nigel Farage in two televised debates ahead of the 2014 European elections. He hoped to reinforce his party's distinctive pro-European message and shore up its core support. But post-debate polling gave Farage 'victory' and the Liberal Democrats lost all but one of their seats in the EP, trailing in fifth place in the popular vote.

Conclusion

The Coalition government could prove to be one of the most significant in shaping the UK's relationship with the EU. However, the key policy changes in this period resulted from developments in the Eurozone and pledges made by the Conservatives rather than government initiatives. The UK has long been an 'awkward partner' in the EU, but became more isolated and less influential under the Coalition, sitting outside of the Eurogroup, opting out of many police and criminal justice measures and seeking reform in other policy areas. This raised fundamental questions about the UK's future relationship with the EU which the Coalition did not and, given the tensions between and within the two parties, could not, address effectively.

The prospect of a referendum on EU membership also moved closer and withdrawal from the EU was no longer unthinkable. Cameron described himself as a 'practical, sensible' Eurosceptic (Kirkup, 2010) early in his premiership, but subsequently paved the way for radical change by pledging to negotiate a new settlement with the EU and hold an 'in-out' referendum. His policy shift was a tactical response to intra-party divisions and the rise of UKIP, but has potentially momentous consequences for the UK and the EU, as well as his party. For Cameron, the risks are that renegotiation delivers little, the Conservative Party splits and the UK leaves the EU. However, in the best case scenario for Cameron, renegotiation and an 'in-out' referendum would resolve Conservative divisions over European integration, give Conservative policy on the EU greater legitimacy and provide a clearer footing for the UK's relationship with the EU.

Before a referendum, the Conservatives will have to resolve key strategic dilemmas. On EU reform, the changes identified by Cameron might be difficult to achieve but are still unlikely to satisfy those Conservative MPs who want fundamental renegotiation. With EMU entry off the agenda, the options facing all major British political parties could boil down to limited influence in a reformed EU or limited influence outside it. An increasing number of Eurosceptics argue that the latter is now preferable and will bring economic benefits (e.g. Lawson, 2013). However, much of British business favours EU reform and opposes withdrawal (TheCityUK, 2013; Confederation of British Industry, 2013). In the near future, the Conservatives might be forced to choose between their historic roles as the defender of national sovereignty and of the interests of property.

References

Adonis, A. (2013) *Five Days in May: The Coalition and Beyond* (London: Routledge).

Booth, S. and Chalmers, D. (2014) What are the Legal Implications of David Cameron's Proposed Reforms to EU Migration? (London: Open Europe). www.openeurope.org.uk/intelligence/immigration-and-justice/legal-implications-david-camerons-proposed-reforms-eu-migration/ (accessed 20 December 2014).

Cameron, D. (2013) EU speech at Bloomberg. London, 23 January.

Cameron, D. (2014) Speech on immigration and the EU. Rocester, Staffordshire, 28 November.

Centre for Economic Policy Research (2013) *Estimating the Economic Impact on the UK of a Transatlantic Trade and Investment Partnership (TTIP) Agreement between the European Union and the United States* (London: Centre for Economic Policy Research).

Confederation of British Industry (2013) *Our Global Future* (London: Confederation of British Industry).

Conservative Party (2010) *Invitation to Join the Government of Britain: The Conservative Manifesto 2010* (London: Conservative Party).

Copsey, N. and Haughton, T. (2014) Farewell Britannia? 'Issue Capture' and the Politics of David Cameron's 2013 EU Referendum Pledge. *Journal of Common Market Studies*, 52, supplement 1: 74–89.

Cowley, P. and Stuart, M. (2010) Where Has All the Trouble Gone? British Intra-Party Divisions during the Lisbon Ratification. *British Politics*, 5: 133–48.

Cowley, P. and Stuart, M. (2012) The Cambusters: the Conservative European Union Referendum Rebellion of October 2011. *The Political Quarterly*, 83: 402–6.

Craig, P. (2011) The European Union Act 2011: Locks, Limits and Legality. *Common Market Law Review*, 48: 1915–44.

Dashwood, A. (2013) The United Kingdom in a Re-Formed European Union. *European Law Review*, 38: 737–56.

European Council (2014) *Conclusions of the European Council 26–27 June*. EUCO 79/14. (Brussels: European Council).

European Scrutiny Committee (2013) *Reforming the European Scrutiny System in the House of Commons*. 24th Report, 2013–14. HC 109. (London: House of Commons).

European Scrutiny Committee (2014) *The Application of the EU Charter of Fundamental Rights in the UK: a State of Confusion*. 43rd Report, 2013–14. HC 979. (London: House of Commons).

Ford, R. and Goodwin, M. (2014) *Revolt on the Right. Explaining Support for the Radical Right in Britain* (London: Routledge).

Fresh Start Project (2013) Manifesto for Change. www.eufreshstart.org/downloads/manifestoforchange.pdf (accessed 20 December 2014).

Goes, E. (2014) The Coalition and Europe: a Tale of Reckless Drivers, Steady Navigators and Imperfect Roadmaps. *Parliamentary Affairs*, 67: 45–63.

HM Government (2010) *The Coalition: Our Programme for Government* (London: The Cabinet Office).

HM Government (2013a) *Decision Pursuant to Article 10 of Protocol 36 to the Treaty on the Functioning of the European Union*. Cm. 8671 (London: Home Office).

HM Government (2013b) *The Coalition: Together in the National Interest. The Mid-Term Review* (London: The Cabinet Office).

HM Government (2014a) *Review of the Balance of Competences between the United Kingdom and the European Union Single Market: Free Movement of Persons* (London: Home Office).

HM Government (2014b) *Review of the Balance of Competences between the United Kingdom and the European Union Economic and Monetary Policy* (London: HM Treasury).

HM Government (2014c) *Cut EU Red Tape – One Year On* (London: Department for Business, Innovation and Skills).

HM Treasury (2014) *European Union Finances 2014: Statement on the 2014 EU Budget and Measures to Counter Fraud and Financial Mismanagement*. Cm. 8974 (London: HM Treasury).

Home Affairs Committee (2014*): Fourth Special Report – Pre-Lisbon Treaty EU Police and Criminal Justice Measures: the UK's 2014 Opt-in Decision: Government Response* to the Committee's *9th Report of Session 2013–14*. HC 954 (London: House of Commons).

Kirkup, J. (2010) 'David Cameron says he is a "Eurosceptic" following EU "deal"'. *Daily Telegraph*, 29 October.

Laws, D. (2010) *22 Days in May: The Birth of the Lib-Dem Conservative Coalition* (London: Biteback).

Lawson, N. (2013) 'I'll be Voting to Quit the EU', *The Times*, 7 May.

Liberal Democrats (2010) *Liberal Democrat Manifesto 2010* (London: Liberal Democrats).

Lynch, P. and Whitaker, R. (2013a) Where There is Discord, Can They Bring Harmony? Managing Intra-Party Dissent on European Integration in the Conservative Party. *British Journal of Politics and International Relations*, 15: 317–39.

Lynch, P. and Whitaker, R. (2013b) Rivalry on the Right: the Conservatives, the UK Independence Party (UKIP) and the EU issue. *British Politics*, 8: 285–312.

Oppermann, K. (2013) The Politics of Discretionary Government Commitments to European Integration Referendums. *Journal of European Public Policy*, 20: 684–701.

TheCityUK (2013) *UK and the EU: A Mutually Beneficial Relationship* (London: TheCityUK).

YouGov (2014) *Political Tracker: Europe (Referendum)* www.d25d2506sfb94s. cloudfront.net/cumulus_uploads/document/2psmw7yj4t/YG-Archives-Pol-Trackers-Europe-Referendum-151214.pdf (accessed 20 December 2014).

17
The Coalition: A Transformative Government?

Matt Beech[1]

Paul Addison concludes his famous study of British politics during the Second World War by stating, 'Such was Mr Attlee's consensus, the new dispensation which began after Dunkirk in 1940, and until recent years seemed to be the natural order of British politics. We were all – *almost* all – Butskellites then' (Addison, 1975: 278). Whether one agrees with Addison that there was a period from 1940 until the election of Margaret Thatcher to the office of the leader of the Conservative Party in 1975, which can meaningfully be understood as a consensus in British politics, or whether we interpret this period in rather less anodyne terms, it is, nonetheless, a fruitful starting point to examine whether the Conservative–Liberal Coalition has been a transformative government. Without an appreciation of post-war British politics one lacks the necessary historical data to measure the 2010–15 Coalition. Addison's thesis is well known; the Labour governments of 1945–50 and 1950–51 set in motion a set of far-reaching social, industrial, foreign and defence reforms underpinned with the economic doctrine of Keynesian demand management, and it is because subsequent Conservative governments did not stray significantly from Labour's post-war policy diet, that it came to be regarded as 'Mr Attlee's consensus' (ibid.). This acquiescence was the pattern of politics until the emergence of the Conservative New Right which directly challenged the so-called post-war consensus. But notions of post-war consensus should not imply a harmonious society. In social terms, class remained English society's great sin and, during the mid-century decades, stark differences between people affected most areas of social intercourse, and yet, through education, social mobility was rising. In economic terms, Britain had experienced approximately a decade and a half of full employment and rising affluence, but as Keith Middlemas points out, 'Popular memory of a long postwar boom was of course an illusion, as debate even in the 1960s about Britain's relative economic decline revealed' (Middlemas, 2001: 216). Signs of social and economic upheaval appeared in the 1960s as a portent of the challenges to come in the significantly disruptive following decade.

Referring to Joseph Chamberlain, Winston Churchill wrote that he 'was the one who made the weather' (Churchill, 1941: 58), and today that phrase has passed into the political lexicon to refer to a politician of such significance and originality that they *transformed* politics. When used to describe a politician this is an exceptionally bold claim. The vast majority, including Prime Ministers, do not get close to such an epithet. But what of governments? An argument can be made that practically all post-war governments made their mark – save the brief administration of Sir Alec Douglas-Home 1963–64 – but the necessary condition is whether a government *transformed* British politics. For example, the Suez Crisis of 1956 instigated by Conservative Prime Minister Anthony Eden, negatively affected the special relationship with the United States and informed the rest of the world that Britain was clearly no longer a superpower; this a notable change, albeit a deleterious one. The Conservative government of Edward Heath 1970–74, experienced huge challenges of governability but left a changed country in that the UK was finally admitted into membership of the European Economic Community. To some this single achievement would suggest political and economic *transformation*. What is quite clear is that a government's impact can be for good or ill and it can be in a particular arena or spread across a range of policy areas. The debate around the *transformational* quality of a government on the politics of Britain is always going to be subject to normative considerations. The best one can hope for is robust evidence to support one's interpretation of political history.

In the post-war era two governments are worthy of Churchill's soubriquet: the Labour governments led by Attlee and the Conservative governments led by Thatcher. Attlee himself was not the pre-eminent figure of the post-war era who 'made the weather', though his longevity in front-line British politics is impressive. That title belongs to Thatcher, with Tony Blair not far behind. Anthony Seldon argues that, 'Blair should be seen in history as Labour's most successful party leader ... But for the Iraq War, he might have been considered one of the great prime ministers, on a par with Attlee and Thatcher' (Seldon, 2007: 650). Speaking of Thatcher, Peter Riddell suggests, 'Unlike all other postwar British prime ministers, she became an icon. The Thatcher myth became embedded in the minds of politicians and the public as much as the reality of the Thatcher years' (Riddell, 2001: 80). She exemplified the philosophy of her administrations. Though more pragmatic than often noted (Young, 1990), the combination of her passion for the battle of ideas with an ability to effectively communicate her values beyond her party's heartlands, and her single-mindedness and dogmatism, resulted in the ideology we know as Thatcherism. Attlee's feats were no less impressive, just different and less personalised. His temperament and class background, and his sometimes barely concealed reticence for policy, implies he was a Prime Minister with a 'hinterland' and a world beyond Westminster: family, cricket and reading. In contrast, Thatcher, more akin to Lloyd-George and Churchill, was a political animal. Major Attlee's great gifts were to keep order and effectiveness in the face of fire. His steadfastness enabled him to manage the invidious, unparalleled conditions of a battle-weary and practically bankrupt Britain. He somehow survived the plots of Herbert Morrison and Hugh Dalton; managed the personalities of Aneurin Bevan and Stafford Cripps; and forged an invaluable, if somewhat unlikely, friendship with Ernest Bevin. In a heavyweight Cabinet full of independent-mindedness, talent and egos, Major Attlee held the line as he did in Gallipoli and then on the Western Front. Thatcher was more of a General; there to inform her senior officers of the invasion plan and demanding utter loyalty with the minimum of fuss.

While Thatcher is the pre-eminent post-war figure, her governments come a close second to Attlee's in their transformational pedigree. In my reading of post-war history, Attlee's Labour government of 1945 had a greater mandate than Thatcher's Conservatives in 1979, and they had the greater task of peace-time reconstruction. Despite three consecutive election victories and the longest prime ministerial tenure of the twentieth century, Beer argues that 'less was accomplished, however than the rhetorical display suggests' (Beer, 2001: 38). When compared directly to Attlee this seems true. Kenneth Morgan illustrates how and why Attlee's governments deserve to be ranked as the most effective:

> The Attlee government was thus unique in its structural cohesiveness and in its legislative vitality. Its legacy lived on in a broad influence over the Labour and progressive left, over political and economic thought and, indeed, over much of British intellectual and cultural life for a full quarter of a century after 1951. (Morgan, 1985: 503)

In an unsurprisingly divergent view, expressed by Cameron on the announcement of Thatcher's passing, he gave the following tribute:

[...] Margaret Thatcher – who rescued our country from post-war decline. They say that cometh the hour, cometh the man. Well in 1979 came the hour, and came The Lady. She made the political weather. She made history. And let this be her epitaph: that she made our country great again. (Cameron, 2013)

While it was predictable to hear such fulsome praise from a fellow Conservative Prime Minister, it does reveal how the legacy of Thatcher and Thatcherism is viewed by the Conservative elite. For Cameron and his supporters – although much more socially liberal than the New Right – share Thatcher's economic liberalism and Euroscepticism (Beech, 2009). Cameron was not merely speaking for himself or his liberal Conservatives but for the foot soldiers and supporters of the Conservative Party, when he declared Thatcher, Britain's political saviour. What is measurable is the extent to which both Attlee and Thatcher's governments survived economic crises and wars fought half a world away; both confronted internal party disputes which threatened their premierships; both recast political debate in Britain. Their respective legislative legacies not only determined the road of travel for their opponents, but also *transformed* British public life for generations to come. Attlee's achieved this through the development of a vast welfare state, including the establishment of the National Health Service, nationalising approximately 20 per cent of industry, a tripartite industrial relations strategy, deciding to acquire the nuclear bomb, driving Britain's membership of NATO, planning for full employment and an economy run on Keynesian principles. This vision transformed the country because it left as a distant memory the 'hungry thirties' – the product of laissez-faire capitalism – and changed the role of British government in the lives of people. In an intentionally different way, Thatcher's administrations cut direct taxation, privatised state-managed and state-owned industries and companies, embarked upon trade union reform, sold off council houses to their tenants, deregulated the City of London and utilised monetarist theory. Her vision, in contradistinction to Attlee's, was to restore personal liberty and roll back the frontiers of government through a re-birthed economic liberal capitalism. Having established the *bona fide* credentials of the two *transformative* post-war British governments, we now turn our attention to the Conservative–Liberal Coalition.

Transformative or reformist?

The true impact of a government and, in this context, its *transformative* character can only be fully understood in the subsequent years. The purpose of the remainder of this chapter is to hypothesise the extent to which the Coalition will be considered a *transformative* or merely a reformist government.

Effects of coalition

First, that the Conservative–Liberal Coalition was formed by agreement (Cabinet Office, 2010) and has lasted a full parliamentary term is a *transformative* event in post-war British politics. This is no mean feat given that the two parties substantially disagree on the European Union, immigration, defence, the constitution and environmental policy (Conservative Party, 2010; Liberal Democrats, 2010). When one considers the contrasting traditions of the two organisations – the Conservative Party as the most successful British political party and the Liberal Democrat Party born of a merger of two parties in 1988 which, until May 2010, had known only the politics of opposition at Westminster – it is significant but not sufficient to make it a *transformative* government. Several related points follow:

1. Voting for third parties such as the Liberal Democrats is no longer seen as a wasted vote because they can realistically hold the balance of power in a hung parliament. For supporters of minor parties the argument from the Conservative and Labour parties of a 'wasted vote' had traditionally been the biggest obstacle in persuading the electorate to give their support.
2. It is a Conservative-led Coalition. The numerical advantage of the Conservatives in the Coalition has meant that the Quad – an inner cabinet comprising Cameron, George Osborne, Nick Clegg and Danny Alexander – has been necessary to facilitate cohesiveness.
3. Coalition has proved to be something of a cautionary tale for the Liberal Democrats. They have suffered great reputational harm from partnership with the Conservative Party. They are perceived to have won few policy battles, largely due to only having a handful of Cabinet Ministers, and to have sacrificed principle. Their victories include the substantial increase of the tax-free threshold, the Pupil Premium, and the 'triple lock' on the basic state pension, and their most famous U-turn was on the £9,000 per year university tuition fees. Liberal Democrat poll rating, according to the YouGov/Sunday

Times poll on 6 February 2015, was 7 per cent, placing them fifth behind the Green Party (Wells, 2015).

4. After five years of Conservative–Liberal Coalition all four nations of the Union have multi-party politics and the British electorate is more divided than at any period in post-war history. The growth of the SNP in Scotland; the rise of UKIP in England which itself is split between Labour urban versus Conservative rural and semi-rural constituencies; the strength of Labour in Wales; and of course the sectarian politics of Northern Ireland reveal this fact (New Statesman, 2015).

Economy

Second, the economic liberalism of Cameron's Conservative-led Coalition evinces a continuity – bar social ethics and foreign policy – with that of the Thatcher and Major governments. This liberalism is the glue that binds the Coalition partners and it is a reasonably successful ideological project. The Coalition has failed in its primary goal to clear the deficit by the end of the parliament and to significantly reduce the cost of the state. Between April and December 2014 the state spent £516.8 billion (Office for National Statistics, 2015: 2). The deficit, though smaller, remains. The Office for Budgetary Responsibility (OBR) forecasts that it will be £91.3 billion in the financial year 2014–15 (OBR, 2014: 5). As Carl Emmerson and Gemma Tetlow of the Institute for Fiscal Studies state:

> Between 2010 and 2012, the outlook for economic growth and tax revenues deteriorated. The coalition government decided not to increase the fiscal tightening planned for this parliament but to extend the period of consolidation into the next. Consequently, the coalition government has borrowed more than planned over this parliament: over the five years from 2010–11 to 2014–15, borrowing is now estimated to have been around £100 billion higher than forecast in the November 2010 Autumn Statement. (Emmerson and Tetlow, 2015: 10)

The politics of austerity has not come in on time or on budget. Its costs are enormous in terms of unemployment, poverty, social upheaval and degradation in the quality of essential public services. The Big Society narrative quietly faded early in the life of the Coalition. But the determination behind the idea to supplant Britain's social democratic state continues unabated.

The Coalition effect on domestic policy

Third, Coalition domestic public policy is a mixed bag of reform with both continuities and discontinuities, rather than a *transformative* politics. Education policy in England has continued along the market-based reforms of the Blair era, although Academies under the Coalition serve a different demographic and Free Schools represent a significant step-change which has been both relatively unsuccessful and unapologetic in seeking to reduce the influence of Local Education Authorities. The NHS has been subject to yet another central government reorganisation with privatisation the modus operandi. As Stuart Hall asserts:

> GPs, grouped into private consortia (part of whose profits they retain), will take charge of the £60 billion health budget. Since few GPs know how or have time to run complex budgets, they will 'naturally' turn for help to the private health companies, circling the NHS like sharks waiting to feed. (Hall, 2011: 720)

Though it has not experienced the level of cuts in percentage terms that other public services have endured since the Spending Review in 2010 (HM Treasury, 2010), the NHS requires constant investment to keep pace with the inflationary rises in medical equipment and drugs. In addition, each year Britain's ageing population is making increasing demands on the health and social care systems which, unless they are progressively funded, will continue to fail to meet public needs and expectations. The lack of sustained funding and overt privatisation in the form of Clinical Commissioning Groups is a discontinuity with the approach of previous governments.

On social issues, as I state in my opening chapter, Cameron's Conservatives are distinct from the mainstream of conservative opinion inside and outside of the Conservative Party. Here the social liberalism of Cameron's Conservatives and Clegg's *Orange Book* Liberal Democrats is in continuity with the liberal-left in British politics and the metropolitan middle classes across the country. The passing of the Marriage (Same-Sex Couples) Act 2013 (HM Government, 2013) could be understood as the final step in a long campaign for equal rights for gay people. This is in continuity with New Labour's gay rights legislation. But, by the Act's historic nature – which changes the definition of marriage – it can also be understood as a radical discontinuity in British family policy. In a sense, this piece of legislation is *transformative* in the minds of its supporters and its opponents but insufficient to make the Coalition a *transformative* government.

The Conservative–Liberal Coalition might well have been expected to push hard for the 'green agenda' but it has proved to be something of an irritant when the main issue has been deficit reduction and the search for economic growth. A less green government than New Labour marks this area as a discontinuity with its predecessors. With the significant net rise in both EU and international immigration to the United Kingdom in recent times, immigration is near the top of most voters' concerns. Rising immigration combined with the politics of austerity, which has impacted job prospects, schooling, social housing and GP and hospital waiting times, and the liberalism of the Conservative–Liberal Coalition, has opened up political space for UKIP to come of age. With no British Bill of Rights to supplant the Human Rights Act and no radical action on the European Convention on Human Rights, despite the amount of anger it seems to cause in the Conservative Party, broad continuity is the story on issues of justice and home affairs. Constitutional issues have continued to separate Coalition partners and, bar the Fixed-term Parliaments Act 2011 (HM Government, 2011), there has been no significant reform let alone *transformation*.

The Coalition effect on the four nations

The future of the Union appears to be intact, for now, with a clear victory for the 'Better Together' campaign in September 2014. Despite the strong 'Yes' vote, the issue of Scottish independence has stepped off centre stage. However, the Edinburgh Agreement had the potential to be *transformative* and, arguably, still could prove to be in the future, as the SNP are presently Scotland's ascendant political party. For Wales there has been continuity in devolution and this can be evidenced in the 2011 referendum through which a public mandate was won for greater primary legislative powers. Northern Ireland's politics remain something of a distinct affair with difficult decisions to be made over reductions in public expenditure and the foundational issues of community cohesion and an end to sectarianism. England is a case-study in continuity governance. The 'English Question' remains unanswered, but for how long? When it finally arrives it surely will be a political headache for the Labour Party.

The Coalition effect on foreign policy

The Coalition's foreign policy has not been *transformative*. As I note in my chapter, it has continued with New Labour's liberal interventionism, albeit with a more tempered approach. Libya, and parliament's veto of Cameron's intention to intervene in Syria, evidence this. Nonetheless, for Conservatives, this idealist approach to international relations is a discontinuity, as is the 0.7 per cent of GDP commitment to international development funding. The cuts to the Ministry of Defence have been notable and have affected Britain's military capability – another discontinuity. The UK's membership of the European Union has witnessed little substantive reform. Cameron's promise of an 'in-out' referendum under a majority Conservative government could, if a majority of the electorate opted for 'out' be classed a *transformative* act in contemporary British politics, but this is a long way off and by no means a foregone conclusion.

In conclusion, the Conservative–Liberal Coalition is a reformist rather than *transformative* government. It has not marked a paradigm shift in British politics but is one largely defined by continuities with some notable discontinuities. And yet, after five controversial and economically stagnant years, the ideological project of Cameron and Clegg has significantly affected the landscape of politics in Britain. The Coalition's politics of austerity (the means) to clear the deficit (the end) might have run out of time in the 2010 parliament, but it could still prove to be the *transformational* act of the era. A pertinent related question is whether Britain's welfare state can ever recover to previous levels of funding, support and provision. For some this might seem a technocratic concern or merely a focus on a particular area of policy, but given the politics of austerity – with contracting welfare provision and increasingly divested state responsibility – there is a great concern that welfare capitalism in Britain is dying, and, rather more quickly in England. Can citizens expect a return to a more collective and solidaristic ethos or have the Conservative–Liberal Coalition – inspired by Thatcher – potentially triumphed where she failed? The answer to this question remains to be seen.

Note

1. I am grateful to Simon Lee for commenting on an earlier draft and to Timothy J. Oliver for discussions about the Liberal Democrats. Any errors are, of course, my own.

References

Addison, P. (1975) *The Road to 1945: British Politics and the Second World War* (London: Jonathan Cape).

Beech, M. (2009) 'Cameron and Conservative Ideology', in Lee, S. and Beech, M. (eds) *The Conservatives under David Cameron: Built to Last?* (Basingstoke: Palgrave Macmillan), 18–30.

Beech, M. (2011) 'A Tale of Two Liberalisms', in Lee, S. and Beech, M. (eds) *The Cameron–Clegg Government: Coalition Politics in an Age of Austerity* (Basingstoke: Palgrave Macmillan), 267–79.

Beer, S. (2001) 'The Rise and Fall of Party Government in Britain and the United States 1945–96: The Americanisation of British Politics?' in James, S. and Preston, V. (eds) *British Politics Since 1945: The Dynamics of Historical Change* (Basingstoke: Palgrave), 18–50.

Cabinet Office (2010) *The Coalition: Our Programme for Government* (London: Stationery Office).

Cameron, D. (2013) Tribute to Lady Margaret Thatcher by Prime Minister David Cameron (London: Cabinet Office). https://www.gov.uk/government/speeches/tribute-to-lady-margaret-thatcher-by-prime-minister-david-cameron (last accessed 29 January 2015).

Churchill, W. S. (1941) *Great Contemporaries* (London: Reprint Society).

Conservative Party (2010) *Invitation to Join the Government of Britain* (London: Conservative Party).

Emmerson, C. and Tetlow, G. (2015) 'Public Finances under the Coalition', in Emmerson, C., Johnson, P. and Joyce, R. (eds) *The IFS Green Budget 2015* (London: Institute for Fiscal Studies), 10–32. http://www.ifs.org.uk/publications/7530 (last accessed 7 February 2015).

Hall, S. (2011) The Neo-liberal Revolution. *Cultural Studies*, 25(6): 705–28.

HM Government (2011) *The Fixed-term Parliaments Act* (London: Stationery Office).

HM Government (2013) *The Marriage (Same-Sex Couples) Act* (London: Stationery Office).

HM Government and Scottish Government (2012) *Edinburgh Agreement* (London: Stationery Office). https://www.gov.uk/government/uploads/system/uploads/attachment_data/file/313612/scottish_referendum_agreement.pdf (last accessed 8 February 2015).

HM Treasury (2010) *Spending Review 2010*. Cm 7942 (London: Stationery Office).

Liberal Democrats (2010) *Liberal Democrat Manifesto 2010* (London: Liberal Democrats).

Middlemas, K. (2001) 'When did Postwar Britain End?' in James, S. and Preston, V. (eds) *British Politics Since 1945: The Dynamics of Historical Change* (Basingstoke: Palgrave), 200–18.

Morgan, K. O. (1985) *Labour in Power: 1945–1951* (Oxford: Oxford University Press).

New Statesman (2015) Politically, the UK is now five nations. 6 February http://www.newstatesman.com/politics/2015/02/politically-uk-now-five-nations (last accessed 8 February 2015).

Office for Budget Responsibility (2014) *Economic and Fiscal Outlook December 2014*. Cm 8966 (London: Stationery Office). http://cdn.budgetresponsibility.independent.gov.uk/December_2014_EFO-web513.pdf (last accessed 9 February 2015).

Office for National Statistics (2015) *Summary of Public Sector Finances, December 2014* (London: ONS). http://www.ons.gov.uk/ons/dcp171780_392612.pdf (last accessed 9 February 2015).

Riddell, P. (2001) 'The Lasting Impact of Margaret Thatcher', in James, S. and Preston, V. (eds) *British Politics Since 1945: The Dynamics of Historical Change* (Basingstoke: Palgrave), 77–92.

Seldon, A. (2007) 'Conclusion: The Net Blair Effect, 1994–2007', in Seldon, A. (ed.) *Blair's Britain* (Cambridge: Cambridge University Press), 645–50.

Wells, A. (2015) YouGov/Sunday Times Poll 5–6 February 2015. http://ukpollingreport.co.uk/ (last accessed 9 February 2015).

Young, H. (1990) *One of Us: A Biography of Margaret Thatcher* (London: Pan).

Index

Compiled by Sue Carlton